THE PEACEMAKERS OF
1864

THE PEACEMAKERS OF 1864

BY

EDWARD CHASE KIRKLAND

AMS PRESS
NEW YORK

Reprinted from the edition of 1927, New York
First AMS EDITION published 1969
Manufactured in the United States of America

105569

Library of Congress Catalogue Card Number: 74-97888

AMS PRESS, INC.
New York, N.Y. 10003

ACKNOWLEDGMENTS

Footnotes and bibliography are not a complete statement of my indebtedness to others in the preparation of this book. With Professor James A. Woodburn, of Indiana University, I had the privilege of a conversation which did much to orientate the material of this volume. Professor Henry G. Pearson, of Massachusetts Institute of Technology, has constantly aided my researches by his generosity and interest. My greatest debt is, however, to Professor Edward Channing, of Harvard University, whose historical common sense and historical wisdom have been to me, as to many others, a real inspiration.

E. C. K.

Brown University,
December, 1926.

CONTENTS

THE PEACEMAKERS OF
1864

THE PEACEMAKERS OF 1864

CHAPTER I

THE PLEBISCITE OF 1864

AFTER all, the Civil War was a war. It is proper, therefore, to memorialize its commanders,—Beauregard and
McClellan, Longstreet and Meade, Jackson and Hooker,
Lee and Grant. Military men should be connected with
military affairs. It is proper, also, to litter important
battlefields with monuments. Gettysburg and Chattanooga were the scenes of great conflicts. And if the defi-
nition of warfare be enlarged, some attention can justly
be bestowed upon its incidental aspects, railroads, hospi-
talization, prisons, and finance. Thus the circle of military history can eventually be circumscribed. But the
history of the Civil War would still be incomplete unless
attention was directed to a conflict not waged upon the
battlefields where the armies met but behind the lines
where a host of various opinions were "as for a battle
ranged" and where the struggle between them, though
not fought with arms, was just as merciless and just as
bitter. The task of reconciling these differences of
opinion, of creating and sustaining a united desire for
war—in short, the problem of public morale—was a vital
factor in the Civil War. It may even be appraised the

1

decisive factor which denied victory to the Confederacy and gave it to the Federal Union.

In the case of the Union, the popular notion has been that the North was one in its allegiance to the policy of Abraham Lincoln. That policy has indeed been made immortal by its literary expression in the Inaugurals and the Gettysburg Address. "Dedicated to freedom," "with malice toward none; with charity for all," "government of the people, by the people, for the people shall not perish from the earth,"—these matchless phrases are imperishable. They have, therefore, become for posterity more than the expression of Lincoln's personal clarity of vision and strength of purpose. By some mysterious process they have been ascribed to every Northerner. The Federal Union was populated by some twenty odd million Lincolns, animated by the same principles and moving toward the same goal, calmly, patiently, and unafraid. In this unified and sanctified host there was no such thing as dissent. Perhaps the tradition of Lincoln's infallibility has done no greater disservice than this.

From the outset opinion in the North was divided upon two questions. In the first place, there was the inevitable divergence between those who believed that the war should never have been fought and those who believed that it should; in the second place, there was the equally inevitable difference of opinion as to what was the legitimate purpose of that conflict. The former quarrel was one waged over the question of peace or war; the latter, once the nation had chosen the arbitrament of the sword, was fought over the choice of war aims and peace terms. Naturally enough, the first of these two questions was the more important in the remorseless days between the election of November, 1860, and the outbreak of the war in April, 1861. In that period the answer given by the nation was confused, ill-informed, and vacillating.

The election of 1860, if it can be interpreted to prove anything, revealed the will of the nation as in favor of peace. Although the southern "fire-eaters" had asserted that the election of Lincoln meant war, such could not have been the desire of an indeterminate number of those who voted for the "Black Republican" president. Seward, during the campaign, had prophesied that there would be no disunion; and Chase coined the political watchwords of "Tranquillity, liberty and Union under the Constitution." [1] Whether or not these utterances were sincere is a matter of indifference; the voters who were attracted by them accepted the good faith of the statements. To this element in the victorious party must be added the large vote cast for two of the minority candidates, Douglas and Bell. The platforms of these men were professedly committed to a peace policy and to the preservation of the Union by compromise and adjustment. In the election itself the combined vote of these two elements carried eleven states. While only three of these states were in the North, impressive minorities were secured there. In fact, the Douglas and Bell parties polled over two-fifths of the total vote throughout the country. Since the remaining three-fifths was divided in a ratio of about two to one between Lincoln (many of whose supporters were for peace) and Breckinridge, the

---

[1] Scrugham, Mary: "The Peaceable Americans, 1860-1861," *Columbia University Studies in History, Economics, and Public Law,* Vol. XCVI, No. 3, p. 45.

"peaceful Americans" certainly constituted a plurality of the nation.[2]

If additional evidence were needed that the people were for the peaceful preservation of the Union, the months after the election, packed as they were with frantic efforts to avert a recourse to arms, would furnish it. It is not necessary to examine in detail the Congressional plans of compromise and the activities of peace conferences; it is sufficient to note their existence. Less formal evidence of the general temper is piled up by the letters, the speeches, and the newspaper editorials of those hectic days before the outbreak of the war. But in this hope for peace there was always one difficulty. There was no accurate knowledge of what price must be paid for the avoidance of war. There was an eagerness to make concessions but an ignorance of what concessions were necessary. There was a desire for peaceful settlement but an unwillingness to be the first to make the sacrifice which that settlement required. The public mood was fluid; the public mind was chaotic. Even those leaders who should have brought light to the multitudes were themselves wrapped in a dusk of uncertainty. Big business men are not ordinarily considered victims of fatal indecision. Yet August Belmont, "the fastidious millionaire" of New York, in December spurns the suggestion that the Union should be dissolved because such a dissolution would be advantageous to New York's commercial preëminence. "I prefer," he wrote, "to leave to my children, instead of the gilded prospects of New York merchant princes, the more

[2] Greeley, Horace: *The American Conflict,* Vol. I, p. 328. In Illinois, the Bell-Douglas vote was 49 per cent of the total; in Indiana, 48 per cent; in Pennsylvania, 47 per cent; in New York, 46 per cent; and in Iowa, 45 per cent.

enviable title of American citizens." Yet in other moods and at other times, he was in favor of the peaceful separation of the two sections.[3] John Murray Forbes, a Boston merchant and railroad builder, who, whatever qualities he might exhibit, never showed a lack of determination, wrote at one time favoring "masterly inactivity," later opposing compromise as debasing and dangerous, and finally preferring to "see the cotton states taken at their word and let off——."[4] And last of all there was William H. Seward, one-time outstanding candidate for the presidential nomination of the Republican Party, now a Senator from New York and regarded as likely to be the most prominent figure in the Lincoln administration. He was following a course of action in favor of compromise, so devious and so perplexing that his contemporaries doubted his sincerity and loyalty and posterity has had difficulty in understanding it. When the opinion of the mass and the leaders of the nation was thus confused, its action was likely to be controlled by the whimsical turn of events or by minorities who had made up their minds.

The minorities were composed of extremists. On the one hand was a group of northern "secessionists" whose distaste for the Federal Union, as it existed, was as strong as that of southern "traitors" and "rebels." These were

[3] Belmont, August: *Letters, Speeches, and Addresses*, pp. 39, 49. Letters to John Forsyth of Mobile, Alabama, December 19, 1860, and to Baron L. De Rothschild, May 21, 1861.
[4] Forbes, J. M.: *Letters (Supplementary) of John Murray Forbes*, Edited by Sarah F. Hughes, Vol. I, pp. 233, 237. Letters to F. W. Brune, January 17, 1861, and to Charles F. Adams, January 20, 1861. Forbes, J. M.: *Reminiscences of John Murray Forbes*, edited by Sarah F. Hughes, Vol. II, p. 103. A letter to Ashburton, March 1, 1861.

the extreme abolitionists. To their mind association with the evil-doers and the unrighteous men of the slav-ocracy was unendurable. William Lloyd Garrison in his famous auto-da-fé of the constitution at Framingham, Massachusetts, reiterated his belief that it was a "covenant with death and an agreement with hell." [5] His disciples were numerous and to them a war to preserve a government, which gave any countenance to the "established institution," seemed peculiarly unholy. Moncure D. Conway, a Virginian, became through a series of religious conversions, a Unitarian; and as a Unitarian, an associate of the New England anti-slavery thinkers and writers. At the outbreak of the war he was preaching in Cincinnati. To him the worship of the Union seemed "idolatry," upon whose altar human sacrifices were offered. On December 2, 1860, he took occasion to preach a vigorous sermon to his congregation in which he attacked nationalism, called treason a fictitious crime, and decried any attempt "to set a mere cold national interest—a question of laws and boundaries—against the integrity of homes and hearts and humanities." [6] A Washington observer records a conversation with Charles Sumner, Senator from Massachusetts, in which the latter said there was little choice "between a war for the Union which was not to be thought of," and a "corrupt conspiracy to preserve" it.[7]

From East to West the abolitionist press echoed the cry of its leaders. The *Ashtabula Sentinel*, the journalistic

[5] Swift, Lindsay: *William Lloyd Garrison*, pp. 306-307.
[6] Conway, Moncure D.: *Autobiography, Memories, and Experiences*, Vol. I, pp. 322-323.
[7] "The Diary of a Public Man," in the *North American Review*, Vol. CXXIX, p. 378.

mouthpiece of Giddings in Ohio, declared that the South should be allowed to depart in peace; [8] and the *New York Tribune* justified the right of peaceful secession if the South desired it.[9] To concede this right to the Southerners was better than to make compromises with them. This group's Pharisaical dislike for association with evil was buttressed by other articles of a distinctive creed. They were advocates of the right of democratic revolution; they were instinctively averse to the employment of military methods under any circumstances. All in all, a war for the preservation of the Union was not to be thought of.

Set over against the abolitionists was another minority which believed in the preservation of the Union at any cost,—even that of war. The decisiveness of their opinions arose not so much from pure idealism as from the clearness with which they saw the realities of the situation and the tempestuousness of their individual temperaments. They were intense realists. Zachariah Chandler, Senator from Michigan, a regular old war-horse, wrote to the Governor of his state that many Northerners were eager for compromise, but, as for himself, he did not think the "Union worth a rush without a little bloodletting." [10] Montgomery Blair, later Postmaster-General in Lincoln's cabinet, gave it as his "deliberate opinion that nothing will do so much to secure real and perma-

[8] Porter, G. H.: *Ohio Politics during the Civil War Period*, p. 52, a quotation from the *Ashtabula Sentinel* of February 13, 1861.

[9] *New York Tribune*, November 9, 1860.

[10] Dilla, Harriette M.: "The Politics of Michigan, 1865-1878," *Columbia University Studies in History, Economics, and Public Law*, Vol. XLVII, No. 1, p. 29.

nent fraternity between the Sections as a decisive defeat" on the field of battle.[11]

The eventual outbreak of the Civil War leads naturally to the conclusion that it was this determined minority which maneuvered the country into the conflict. Such a conclusion is too simple a one. Events affirmed the anticipations of this minority, partly through chance, partly through the fact that their ideas grasped the reality of the situation, and partly because they found an ally in whose hands lay the power of deciding for peace or war, Abraham Lincoln. It is not customary to associate Lincoln with warmongers. He is the man of peace, bowed down with the burden of a great war. But his alliance with the group which thought war necessary was inevitable. It sprang, primarily, from his allegiance to the Union. This allegiance was fundamental and vital. It was not based upon a mere shallow patriotism, for he saw a destiny for American nationalism to fulfill. This nation was to bring liberty and hope to the whole world; it was to give a promise that all men should have an equal chance. Lincoln came to see that the achievement of this destiny was threatened by the possibility of disunion. That eventuality he determined to avert. As to how far he would have to go to prevent secession, he was at first uncertain. He had early decided that slavery must be placed on the road to eventual extinction by denying it the possibility of expansion into the Federal territories. Any compromise on this crucial question would simply prolong the existence of a condition which threatened the life of the Union. But he was not positive that this deci-

[11] Fox, G. V.: *Confidential Correspondence of Gustavus Vasa Fox,* Vol. I, p. 4, Montgomery Blair to G. V. Fox, January 31, 1861.

sion meant war. Gradually, however, that recognition
was forced upon him. His first Inaugural, while conciliatory in tone, showed that he realized the obligation
of his oath of office to preserve the Union; his delivery
laid emphasis upon the point that, for the fulfillment of
his oath, he must "hold, occupy, and possess the property
and places belonging to the government——" of the
United States.[12]

These apparently insignificant words were the hint
of a momentous decision. The question of the Federal
forts—particularly Fort Sumter—situated in the seceded
states, had now transcended their mere military importance. Their retention or surrender was an earnest of
the purposes of the potential combatants. If the Republican administration made efforts to carry supplies
and reinforcements to these fortresses, the South threatened to flare forth in rebellion; if the Republican administration pursued an opposite policy, there was the
promise, if not the possibility, of reconciliation. In short
the forts were the chip on the shoulder of the belligerent South. After a month of indecision, Lincoln determined to make an attempt to relieve Fort Sumter. Although he was convinced that his duty compelled him to
hold these forts, he could not forget that, should his
attempt mean war, the nation had in November con-
fusedly voted for peace. A jest of his revealed the
gravity underlying the surface humor. In New York
some time before, he had breakfasted with a large number of wealthy men. Another guest, deficient in good

[12] Lincoln, Abraham: *Complete Works of Abraham Lincoln*, edited
by John G. Nicolay and John Hay (1905 edition), Vol. VI, pp. 169-185;
"The Diary of a Public Man," in the *North American Review*, Vol.
CXXIX, p. 384.

taste, had remarked that probably nowhere else could
one find so many millionaires.   Lincoln replied that he,
too, was a millionaire, for he had had a minority of a million votes in the last election.[13]   The President finally saw
that all this baffling contradiction of duty with actuality
could be solved in only one fashion.   It was necessary
to have for war, if war must come, an issue which had so
great an emotional content that all the differences and
uncertainties of the popular mind would be swallowed up
in loyalty.   When the Southerners fired upon Fort Sumter, following Lincoln's attempt at its relief, they gave
him the issue which he desired.   They had called in question the orderly processes of the law and of the Constitution; they had assaulted the flag of the nation.   At
once all the latent patriotism of the North swept away
divergences of politics and principles.   There was a
veritable revolution in sentiment.   A call for a gigantic
Union meeting in New York was signed by men of all
parties; fifty thousand people packed the square; men
of all political beliefs addressed the gathering; and even
Fernando Wood, who had been notorious for his sympathy
toward the South, made a speech in which he called "upon
every man, whatever had been his sympathies to make one
great phalanx in this controversy, to proceed . . . to
conquer a peace." [14]

Three months later, under the shadow of the disaster
of Bull Run, the two houses of Congress passed by im-

[13] "The Diary of a Public Man," in the *North American Review*, Vol.
CXXIX, p. 138.

[14] *New York Tribune*, April 22, 1861.   An explanation of Wood's sudden Union sympathy is found in the *New York Tribune*, November 29,
1861.   This report asserts that General Dix and a committee called upon
Wood previous to the meeting and informed him that he would not be
allowed to utter pro-secession sentiments.

mense majorities the Johnson-Crittenden resolution. After a reiteration of the causes of the conflict, it closed with a statement of the objects for which the war was fought: "this war is not prosecuted upon our part in any spirit of oppression, nor for any purpose of conquest or subjugation, nor for the purpose of overthrowing or interfering with the rights or established institutions of those states, but to defend and maintain the supremacy of the Constitution and all laws made in pursuance thereof, and to preserve the Union, with all the dignity, equality, and rights of the several states unimpaired; that as soon as these objects are accomplished the war ought to cease." It is important to note the silences as well as the assertions of this statement of war aims. There is no mention of emancipation or abolition; on the contrary, "the established institutions" of the states are not to be altered or tampered with; there is no thought of the ruthless subjugation of the rebellion for the rights and dignity of the states are to be unimpaired. The Civil War is to be fought only for the preservation of the Union. Here speaks the success of Lincoln's conservative policy. Against this resolution only five votes were cast in the Senate; in the House only two Representatives were found opposed to the affirmative majority of one hundred and seventeen. Not only was the nation united for war, it was also committed to a common war purpose.[15]

Yet three years later, in August, 1864, President Lincoln wrote an extraordinary secret memorandum. "This morning, as for some days past, it seems exceedingly prob-

[15] *The American Annual Cyclopædia* (Appleton's), 1861, pp. 241-244. This quotation is the wording of the resolution as passed in the Senate. In the House of Representatives, the resolution had a slightly different wording.

able that this administration will not be re-elected. Then it will be my duty to so coöperate with the President-elect as to save the Union between the election and the inauguration as he will have received his election on such grounds that he can not possibly save it afterwards."[16] Were these the words of a frightened and hysterical man? On the contrary, Lincoln's political clairvoyance and his uncanny understanding of men in the mass has never been questioned. It is easier to believe that in the summer of 1864 the course of events actually pointed to the President's defeat. In fact, the three years of inconclusive warfare were beginning to bear fruit. Within the nation, so blithesomely harmonized in 1861, criticism and discontent welled up from the depths of long suppressed opposition. Temporarily the military situation sank into a subordinate position; the nation concentrated its attention instead upon a presidential campaign, just as vital as that of 1860, which was to pose again the two old questions. Should the war continue? If it did, for what purposes should it be fought? These questions were to receive an answer in 1864. It was the year of great decisions.

By no means the least important aspect of that decisive year was the conflict which Lincoln was waging with a powerful group within the Republican party. The names applied to this group by both friends and enemies —"Radicals," "Vindictives," "Jacobins"——suggest that it was composed of extremists. They were men of drastic principles. For years they had sought an outlet for their explosive natures and for years it had been denied them;

---

[16] Nicolay, John G., and Hay, John: *Abraham Lincoln, a History,* Vol. IX, p. 251.

now the war which inevitably placed a premium upon strength for strength's sake gave them their opportunity. For that opportunity they had able leaders. In the Senate, they were grouped around Trumbull of Illinois, Wade of Ohio, and Chandler of Michigan. In the House they were led by Thaddeus Stevens of Pennsylvania. Even in the council of the President, they had their spokesman —at first Chase, and then Stanton. An examination of their actions and a perusal of their utterances leaves it certain that the leaders and the members of this Republican group were those to whom a merciless war had become almost an obsession.

These bitter-enders were almost sickened by the war policy of Lincoln. That war policy was a conservative one. In accord with the Crittenden resolution, it focused solely on the preservation of the Union and ignored the question of negro slavery. In this emphasis expediency and the temperament of Lincoln both had a part. Lincoln had a profound passion for the Union. In regard to the slave, he often seemed indifferent. Undoubtedly his spontaneous feelings on the subject of slavery made him sympathetic with the conservative classes. Although he was determined to put slavery on the road to ultimate extinction by excluding it from the territories and by denying it imperialistic expansion, he was not an abolitionist. Steeped in the tradition of the law, inspired by reverence for the Constitution, his attitude toward slavery would naturally be considered tender by extreme men. His practical policy for the subject was accurately expressed by a bill passed through Congress in April, 1862, for the emancipation of the slaves in the District of Columbia. There was to be compensation, ranging from

one hundred to three hundred dollars a slave, to such
owners as were loyal to the Union; and an amendment
provided an appropriation for transporting the negroes,
so freed, to some tropical region.[17]   In contrast to most
Northerners, Lincoln saw that the question of the negro
was more than the question of slavery.   The freed colored man was a problem.   The former master would regard him as a threat and a danger; he could never accept
his former slave as an equal in society, in politics, in
labor.   Such a situation was bound to produce friction
and ill-feeling.   It is significant that Browning, com-
monly regarded as the President's spokesman, introduced
the amendment for colonization and that a year earlier
the President had been in cabinet meeting an ardent advocate of the so-called "Chiriqui grant"—an area in
Costa Rica to be purchased by the government as a refuge
for the freed slaves.[18]   So much for Lincoln's conception
of the problem.   As a matter of expediency, he was also
determined to keep the slavery question out of the war
aims of the Northern government.   Only in this fashion
could he bind to the Northern cause the important border
states whose devotion to the Union was delicately balanced against their property interest in slaves; only in
this fashion could he unite to the Union that vast body
of conservative opinion which had been won through the
Southerners' attack upon Fort Sumter and had been
then tied fast by the Crittenden resolution.

With the sarcasm of contradiction the bitter-enders
called Lincoln's procedure waging a war on peace principles.   So far has the process of the deification of Lin-

[17] *Statutes at Large,* Vol. XII, pp. 376-378.
[18] Welles, Gideon: *Diary of Gideon Welles,* Vol. I, pp. 123-150.

coln gone, that it is difficult to credit the extremes to which their criticism mounted. One of Trumbull's correspondents grew particularly bitter when the presidential message of December, 1861, showed that no stringent measures were to be followed toward slavery. He described it as "a tame, timid, time serving commonplace sort of an abortion of a Message, cold enough with one breath to *freeze* h—l *over*." [19] The summer of 1862 with the disasters to McClellan's army saw this criticism gain in fury. Wade expressed it when he said that the country was going to hell and that the scenes of the French Revolution were nothing to those which were to be enacted in this country.[20] Naturally the policy of such critics was one of "thorough." They were abolitionists, but of the militant rather than the pacific variety. Whatever may have been the considerations which made it desirable to ignore the question of the slave in the conduct of the war, they were bent upon its reintroduction. This should not be a war for mere "Union-saving," a phrase often used with contempt, but a war for freedom. Let such a war alienate conservative patriots, commercial interests, and border states; it would enlist the devotion of abolition theorists and anti-slavery fanatics; it would secure the reasoned assent of practical men who saw in the slaves of the South a reservoir of man power which made possible a more effective Southern resistance. Finally it must be observed that negro slavery was the outstanding difference between Northern and Southern civilization and that it was one of the fundamental causes for

[19] Cole, Arthur C.: *The Era of the Civil War, 1848-1870, The Centennial History of Illinois,* Vol. III, p. 293, note 14, letter from Shubal York to Trumbull, December 5, 1861.

[20] Julian, George W.: *Political Recollections, 1840-1872,* p. 220.

the dangers which threatened American nationalism. To eradicate this difference by radical measures was charmingly logical. Such was the case of the bitter-enders, they pressed to the attack.

Until the year of a presidential election might make it possible for them to supplant the lenient Lincoln with someone of their own hot temper, the recourse of these extremists was Congress. Over this body, restive under executive domination, they exerted throughout the war a considerable measure of control. From it they had secured in December, 1861, the creation of the Congressional Committee on the Conduct of the War. This committee had its origin in a determination to investigate the disasters of Bull Run and Ball's Bluff; a congressional debate amplified its functions into an inquiry "into the conduct of the present war," and the appointment of its members delivered it into the hands of the radicals. The Senatorial representatives were Wade and Chandler and Andrew Johnson—the first two were the most violent of radicals—and the House delegation contained Julian and Covode as fit partners for the Senatorial pair. The extremists thus constituted a majority of the committee. Its powers were in exercise as large as the committee could obtain without opposition. They investigated all the military departments, although the propinquity of the Army of the Potomac made it especially accessible for their scrutiny, and all military affairs in general; and then they added non-military matters such as war contracts, trade regulations in the Mississippi region, and the return of slaves to their rebel owners. They employed these functions in the most exasperating manner. Although not a single member of the committee had the slightest military training, they endeavored to censure commanders and discipline officers, to make military suggestions, and to influence appointments. Critics asserted that the procedure of the committee was characterized by partisanship and arbitrary methods. The sessions were secret, the defendant was allowed no counsel; often no record of the meetings was kept and the witnesses were carefully hand-picked.[21]

As if the creation of such a tribunal was not enough of a challenge to the executive, a year later a Senatorial cabal tried to reconstruct Lincoln's cabinet with those who would vigorously suppress "a causeless and atrocious rebellion," and who would counteract the weakness of the President and his present advisors. Both these attempts at congressional usurpation increased the burden which Lincoln was bearing and that burden was not perceptibly lightened by the fact that he was able to withstand successfully this congressional pressure. Lincoln, however, became convinced through this experience that the slavery issue which the bitter-enders were pressing possessed ominous political complications. In spite of the hazards which action involved, he saw that he must do something to deal with the situation. He devised a double policy.

[21] Criticisms of the committee are voiced in Hurlbert, W. H.: *General McClellan and the Conduct of the War,* p. 160; Swinton, William: *Campaigns of the Army of the Potomac,* p. 89; Meade, George: *The Life and Letters of George Gordon Meade,* Vol. I, p. 324; Vol. II, pp. 169-171, 179; Franklin, W. B.: *A Reply to the Report of the Joint Committee of Congress on the Conduct of the War, submitted to the public on the 6th of April, 1863,* p. 5. Both Franklin and Meade had little cause to be friendly with the Committee on the Conduct of the War. Meade had not been regarded by it with favor, and Franklin had been made responsible for the disaster at Fredericksburg. The best idea of the committee and its labors can be obtained by glancing through the great number of volumes which contain its reports.

In the first place, he endeavored to bring about voluntary abolition in the border states. The advisability of such action was obvious. If abolition were accomplished there, these states would not be alienated by any further measures which Lincoln might be compelled to take under radical pressure; the whole irritating problem of using the army to maintain the rights of loyal slave owners would be obviated; and the last tie of interest which bound the border states to the Confederacy would be destroyed. To accomplish his purpose he recommended to Congress that aid should be furnished to the states which would free their slaves; he urged such action upon the border state representatives on two occasions and on both he found their sentiment lukewarm or divided. This part of his policy was a temporary failure. By July, 1862, however, Lincoln seems to have decided on the second feature of his policy—the emancipation of the slaves in the rebel states on the plea of military necessity. The first hint of the new policy he gave to Seward and Welles on a carriage ride on July 13. He opened preliminary discussions with the whole cabinet on July 22 and postponed a decision until a more favorable military situation should arise. Throughout the month of August he dissembled his intentions in spite of the furious attacks and unrelenting pressure of the abolitionists. At last the victory of Antietam gave the proper occasion, and on September 22, 1862, the preliminary emancipation was issued. Its essentially conservative nature must be observed. It proposed a renewal of the plan of compensated abolition; the continuance of the effort at voluntary colonization; a promise to recommend ultimate compensation to loyal owners; and the military emancipation of all slaves in the states still in rebellion on January 1, 1863. Three months later, since the rebellion had not ceased, the proclamation was issued in its final form.

About this momentous document, there was a thick atmosphere of ambiguity. People asked themselves whether it would apply after the cessation of the war and of the attendant exercise of war powers; others questioned if the President could legally issue such a proclamation; still others suspected Lincoln's sincerity. Did he intend that henceforth the abolition of slavery was as essential for peace as the restoration of the Union? Finally everyone was interested in the response of the nation. Did the new issue meet with such national support that the war would not be ended unless the slave was freed? Did emancipation become a part of the national purpose for the accomplishment of which the nation was prepared to make sacrifices?

The abolitionists hailed the emancipation proclamation with indescribable enthusiasm. Moncure D. Conway was inspired with the exaltation of a new religion and was moved to compose an Advent poem or hymn for the "Commonwealth." [22] More robust, John A. Andrew, Governor of Massachusetts, preferred to sing hymns. Just after the preliminary proclamation Edward Kinsley, a friend, called upon him in the council chamber of the Massachusetts capitol. If there had been an onlooker, he would have witnessed these two singing *Coronation* and *Praise God from Whom all Blessings Flow*, and then would have seen Andrew marching around the chamber while Kinsley chanted the verses of *Old John Brown* and

[22] Conway, Moncure D.: *Autobiography, Memories, and Experiences,* Vol. I, pp. 370-371.

both shouted out the chorus.[23]   Lincoln had indeed conciliated the abolitionists.   The tale of his conservative
supporters is a different one.   Some accepted the proclamation as necessary from a military point of view.   But
it is significant that when a Governors' conference, meeting in September at Altoona in Pennsylvania, drew up
a paper endorsing the President, the Governors of New
Jersey, Delaware, Maryland, Kentucky, and Missouri refused to sign it because they disapproved of the emancipation proclamation.[24]   Finally the congressional elections of 1862 went heavily against the administration.
This defeat can be ascribed to many causes: the military
reverses, the usual off-year reaction, and important local
issues; but the emancipation proclamation had alienated
a portion of national public opinion.[25]   This coolness
on the part of the country was reflected in the mind of
the President.   In December, 1862, Lincoln engaged in
an exchange of letters with the Southern sympathizer,
Fernando Wood of New York.   The latter had written
the President that the South would probably make peace
if it were granted a political amnesty.   Lincoln in his
reply discounted Wood's sources of information and then
added that if "the people of the Southern States would
cease resistance, and would reinaugurate, submit to, and

[23] Pearson, H. G.: *The Life of John A. Andrew, Governor of Massachusetts, 1861-1865*, Vol. II, p. 51, note 1.

[24] Nicolay, John G., and Hay, John: *Abraham Lincoln, a History*,
Vol. VI, p. 167.

[25] Julian, George W.: *Political Recollections, 1840-1872*, p. 230; Nicolay, John G., and Hay, John: *Abraham Lincoln, a History*, Vol. VI,
p. 172; *New York Tribune*, October 27, 1862, November 5, 6, 1862;
Porter, George H.: "Ohio Politics during the Civil War Period," *Columbia University Studies in History, Economics, and Public Law*, Vol.
XL, No. 2, pp. 105-106, note 2.

maintain the national authority within the limits of such
States under the Constitution of the United States, I
say that in such case the war would cease on the part of the
United States. . . ." [26]   On the very eve of the final
emancipation proclamation, this statement is very significant.

Twelve months later Lincoln was again to state the issues of the conflict. The occasion was the annual message
sent by the President to Congress; at the time of its delivery, the decisive year of 1864 was right at hand. The
discussion of slavery came toward the end of the message.
"While I remain in my present position, I shall not
attempt to retract or modify the Emancipation Proclamation; nor shall I return to slavery any person who is
free by the terms of that proclamation, or by any of the
acts of Congress." [27]   Here was another public profession
of his adherence to the policy of emancipation. Yet this
assertion of allegiance had something rather equivocal
about it. To be sure the proclamation was then in operation; at that precise moment, slaves were undoubtedly
being freed under it. Yet the rebel states were still
unconquered; hosts of enslaved negroes had not yet been
freed by Northern armies. And was the emancipation
proclamation binding after peace had come? A year
later, Lincoln was to give it as his personal opinion that it
was not. The message of 1863, therefore, did not in
reality mark a great departure from the statements which
Lincoln had made twelve months earlier to Wood.

[26] *Lincoln, Abraham: Complete Works of Abraham Lincoln,* edited
by John G. Nicolay and John Hay (1905 edition), Vol. VIII, pp. 142-
144, Lincoln to Fernando Wood, December 12, 1862.
[27] *Lincoln, Abraham: Complete Works of Abraham Lincoln,* edited
by John G. Nicolay and John Hay (1905 edition), Vol. IX, p. 249.

The same address to Congress called a halt to the further severities which the bitter-enders were planning to
inflict upon the South before it could have peace. The
temper in which these measures were designed is suggested
by a remark made by Thaddeus Stevens to a meeting at
Stanton's home which was attended by members of the
Committee on the Conduct of the War and by a few other
choice spirits. At this conference Stevens exploded, "He
was tired of hearing d——d Republican cowards talk
about the Constitution; that there *was* no Constitution
any longer so far as the prosecution of the war was concerned and that we should strip the rebels of all their
rights, and give them reconstruction on such terms as
would end treason forever." [28] Inspired by such a spirit,
the extremists had passed through Congress a series of
punitive measures. In 1861 and 1862, acts had been
passed for the confiscation of property, including slaves,
owned by the Confederates. Since no Federal Courts, to
which were entrusted the execution of these acts, existed
in the Southern states, they were not of wide application.
The debate upon these measures, nevertheless, showed
what the bitter-enders were after. They thrust aside
such technicalities as international law and rebel status
and talked about meting out justice to black-hearted
traitors. Convinced that the confiscation acts were not
enough, supplementary measures of an oppressive nature
were passed. Perhaps in the hope that the South could
be forced to contribute to the cost of the war, a direct tax
was levied upon Southern districts in insurrection; as the
Northern troops advanced, special tax commissioners advanced also and levied assessments upon the seized terri-

---

[28] Julian, George W.: *Political Recollections, 1840-1872*, p. 213.

tory. When these taxes were not paid, the property was seized and sold at tax sales.[29] Extensive seizures were made in Tennessee, Virginia, and South Carolina.[30] Robert E. Lee's estate at Arlington first came into the hands of the Federal government through its confiscation for an unpaid tax of $92.07. It is upon this property that the National Cemetery has been built.[31] An act of March 12, 1863, gave a final elaboration to this general policy. Under its terms the Secretary of the Treasury was authorized to collect and sell captured and abandoned property of a non-military nature.[32] The Treasury Department created for this purpose a tremendous organization of general agents, supervising agents, local agents, agency aids, and customs officers—a hierarchy which was supplemented by private contractors. This vast bureaucracy soon became notorious for both its efficiency and corruption.[33] Later acts gave to the Treasury the management of deserted houses and plantations which were to be confiscated or returned after the war depending upon the loyalty or disloyalty of the owner.[34]

By the end of 1863 the problem of the Southern States was a more extensive one than the confiscation of property and the collection of tribute. The progress of the Union armies and the reoccupation of the territory lately in rebellion made necessary the formulation of some policy

[29] *Statutes at Large,* Vol. XII, pp. 422-426.
[30] *The Congressional Globe,* 42nd Congress, 2nd Session, p. 3387.
[31] Hosmer, J. K.: *The Appeal to Arms, 1861-1863,* pp. 172-173.
[32] *Statutes at Large,* Vol. XII, pp. 820-821.
[33] *House Documents,* 38th Congress, 2nd Session, Executive Documents, Vol. VII, No. 3, Report of the Secretary of the Treasury on the State of Finances for the Year 1864, pp. 294-296; *ibid.,* 39th Congress, 2nd Session, Executive Documents, Vol. XI, No. 97, p. 3.
[34] *Statutes at Large,* Vol. XIII, pp. 375-378.

for treating these redeemed regions. The word "reconstruction" was in the mouths of politicians. To the bitter-enders, such a process involved the annihilation of the rights of the states and their readmission into the Union on extremely stringent terms as to slavery, the position of the freed black, and the punishment of rebels. If the exact details of their policy were unknown, the legislative measures already passed by Congress, the harsh utterances of the radical leaders, and the unrestraint of their tempers were earnest enough of what could be expected. Accordingly Lincoln in his December message to Congress decided to challenge this spirit before it gained accurate expression and acquired momentum. He advanced a plan for reconstruction to be executed under presidential auspices. By its provisions all participants in the rebellion, except certain excluded classes, were to be pardoned by the President and restored to all their rights of property, except in slaves, if they would take an oath of allegiance to the Constitution and Union and would accept the acts of Congress and of the President in regard to slavery. Furthermore if "a number of persons, not less than one-tenth in number of the votes cast in such State at the presidential election" of 1860, will take the oath and reëstablish the government of the State according to the terms of the oath, the executive will then guarantee their new government against invasion and domestic violence; and Congress will determine whether or not it will readmit representatives from these reconstructed states. Then followed a defense of his policy.[35] The message, however, had an importance

[35] *Lincoln, Abraham: Complete Works of Abraham Lincoln,* edited by John G. Nicolay and John Hay (1905 edition), Vol. IX, pp. 218-223.

greater than any of its details. On the eve of a presidential election, Lincoln had there drawn up a definite statement of his war and peace policy. The aims he expressed differed from those stated by the Crittenden resolution when the war began. Lincoln had been forced to place a modified emphasis upon freedom for the slave. But the spirit of the administration was still conservative. It refused to be hurried along by the passions of war; it yet hoped to settle the questions of peace with charity rather than with punishment. As to whether this presidential policy had a chance of victory, the year 1864 would decide.

In the Republican party, the use of a common party label did not mean loyalty to a common ideal. The same generalization was even more true of the Democrats. The emotional outburst, set off by the Southern attack upon Fort Sumter, had swept them into support of the Union and this unanimity of purpose was strengthened by the disasters which the Union cause suffered in the summer of 1861. But it was hardly to be expected that the three years of a Civil War, which had shattered the unity of the Republicans, should leave unaffected an alliance between two logically hostile parties. Soon the tide of Democratic support began to recede and to carry with it the erstwhile allies of the Northern cause. In its ebb, it left a residuum—the War Democrat. This group was naturally a small one. Its importance derived from the talent of its leaders and from the power which it held in states where the balance of party strength was peculiarly precarious. With the exception of a few men whose conversion was so intense as to carry them into the ranks of the bitter-enders, the War Democrats supported the war because they believed it was necessary for the preservation of the Union. They were bound to the Northern cause, as were the border states, by the conservative policy of Abraham Lincoln. They were Lincoln men. As such they were enemies of the Republican radicals. Consequently in 1862 the extremists were in favor of abandoning attempts at fusion with their unwelcome Democratic allies and were for going it alone.[36] In Ohio the *Ashtabula Sentinel* demanded a return to the old party system on the ground that the coalition movement had freed the President, elected on a Republican platform, from any responsibility to his own party.[37] But the votes of the irritating War Democrats could not be despised even by Republican hot-heads and the recurring election years always cooled their fevered comment.

That any Democrat should support a Republican war is more surprising than that the majority did not. In general the Democratic party in the North behaved in a normal fashion; it did not remain in alliance with its opponents. The reasons for its action are to be found in human nature and in circumstances. In the first place the cries of "support the War" and "be a patriot" do not have strength enough to iron out all differences of opinion and of principle. Particularly was this true of the Civil War where the issues were so vital and so fundamental. In the second place, Democratic support of the

[36] Brummer, S. D.: "Political History of New York State during the Period of the Civil War," *Columbia University Studies in History, Economics, and Public Law*, Vol. XXXIX, No. 2, pp. 191-194; Dilla, Harriette M.: "The Politics of Michigan, 1865-1868," *Columbia University Studies in History, Economics, and Public Law*, Vol. XLVII, No. 1, pp. 26-27.

[37] Porter, G. H.: *Op. cit.*, Editorial, January 8, 1862.

war would have involved a reversal of the habits of party action—habits which had been built up through years of partisan conflict. This emotional factor was bound to drive the average Democrat into outright opposition to the Republicans or else to convert him into a petty critic and bickerer.

From the beginning of the war, the operation of these factors involved a majority of the Democratic party in a fatal contradiction. The latent patriotism of the average Democrat made it inevitable that he should cherish some patriotic feelings and that he should announce them. From the standpoint of party expediency, it was also wise to avoid the taint of treason. The Democratic party of the North, therefore, was not backward in condemning the right of secession and of asserting a zeal for the restoration of the Union. The habit of partisan action had to find its outlet in criticism of the methods by which these laudable ends were being accomplished. The suspension of *habeas corpus*, the arbitrary arrests which followed, the restraints upon newspapers and upon speech were all regarded as unwarrantable interferences with the rights of the citizen and as evidence of the intention of the party in power to convert the North into a military despotism. Undoubtedly a great many Democrats bore a high devotion to these "freedoms" of the constitution, but a large share of their hostility to the arbitrary measures which violated them can be ascribed to the fact that the Republicans did it. To support the war and to criticise its conduct was a distressing straddle. It became unpleasantly obvious when a draft had to be inaugurated to increase the Northern armies. Although resistance to the draft was not confined to New York City, it was upon

that metropolis that all attention was focused. Horatio
Seymour had been elected Governor of the state in the
Democratic tidal wave of 1862 and his opposition to the
draft was outspoken. What would be his attitude if the
act were actually put into operation? The draft riots
in New York City made definite action on his part inescapable. An epistolary debate with Lincoln gave him an
opportunity to elaborate the theoretical bases for his opposition. But in both word and deed, Governor Seymour
showed only timidity, uncertainty, and equivocation.[38]
An intelligent man in his situation, trying to do what he
did, could not display any other qualities. Seymour was
faced with a dilemma. On the one hand he avowed his
loyalty to the Union and admitted the necessity for the
war; on the other hand he was found opposing measures
like the draft which were absolutely essential to its prosecution. The plight of Horatio Seymour was the plight
of all similarly minded conservative Democrats.

But a release from this contradiction was even then at
hand. Lincoln suddenly did the Democrats a tremendous
service. The emancipation proclamation, which he had
issued to cure the diseases in his own party, gave the
party of opposition a real principle. The war had been
declared for the preservation of the Union: now it had

---

[38] The draft and the controversy attendant upon it can be traced in
New York Tribune, July 15, 18, 1863; August 19, 1863; *New York
Herald,* July 24, 1863; August 11, 29, 1863. These references are to
proclamations, letters, speeches, and messages of Governor Seymour.
Lincoln, Abraham: Complete Works of Abraham Lincoln, edited by
John G. Nicolay and John Hay (1905 edition), Vol. IX, pp. 58-61, 69-
70; Nicolay, John G., and Hay, John: *Abraham Lincoln, a History,*
Vol. VII, pp. 13-27, 32-45; Fry, James B.: *New York and the Con-
scription of 1863, a chapter on the history of the Civil War.*

been transformed into a "nigger crusade"; this transformation had taken place after the support of loyal men had been obtained for a war fought for other principles. Hypocrisy and perfidy could go no further. The betrayed conservatives declared that the Crittenden resolution was the only true end of the war; to disregard it was to commit a breach of the public faith. The withdrawal of Democratic support from a war waged for freedom and emancipation was certainly justified.[39] So far their case had logic in it. But the Democrats were unwilling to stop with a case based upon obvious reasonableness. Their bitterness made the slavery issue a postulate for a chain of reasoning which led them into strange assertions. Since the adoption of abolition principles had perverted the true war aims of the North, it was this perversion which alone stood in the way of obtaining peace. There would be peace, therefore, if emancipation were repudiated. If the North could approach the South with the offer of a compromise based upon the "Union as it was and the Constitution as it is," the South would yield and

[39] Carpenter, S. D.: *Logic of History, Five Hundred Political Texts— being concentrated extracts of abolitionism; also results of slavery agitation and emancipation, together with sundry chapters on despotism, usurpation and frauds.* This book is a digest of the sayings and doings of the Northern disunionists for the last sixty-five years, the editor says in his preface. It has been compiled for the use of "Copperheads" and "Traitors" in order that they might answer the arguments of their opponents. The general theme of the book is an attempt to show that there is a vast conspiracy to destroy the Union in order to free the slave. After the war began, there came a gradual increase in the power of the abolitionists and they finally controlled the President. The emancipation proclamation was the result. Carpenter favors, however, the legitimate ends for which the war was at first fought. The whole book is an admirable statement of the conservative Democrat position.

a national convention would be held to reconcile the remaining differences. If the extremists with their principles of confiscation, emancipation, and reconstruction could only be defeated, the Union might be saved without further fratricidal bloodshed and without the continuance of misrule, anarchy and despotism in the North. Although such a belief is understandable, it was not in accord with the facts of the situation. It had the fatal weakness of entirely ignoring the fundamental cause of the war, the desire of the South for complete independence.

But another cause than mere partisan bitterness was responsible for the elaboration of this formula by Democratic conservatives. That cause was to be found in the growth within the Democratic party of a group of extremists who were threatening to seize the Democratic organization and to convert it into an out-and-out peace-at-any-price party. These were the true Copperheads. To define accurately the term Copperhead is impossible, for that opprobrious epithet was applied indiscriminately by "loyal" persons to all those who opposed the methods and aims of the war. There was no allowance by such accusers for gradations of belief or shades of opinion. It was far easier to speak of "traitors" and to label all such, "Copperheads." Removed from the heat of the conflict, it is easy to see that the deeds and speeches of many Copperheads were not treasonable. If the term is to be used with precision, it must be applied only to those who advocated a complete reversal of the Northern policy and the use of vigorous measures to bring about that end. Such extremists were not localized in any part of the country. There were Copperheads in Massachusetts and in Michigan.[40] But the centers of Copperhead strength were logically those areas which were bound before the war most closely to the South by ties of sentiment, politics, and commercial advantage. Excluding the border states, these were New York City and the southern portions of Ohio, Indiana, and Illinois.

During the campaign of 1860 and the days which intervened between that election and the declaration of war, the city of New York was a comfort and a strength to the secession leaders. The opposition to Lincoln's election was led by the wealthy merchants and bankers whose commercial interests would be jeopardized either by peaceful secession or military coercion. The *New York Herald*, for instance, said that a Republican victory would be a blow at the commercial and financial prestige of the city and urged those upon whom the blow would fall to unite in order to secure Lincoln's defeat.[41] Nor was the clamor stilled after the nation had cast its ballots. Rather it was marshalled and directed by the prince of rascals, Fernando Wood. Fernando Wood was an ex-Philadelphian who in New York had progressed through various employments—a wine and cigar merchant, a ship chandler, and a grocer—into politics. In this field it is impossible to accuse the man of principle. His genius which transformed political manipulation from a clumsy

[40] Ware, Edith E.: "Political Opinion in Massachusetts during the Civil War and Reconstruction," *Columbia University Studies in History, Economics, and Public Law,* Vol. LXXIV, No. 2, pp. 120-132; Moore, Charles: "A Sketch of the Life of Sullivan M. Cutcheon, with particular reference to Michigan political history during the War of the Rebellion" in the *Collections and Researches made by the Michigan Pioneer and Historical Society,* Vol. XXX, p. 104.

[41] *New York Herald,* September 24, 1860, November 6, 1860; *New York Tribune,* November 8, 1860.

and crude procedure into an exact science was well
adapted to emerge triumphant from the factional dis-
order which characterized metropolitan politics. In 1859,
aided by a constituency which to the minds of the well-
born and the well-to-do was "disreputable" and by the
unscrupulous talents of his brother Benjamin, he had been
elected Mayor of the city.[42] Since the up-state Democratic machine, the Albany Regency, stood in the way of
Wood's aspirations to play a larger rôle in state and
national politics, he had allied himself with the Southern
Democracy. This relationship was responsible for the
curious actions of the Mayor in January, 1861. On the
very brink of the war, he proposed to the Common Council the possible secession of New York City and he sent to
the secessionist, Robert Toombs, a letter of apology for
the seizure by the city police of some rifles shipped to
Savannah. If he had had the power, he wrote, he would
gladly have punished the offenders.[43] This exuberance
subsided, however, before the enthusiasm engendered by
the outbreak of the war and the great Union mass meeting
after the attack upon Fort Sumter witnessed the incon-

[42] *New York Tribune,* November 30, 1861, December 2, 1861, November
1, 1862; Myers, Gustavus: *The History of Tammany Hall,* pp. 178-
180, 207-231; Breen, Matthew P.: *Thirty Years of New York Politics
Up-to-date,* pp. 28-81. The above references contain many illustrations
of Wood's methods in politics. Myers considers him a fit successor to
Aaron Burr and a fit predecessor of Tweed. He was connected first
with Tammany Hall and then with Mozart Hall, a rival to the former
which he created.

[43] *New York Herald,* January 8, 1861, February 10, 1861; "Diary
of a Public Man," in the *North American Review,* Vol. CXXIX, p. 140.
The latter reference gives Lincoln's famous reply when he was informed of Wood's plans for secession: "And as to the free city business, well, I reckon, it will be some time before the front door sets
up housekeeping on its own account."

gruous spectacle of Fernando Wood calling upon the
North to conquer a peace. A short time later, when the
tide of loyalty had ebbed, Wood found it convenient to
forget his patriotic exhortation. He began to attack the
government. The *Daily News,* his brother's paper, was
guilty of such treasonable utterances that the government
suppressed it and sent its editor to Fort Lafayette.[44] If
this experience was not sufficiently salutary, a political
defeat was. In 1862 Wood had a recurrence of Union
feeling. Then materialized an impulse which was to send
him again along the path of converting the Democratic
party into a peace organization. That impulse came
from the West.

The sympathies of the Ohio Valley were enlisted in
many ways with the South. The former region had been
settled largely from the South, especially the Southern
Piedmont, and its political and sentimental ties were,
therefore, in Dixie. Commercially the Ohio region had
just been brought into close alliance with the North.
Before 1850 the larger market for its products had been
to the southward and the ease of transportation along
natural waterways had facilitated the growth of this com-
merce. But in the decade before 1860 the competition of
the railroads and of the Lakes and Erie route was helping
to create in the East and in Europe the real market for
western products. Besides this growing economic relationship, there were other factors—the love of the Union
and the preference for free labor—which bound the inhab-
itants of the Ohio Basin to the North. The region, then,

[44] *The American Annual Cyclopædia* (Appleton's), *1861,* pp. 328-330.
Benjamin Wood's ideas as to peace and war can be obtained in de-
lightful fashion from a novel written by him in 1862 entitled, "Fort
Lafayette or Love and Secession, A Novel," New York, 1862.

was one delicately balanced in its sympathies between the
two parties to the Civil War. Lincoln had seen that it
would join the North only on a conservative platform.
He had done his best, therefore, to swing the southern
portion of Ohio, Indiana, and Illinois to a support of the
Union cause. But in spite of his efforts, this debatable
region, along with the border states, was the center of the
most extreme opposition to the Civil War. Here the
peace party recruited its most numerous following and
developed its most vigorous leaders.

The evolution of the peace party in the West from
comparative quiescence at the outbreak of the Civil
War to militant agitation in 1864 centered around several interesting characters. Of them all, Clement Laird
Vallandigham was the most famous and the most influential. Although he professed to be an ardent supporter of
the Union, he actually was a leading exponent of sectionalism. Before the war he had declared against any
attempt to coerce a seceding state and had introduced
into Congress, as a method of solving the conflict between
the slave and free states, a plan modeled upon the Calhoun
notion of dividing the Union into several sections among
which a balance of power was to be preserved through the
operation of concurrent majorities. For a time after the
outbreak of the war, Vallandigham's voice was still but,
when the disintegration of the national purpose set in, he
came forward with a party program. The best means to
preserve the Democracy was not in his mind to ally it with
the Republicans but to give it a policy definitely opposed
to the war. The details of this policy were formulated in
May, 1862, in an address issued by Vallandigham to the
people of the country. While this document stressed the

necessity of preserving "The Constitution as it is and the Union as it was," its chief emphasis was elsewhere. The proper way of dealing with sectionalism was through the ballot box and "the rights and established institutions" of states should not be interfered with. These assertions were quite daring for the early part of 1862. To this address were affixed the signatures of fifteen Democratic members of Congress. The geographical distribution of the signers was significant. Only four Democratic Congressmen from the West refused to support the principles of the address; only three Easterners had attached their names. The state represented by the largest single delegation was Ohio.[45]

The next two years were to demonstrate that peace principles were palatable to that state and to other western regions. The first definite evidence of that fondness came in the campaign of 1862. In Ohio the Democratic party carried fourteen out of nineteen districts. Vallandigham, although defeated in his own district, was already mentioned enthusiastically as a candidate for the presidency.[46] In Illinois the southern section was turbulent with proposals for separation from the state and for the formation of military companies to fight for the South.[47] Resolutions, urging an armistice and a national convention at Louisville, passed the Illinois House the next year, and a gigantic mass meeting at Springfield

[45] Vallandigham, James L.: *A Life of Clement L. Vallandigham*, pp. 204-207. The western signers were distributed as follows: six from Ohio, three from Illinois, two from Indiana, and one from Oregon. Two of the eastern signers came from Pennsylvania and one from New Jersey.

[46] Porter, G. H.: *Op. cit.*, pp. 136-137, a quotation from the *Crisis;* 144-145.

[47] Cole, Arthur C.: *Op. cit.*, p. 302.

declared: "The further offensive prosecution of this war tends to subvert the constitution and the government, and entail upon this Nation all the disastrous consequences of misrule and anarchy." [48] Encouraged by the Democratic victories of 1862 to embark upon a bolder policy and embittered by his own defeat, Vallandigham plunged into an extensive effort to organize the peace party. His tone was now more belligerent. He came East in March and addressed a small gathering in New York City. On that occasion he hinted at the possibility of some other means than the ballot box to bring the administration to terms. "When an attempt is made to deprive us of free speech and a free press, the hour shall have come when it shall be the duty of freemen to find some other efficient mode of redress." [49] Fernando Wood found such sentiments agreeable and in April he engineered a mass meeting, one of whose resolutions declared for peace "as the only mode left to us to restore the Union." In an address at the same gathering, Wood himself urged as a successor to Lincoln a Democrat who would cease hostilities and seek a conference for peace. The success of such a conference was apparently taken for granted since Wood was silent as to the proper procedure in case it failed. [50]

Vallandigham, meanwhile, had returned to Ohio where events were rushing toward some sort of climax. Before a large meeting at Hamilton, he advocated resistance to the government when the party in power sought to perpetuate itself by despotic means. Pendleton, who spoke after Vallandigham, threatened to meet the mob violence

[48] Cole, Arthur C.: *op. cit.,* pp. 298-300.
[49] *New York Tribune,* March 9, 1863.
[50] *Ibid.,* April 8, 1863.

of the Union men with mob violence on the part of his supporters.[51] Such words to loyal ears sounded like the threat of open rebellion. Among those intimately concerned with the menace of rebellion was General Ambrose Burnside, sometime commander of the Army of the Potomac and now Commander-in-Chief of the Department of the Ohio. Of his loyalty there could be no question. The Committee on the Conduct of the War had certified to it.[52] Now he was confronted, not with Confederates entrenched on the heights of Fredericksburg, but with their civilian allies mouthing treason in a state of the Federal Union. In both cases his strategy was disastrous. Without consultation with his superiors he issued General Order Number 38. One of its provisions declared, "The habit of declaring sympathies for the enemy will no longer be tolerated in this department. Persons committing such offenses will be at once arrested, with a view to being tried as above stated, or sent beyond our lines into the lines of their friends." [53] Vallandigham did not delay in supplying the overt act. Speaking on May 1 before a crowd of over twenty thousand people at Mount Vernon, Ohio, he attacked the general conduct of the war, advocated peace, and characterized Burnside's order as a "base usurpation of arbitrary authority." [54] A few days later he was arrested, brought before a mili-

[51] Vallandigham, C. L.: *The Record of the Hon. C. L. Vallandigham,* p. 246.

[53] *Report of the Joint Committee on the Conduct of the War, 1863,* Part 1, pp. 54-60, 103; Julian, George W.: *Political Recollections, 1840-1872,* p. 225.

[53] Poore, Benjamin Perley: *The Life and Public Services of Ambrose E. Burnside—Soldier—Citizen—Statesman,* p. 207.

[54] *Official Records of the Union and Confederate Armies,* Series II, Vol. V, pp. 634-644.

tary tribunal, and sentenced to imprisonment for the remainder of the war. There was a brief stay for *habeas corpus* proceedings but it was futile. The execution of the original sentence, however, did not take place. Lincoln intervened and substituted the alternative penalty, exile in the South.[55] In this fashion some element of humor might be injected into what promised to be a serious business.

The results of Burnside's action were not to be averted so easily. Whatever may have been the theoretical wisdom of General Order Number 38, it gave the peace party a fighting issue. Previously the suppression of free speech, the suspension of *habeas corpus,* and the formula of a military court were mere abstractions; now they were personified in the leader of the peace Democracy. Vallandigham became a martyr. The cause of peace was thereby advanced for the crowd is always more easily influenced by a personality than a principle. A symbol has a greater appeal than a theory. The repercussions of the arrest spread throughout the country. In New York there was a deal of wild talk. At a mass meeting in Albany a letter from Governor Seymour was read which asserted that Vallandigham's arrest is "revolution" and establishes military despotism.[56] Before a similar gathering in New York City, the speakers were even bolder. McMaster, the editor of the *Freeman's Journal,* for statements in which he had been recently imprisoned in Fort Lafayette, said that the war had failed, that it would

[55] *Official Records of the Union and Confederate Armies,* Series II, Vol. V, p. 657.
[56] Vallandigham, James L.: *Op. cit.,* pp. 288-290, a quotation from the *Atlas and Argus* containing the letter of Horatio Seymour; *New York Tribune,* May 18, 1863.

always fail, and the South could never be conquered. Edward Blankman was cheered when he threatened Lincoln, "the George III of the present day," with his Cromwell or Brutus.[57] This emotional outburst was supplemented by a meeting under Fernando Wood's guidance, which demanded a suspension of the war and the summoning of two conventions—one North and one South —for the purpose of reconciliation.[58] When he was unable to force this policy upon the Democratic party of the state, he repudiated the party's platform.[59] In Ohio the persecution of Vallandigham delivered the Democracy into the hands of the peace men. His arrest swept away the last vestiges of opposition, all rival candidates were withdrawn, and at a gigantic mass meeting at Columbus, Vallandigham and Pugh were nominated to head the state ticket in the campaign of 1863.[60] The Republicans were so desperate that they nominated a War Democrat for the governorship. The Ohio campaign thus became an index of the strength of the peace movement. The nation watched with interest. An enormous total vote reflected the importance of the issue. Brough, the candidate of the Union party, received 288,374 votes and Vallandigham 187,492.[61] The peace drive was defeated. In spite of the outcome the election was a painful

[57] Vallandigham, James L.: *Op. cit.*, pp. 290-293, a quotation from the *World; New York Tribune,* May 20, 1863.

[58] *New York Tribune,* June 4, 1863; *New York Herald,* June 4, 1863.

[59] *New York Tribune,* November 3, 1863.

[60] Porter, G. H.: *Op. cit.*, pp. 167-168, 170; Vallandigham, James L.: *Op. cit.*, pp. 302-304.

[61] Greeley, Horace: *The American Conflict, a History of the Great Rebellion in the United States of America,* 1860-1863, p. 509, notes 54, 55, 56.

surprise to Lincoln.[62] Vallandigham's vote was impressive in itself and it was 3,000 larger than the Democratic vote of 1861. The national administration might have been even more disheartened if it had foreseen the further results of the Ohio election. The peace party was now convinced that it was impossible for it to obtain their ends by open and legal methods; it was driven into the adoption of other means. There was a recrudescence of the secret society movement.

Secret societies, whose purpose was opposition to the war aims and the war methods of the government, had been in existence before 1863 and 1864. They had existed under various names at various times,[63] but all of them had apparently developed from one parent organization, the Knights of the Golden Circle. The Knights of the Golden Circle had been founded before the Civil War to effect the conquest of Mexico and to "render it subservient to the march of American civilization." It was the creation of Dr. George W. L. Bickley, a practicing physician and professor of *Materia Medica* in the Eastern Medical College of Cincinnati, and under his direction the membership had been recruited largely in the Southern states. With the advent of the Civil war the purpose of the order was no longer the conquest of Mexico. It became the ally of the Confederate cause.[64]

[62] Welles, Gideon M.: *Diary of Gideon Welles*, Vol. I, p. 470.

[63] *Official Records of the Union and Confederate Armies*, Series II, Vol. VII, pp. 931-932. Among the various names were: Mutual Protection Society, Circle of Honor, and Circle or Knights of the Mighty Host. In Missouri it was known as the Corps de Belgique; in Chicago, the Democratic Invincible Club; in Louisville, the Democratic Reading Room.

[64] Fesler, Mayo: "Secret Political Societies in the North during the Civil War," in the *Indiana Magazine of History*, Vol. XIV, pp. 190-191, 198-199.

Another doctor, William A. Bowles of Indiana, whose wife came from New Orleans and owned slaves, was responsible for the introduction of the order into his own state.[65] From there it spread into all the Middle Western states. The Knights of the Golden Circle was always a loose organization and lacked leaders of initiative; and, in spite of many acts of violence traceable to its activity, it is probable that the majority of its small membership were not traitors but simply opponents of the policies of the government.[66]

In the spring of 1863 the Knights of the Golden Circle underwent a transformation at the hands of Phineas C. Wright, formerly a resident of New Orleans, now a resident and lawyer of St. Louis. The legal discipline, however, did not crush his exuberant fancy. He possessed in an unusual degree the American genius for organizing fraternal and secret societies. His imagination made it easy for him to devise a mysterious hierarchy with suitable titles and degrees and his gift for turgid thought and rhetoric made simple the elaboration of a luxuriant ritual.[67] The new organization was christened the Order of American Knights. There were five degrees, the first three of which—the Vestibule, the Temple, and the Inner

[65] Foulke, William D.: *Life of Oliver P. Morton, including his important Speeches,* Vol. I, pp. 279-280.

[66] Foulke, William D.: *Op. cit.,* Vol. I, pp. 273-278. The "battle of Pogue's Run" at Indianapolis, May 20, 1863, showed the weakness of the Knights of the Golden Circle. At a great mass meeting for peace, engineered in part by the desperate members of the order, the crowd was broken up by eight or ten soldiers, and a search for weapons carried on by a small squad of soldiers. The whole episode is so ridiculous that it is a wonder that the order was ever taken seriously.

[67] Marshall, John A.: *American Bastile, a History of the Illegal Arrests and Imprisonment of American Citizens during the late Civil War,* pp. 218, 227.

Temple—were open to all members.[68] The instructions which the Neophyte received on his journey through these degrees were of a state's rights nature; the oaths which he took illustrate the nature and the appeal of the order. For the second degree, after he had listened to a discussion on slavery, rather Southern in tone, he took an oath, "to take up arms in the cause of the oppressed—*in my country first of all*—against any Monarch, Prince, Potentate, Power, or Government usurped," which is waging war against a people who have founded a government based *upon the eternal principles of Truth*.[69] The candidate then received further instruction in state's rights principles and the proper attitude toward slavery and promised ever to "cherish the sublime lessons which the sacred emblems of our order suggest, and will, so far as in me lies, impart those lessons to the people of the earth, where the acorn falls from its parent bough, in whose visible firmament the Orion and Arcturus ride in their resplendent glories, and where the Southern Cross dazzles the eye with its coruscations of golden light, fit emblem of truth." [70] All this wordiness does not sound dangerous, and the mentality which is fascinated by the hocuspocus of Orion, Arcturus, and the Southern Cross, is not one which characterizes traitors. In fact the membership was composed largely of ignorant Democrats who were attracted by the glitter of a secret order and thought

[68] *Official Records of the Union and Confederate Armies*, Series II, Vol. VII, pp. 643-644.

[69] Pitman, Benn (Editor): *The Trials for Treason at Indianapolis, disclosing the plans for establishing a North-Western Confederacy*, p. 300.

[70] *Official Records of the Union and Confederate Armies*, Series II, Vol. VII, p. 294.

it a legitimate means for remedying their grievances and for securing protection against the draft or military arrest.[71] The last two degrees—The Grand Degree and the Supreme Degree—were conferred upon state and national officers, and it was these officers alone who knew of the more extreme military and treasonable plans of the secret orders.[72]

Phineas C. Wright organized lodges in Missouri, Illinois, and Indiana, and then went East in January, 1864, to become a member of the editorial staff of Wood's journal, the *Daily News*. Here he organized the New York Knights with James A. McMaster of the *Freeman's Journal* as Grand Commander.[73] At about the same time two leaders of the organization visited Vallandigham in Canada, whither he had returned from his burlesque Southern exile, inducted him into the order and requested his permission to promote his candidacy for the office of Supreme Commander. He consented and suggested certain changes in the organization. The name became the Sons of Liberty, and the ritual, less rhetorical, demanded

[71] *Official Records of the Union and Confederate Armies,* Series II, Vol. VII, pp. 629-631, 634, 639.

[72] House of Representatives, 39th Congress, 2nd Session, Executive Documents, No. 50, pp. 542-545. The impossibility of securing a general uprising, a plan several times proposed and attempted in the summer of 1864 by the leaders of the organization shows that the rank and file had little knowledge of or sympathy with the designs of the men at the head of the orders. Brigadier-General Carrington in the course of a report written in the course of that year submitted evidence "of the purpose of some of the worst of these men to do mischief, independent of the general plan of the order." *Official Records of the Union and Confederate Armies,* Series I, Vol. XXXIX, Part II, p. 293.

[73] House of Representatives, 39th Congress, 2nd Session, Executive Documents, No. 50, pp. 519, 522; *Official Records of the Union and Confederate Armies,* Series II, Vol. VII, p. 933.

of candidates for the Vestibule Degree simply allegiance to the Jeffersonian doctrine that the Federal government was one of delegated powers; of candidates for the First Degree, the promise to resent the exercise of unconstitutional "war powers"; and of candidates for the Degree of First Conclave, a subscription to the Kentucky and Virginia Resolutions of 1798 and 1799.[74] The romantic glamor of secrecy makes it difficult to estimate the extent of this movement. It must be remembered that the exposure of the order was partisan, and that the exposure was exploited for partisan purposes. To exaggerate the number of these "traitors" was good politics for the Republican "saviors" of the country. This factor, coupled with the credulity of Judge Advocate General Holt, who supervised the investigation, perhaps quadrupled the number of "Knights" and "Sons" of all varieties. Many professed to believe that the total membership reached 500,000 men.[75] But these large numbers never mate-

[74] Pitman, Benn: *Op. cit.*, pp. 302, 304, 306-307.

[75] A few estimates will illustrate the variations in the number of members in the orders. The testimony of Charles E. Dunn, Second in Council in the State of Missouri, places the numbers in Illinois at 100,000; Indiana, 125,000; Ohio, 40,000; Michigan, 20,000; and Missouri, 10,000. The total of these states was therefore 295,000. He was uninformed as to the other states. (*Official Records of the Union and Confederate Armies*, Series II, Vol. VII, pp. 629-630.) Vallandigham informed Thompson in June, 1864, that there were 85,000 Sons of Liberty in Illinois, 50,000 in Indiana, and 40,000 in Ohio. (Castleman, John B.: *Active Service*, p. 144.) Judge Advocate General Holt quotes as "much nearer the correct total" Vallandigham's estimate given by him in an address at Dayton. This total was near 500,000 men, divided as follows: in Indiana from 75,000 to 125,000; in Illinois, from 100,000 to 140,000; in Ohio, from 80,000 to 108,000; in Kentucky from 40,000 to 70,000; in Missouri from 20,000 to 40,000; and in Michigan and New York about 20,000 each. (*Official Records of the Union and Confederate Armies*, Series II, Vol. VII, p. 935.) A letter from J. W. Tucker to Jefferson Davis on March 4, 1864, says that the total number

rialized when they were needed. In the summer of 1864 James A. McMaster was investigating the order in the West. He was certainly no hostile critic. After attending a meeting of the Supreme Council in Chicago, he called it a "humbug" and after visiting the order in the counties of Illinois, where it was supposed to be particularly strong, he declared that the strength of the organization was a "myth." [76]

Whether organized in societies or not, the peace Democrats were, nevertheless, a factor to be considered. They bore to the Democracy the same relation as the bitterenders bore to the Republicans. Vallandigham had almost as little use for the contradictions of August Belmont, a conservative Democrat, as Benjamin Wade had for the equivocal leniency of Abraham Lincoln. Like his Republican prototype, the extreme Democrat wished to impose his radical principles upon his own party. He wished to sweep away compromise and evasion, and substitute in their place a frank and daring avowal of a peace-at-any-price policy. At last opportunity was at hand for the attainment of that desire. The Democratic National Convention would have to nominate a presidential candidate and write a party platform in the decisive year of 1864.

The first clarification of the tangled issues of that year took place within the Republican party. If sheer noise

is 490,000 divided as follows: in Illinois, 110,000; in Indiana, 120,000; in Ohio, 40,000; in Iowa, 15,000; in Pennsylvania, 40,000; in New York, 40,000; and in New Jersey, 15,000. (Davis, Jefferson: *Jefferson Davis, Constitutionalist, His Letters, Speeches, and Papers* (Edited by Dunbar Rowland), Vol. VI, pp. 204-205.

[76] House of Representatives, 39th Congress, 2nd Session, Executive Documents, No. 50, p. 520.

were a measure of strength, the bitter-enders would have been powerful indeed. The first part of the year saw them in full blast against the President. The Committee on the Conduct of the War was reorganized and inspired with a new hostility. A bill, sponsored by Henry Winter Davis, a new recruit to the ranks of the extremists, was designed to thrust aside the executive plans of reconstruction and substitute harsher measures. A few were covertly nursing an intrigue to nominate another candidate for the presidency. In February, 1864, it was prematurely discovered that the object of their affection was none other than Salmon P. Chase, Secretary of the Treasury. So great was his desire for office and so exaggerated his notion of his own indispensability, that he saw no impropriety in being at one time a member of Lincoln's official family and a rival for the presidential nomination. Thoughts of official decency were not apt to bother the radicals. It sufficed for them that Chase had always been a man of extreme principles and that he had supported extreme measures.

Suddenly the anti-Lincoln movement subsided. To be sure a faction of a faction determined to secede from the party and nominate candidates in sympathy with its radical principles. This group found its chief strength in Missouri where the last vestiges of party solidarity had crumbled away in the unscrupulous warfare of extremists and conservatives; and in New York where the intensity of party strife over patronage, personalities, and principles almost rivaled that of the border state of the West. There were numerous calls for the convention which finally met in Cleveland on May 31, 1864. Of the motley crew of self-appointed delegates, the larger portion came from the West. The platform which they adopted demanded the immediate freedom of the slaves, the preservation of the Union, the assertion of the Monroe Doctrine, Congressional rather than executive reconstruction, a single term for president, and the confiscation of the lands of the rebels for distribution among the soldiers and actual settlers. Having thus appealed to all possible sources of radical discontent, the convention nominated for president John C. Fremont, the "Pathfinder," author of the Missouri emancipation proclamation and Major-General in the army; and for vice-president, John C. Cochrane of New York, whom the sarcastic Secretary of the Navy said had been everything—"a Democrat, a Barnburner, a conservative, an Abolitionist, an Anti-abolitionist, a Democratic Republican, and now a radical Republican." [77] But the great bulk of the bitter-enders did not ally itself with such "cranks" and "turn-coats." They had made up their minds to accept Lincoln. Why did strong warriors suddenly grow so weak?

Simply because they discovered that Lincoln, not they, represented the people who had the votes. They admitted their humiliation ruefully. When a caller at the White House in April found that even the occupants of the President's waiting room were "roasting" Lincoln, he asked the hottest critic, Henry Lane Wilson, Senator from Massachusetts, why he did not oppose the President. Senator Wilson replied that the whole North stood with

[77] *New York Tribune,* May 31, 1864, June 1, 1864; Nicolay, John G., and Hay, John: *Abraham Lincoln, a History,* Vol. IX, pp. 29-43; Welles, Gideon: *Diary of Gideon Welles,* Vol. II, p. 43.

the President and would renominate him and "bad as that would be, the best must be made of it." [78]   Another radical, returning disappointed from the Republican convention, said of the choice of Johnson as Vice President that his "nomination, however, like that of Mr. Lincoln, seemed to have been preordained by the people." [79]   The bitter-enders, confronted by this tide of popular support, abandoned their gestures and their rhetoric and climbed aboard the glittering band-wagon.   The Republican National Convention in June, 1864, was a love feast.   The delegates could not wait for parliamentary forms to renominate the President; they chafed at roll-calls and rulings by the Chair; there were countless attempts at a choice by acclamation.   Finally, with only scattering opposition, the convention (to paraphrase the nominating sentences of Cook of Illinois) "again presents to the loyal people of this nation, for President of the United States, Abraham Lincoln.   God bless him." [80]

This nomination was more than a personal triumph. It was an earnest that the party, which was committed to the continuation of the war, was to be led by an advocate of peace without punishment.   In spite of this assurance, the outcome of the election was not yet settled.   There was an alternative to Lincoln in the nominee of the Democratic party.   At present that alternative was but an apparition for the warring factions of the Democracy had come to no agreement.   The conservative Democrats were pursuing a policy of expediency.   They believed that the pos-

[78] Riddle, Albert G.: *Recollections of War Times Reminiscence of Men and Events in Washington, 1860-1865*, pp. 266-267.

[79] Julian, George W.: *Political Recollections, 1840-1872*, p. 243.

[80] Johnson, Charles W.: *Proceedings of the First Three Republican National Conventions of 1856, 1860, and 1864*, pp. 227-235.

sibility of party success rested primarily upon the military situation. If the northern armies were victorious, Lincoln would be reëlected whoever his opponent might be. So much was obvious. If the Union armies met with reverses, popular discontent with the administration might be so great that the election of 1864 would result in a Republican defeat. If such were to be the case, the conservatives wished as a candidate a man who would shear away from the Northern cause its radical excrescences of emancipation and confiscation and who would seek a peace on the old basis of the preservation of the Union. They were, therefore, eager to postpone the nominations until the summer military campaign had proved itself a success or a failure. To the peace men within the Democratic ranks all times and all occasions were alike. There was a need for an immediate declaration of a thoroughgoing peace policy.[81] No better occasion for the statement of that policy existed than the convocation of the National Convention at the time originally set for it, June, 1864. Thus the battle was joined. In the preliminary skirmishes the conservative Democrats won. The papers of June 23 carried an announcement from the National Committee, signed by August Belmont, postponing the Convention until August 29.[82] For two months, at least, the peace Democrats were denied the chance of immediately converting their party to the pacifist cause.

While in the midst of this checkmate, the nation was astounded to discover that peace negotiations with the

[81]Birdsall, D. C.: "McClellan and the Peace Party," in the *Century Magazine*, Vol. XVIII, pp. 638-639.
[82]*New York Tribune*, June 23, 1864.

Confederacy were being conducted, not by disgruntled members of an opposition party but by the editor of the most influential Republican newspaper in the North. The midsummer madness, which had so often before affected the Union cause, again fell upon it.

CHAPTER II

THE PEACE MISSIONS OF TWO NORTHERN JOURNALISTS

By July 1864 Canada harbored a small group of bizarre personages assembled from the Federal Union and from the Confederate States of America. There were Northern traitors and politicians, Southern gentlemen and representatives, intriguers and conspirators of unknown allegiance, Confederate soldiers, escaped from Northern prisons, spies, adventurers, and an imbecile from Europe and Colorado. They came for different motives and by different paths. But suddenly the raveled threads of their separate purposes were tied together by the unexpected arrival of Horace Greeley, editor of the *New York Tribune*. His presence united these diverse characters into peace negotiations of significant importance.

The reasons which compelled Greeley to become a conspicuous peacemaker must not be sought in the immediate situation of June and July, 1864. That situation simply brought to the surface the fundamental forces which animated a personality which has baffled both contemporaries and posterity. This perplexity has been occasioned by the contradictions of the man. A popular biography of Horace Greeley prints an illustration of the arrival of young Greeley in New York City, a young apprentice in search of work. It is the conventional picture which contrasts the gawky country boy, clad in ill-

51

105569

fitting clothes and carrying a cloth bundle, with the new
and strange surroundings of the big city.[1] This sense of
incongruity, Greeley always created to the end of his
days. His clothes, particularly his cravat, were usually
carelessly arranged; he shuffled as he walked; and the
large ill-formed face with its pale blue eyes and its fringe
of white hair around the chin, completed the picture of
rusticity. He never lost, as he once put it, his "ver-
dancy." There was always about him a lack of sophisti-
cation and of self-consciousness, a bewildering naturalness
and straightforwardness, and, if you will, a certain child-
ishness. Yet this man was the successful editor of a great
metropolitan newspaper. No wonder that such a personality amused and baffled more disillusioned and more
complicated people.

The contradictory character of Greeley was fashioned
by two influences. The first was the narrowness of his
early life. The Greeley family knew all too well "the
manly, American sort of poverty." First they had tried
through ceaseless industry to wring a living from a hard-
scrabble farm in New Hampshire; then they moved to
Vermont where the father failed to earn adequate support
as an agricultural laborer; and finally they sought a
refuge, as other Americans had done, in the promise which
the West offered them. But when the family moved to
Western Pennsylvania, there to hew out a farm from the
wilderness, Greeley was left behind as an apprentice to a
local newspaper.[2] Then followed years of wandering ap-
prenticeship, of poverty, of varied and often bitter expe-

[1] Ingersoll, L. D.: *The Life of Horace Greeley*, p. 54.
[2] Greeley, Horace: *Recollections of a Busy Life*, pp. 48-50, 55-56,
61-62.

rience before Greeley started on his great career as an editor and publisher. A life lived so near the mere level of existence left an ineffable impression upon the mind of a delicate child and a sensitive youth. For to read the record of Greeley's life is to become increasingly aware of the influence which his health had upon him. In his boyhood days he was made ill by the sight of falling rain; in the letters which he wrote in the full years of his manhood, there is frequent reference to his fearful headaches and to his nervous exhaustion. Even in trivialities these physical weaknesses shaped his thoughts and directed his acts. At the age of five he took a few puffs at the stub of a black cigar which had been left by some guest at a New Year's party, and he was made deathly sick. Years later he wrote without a trace of humor, "From that hour to this, the chewing, smoking, or snuffing of tobacco has seemed to me, if not the most pernicious, certainly the vilest, most detestable abuse of his corrupted sensual appetites whereof depraved man is capable." [3] He disapproved of checkers, chess, cards and backgammon because they tended to impair the digestion and excite headaches.[4] It is equally significant that he chose walking as his favorite sport and that he wrote down in true scientific fashion the proper rules for pedestrians.[5] Finally it is the same factor which turned the Greeley family into a family of amateur dietitians. They early fell under the influence of Sylvester Graham, a Presbyterian minister, who advocated a vegetarian diet, eschewed the stimulants —coffee and tea—and finally gave his name to a process

[3] Greeley, Horace: *Op. cit.*, p. 98.
[4] *Ibid.*, p. 118.
[5] *Ibid.*, pp. 76-77.

of milling grain.   For a time Greeley joined an eating
club run on the "Graham System" and the vagaries of
the Greeley table were always a source of wonder to his
guests.[6]   Since the weakness of Greeley's body underlay
so many of his derided notions, it is logical to assume that
it was the cause of more fundamental traits—his nervous
excitability, his volatile temperament, his intense alterna-
tions of joy and despair.

The hardships of Greeley's early life and his heightened
sensitivity combined to create in Greeley's character a
great human sympathy and a wide human generosity.
Deprivation and want, true or fictitious, always appealed
to him.   He was forever loaning money; he was a notorious easy-mark.   In fact he did not wait to be asked.
In a letter to a friend, he once wrote, "Won't you have
some money?   I earn a great deal and two-thirds of it
goes every way to all manner of loafers—why not you?
I would rather send you $50 than not if you will let
me—say so and I will do it.   I long ago quit wanting
to be rich—I never did want to live extravagantly.   I
own a house; some mining stocks which mean to be good
some time; and a quarter of the *Tribune* which *pays*, not
to speak of any number of I.O.U.'s that *don't* pay
and won't—they'd see me in heaven first." [7]   It was this
generosity, this sensitiveness to the human need which
drove Greeley into the field of socialism.   His observation
of the lot of the poor, the destitute, and the unemployed
during the panic years of 1837-1838 had touched his
heart.   He read the works of Fourier, St. Simon, and

---

[6] Greeley, Horace: *Op. cit.,* pp. 103-105.
[7] *Proceedings at the Unveiling of a Memorial to Horace Greeley at
Chappaqua, New York,* February 3, 1914, p. 198.

Owen; his paper published articles on Fourierism by A. Brisbane, a wealthy radical; Greeley devoted time and energy to the North American Phalanx at Red Bank, New Jersey, a socialistic experiment conducted on the same lines as Brook Farm. It is only fair to add that if this picture puts Greeley solely as an aspiring idealist, he wrote a little later that he supported socialism simply to attract the progressive elements to the Whig party.[8]

These socialistic activities were but concrete manifestations of Greeley's spontaneous and optimistic belief in the future of the world and of mankind. In its narrower aspects this faith degenerated into a complacent acceptance of mere material progress. Greeley scorned the "good old days" before the use of the railroad. He rhapsodized at the sight of the mechanical inventions at the European exhibitions he visited.[9] Always most dear to his heart was agriculture and he foresaw that occupation transformed from a "mindless, monotonous drudgery" into an "ennobling, liberalizing, intellectual pursuit." The bucolic Utopia will arrive when farming is performed by large bands rendered picturesque by uniforms and inspired by music.[10] In its larger aspects, Greeley's hope for the perfectibility of men and the progress of the universe was translated to the plane of a religion which explained suffering as transitional and disciplinary and evil as preparation for the greater holi-

---

[8] Barnes, T. W.: *Memoir of Thurlow Weed*, pp. 92-93, Greeley to Weed, February 19, 1841.

[9] Greeley, Horace: *Op. cit.*, pp. 269-270.

[10] Greeley, Horace: *Op. cit.*, pp. 293-294; Ingersoll, L. D.: *Op. cit.*, p. 268.

ness and happiness which was to follow. The lines of Tennyson were a precise summary of his ideals.

"Oh yet we trust that somehow good
Will be the final goal of ill." [11]

He had the true background for a rampant reformer.

Greeley's personality impressed itself upon the country through the medium of the *New York Tribune*. Although he took to newspaper work from his youth, his first real editorial adventure was the *New Yorker*, a weekly journal devoted to literature, digested news, and summarized election returns.[12] Then followed various campaign and political sheets. In 1841 the *New York Tribune* published its first issue. In New York there were already many papers but most of them were expensive six-penny sheets and hence were not for the ordinary reader. The *Tribune's* only rivals in its own field were the *New York Sun* and the *New York Herald*—the first was hardly a journal in the complete sense of the word, and the latter had degenerated into a medium of indecency and sensationalism under the able leadership of James Gordon Bennett. Into this vacuum the *Tribune* rushed to, "labour to advance the interests of the People and to promote their Moral, Social and Political well-being. The immoral and degrading Police Reports, Advertisements and other matter which have been allowed to disgrace the columns of our leading Penny Papers, will be carefully excluded from this, and no exertion spared to render it worthy of the hearty approval of the virtuous and refined, and a welcome visitant at the family fire-

[11] Ingersoll, L. D.: *Op. cit.,* pp. 71-73.
[12] *Ibid.,* pp. 94-99. The first issue was published in 1834.

side." [13] For a short while, indeed, it seemed that the *Tribune* would not survive to fulfill its worthy purposes; the first week it lost $433; it had only 500 subscribers and took in only $92. The assets of the editor were $2000.[14] But friends furnished funds to carry him over the crisis,[15] and by 1856 there were over 280,000 subscribers and a few years later the annual receipts were over $500,000.[16]

For an idealist and a reformer, this was a tremendous practical success. To what can it be attributed? The *Tribune's* financial security and policy can be safely ascribed to others; [17] but its success, as a newspaper, must be given to Horace Greeley. He determined its policy. In the collection of news, he utilized the best methods available; there was a well organized bureau at Washington; his news columns were supplemented by an able array of special correspondents. Thomas Hughes, the author of *Tom Brown*, wrote his London letters; from New England, he brought Margaret Fuller, the versatile transcendentalist, to describe the conditions of the New York poor; from Spain Emilio Castelar, who later became the Premier of that country, was correspondent; and then at

[13] Ingersoll, L. D.: *Op. cit.*, p. 111. This is one paragraph of the announcement of the publication of the *Tribune* in the *Log Cabin* of April 3, 1841.

[14] *Ibid.*, pp. 114-115; Greeley, Horace: *Op. cit.*, p. 139.

[15] Pike, James S.: *First Blows of the Civil War*, p. 349.

[16] *New York Tribune*, February 1, 1864.

[17] Ingersoll, L. D.: *Op. cit.*, pp. 114-115. A great deal of the financial success of the *Tribune* was due to Thomas McElrath who had been one of the partners in the publishing house for which Greeley worked when he first came to New York. It was he who loaned money to the *Tribune* in its days of difficulty. He also owned twenty-five shares out of the one hundred shares of *Tribune* stock. Greeley likewise owned twenty-five shares. The other shares were distributed among editors and workmen.

home he enlisted as assistant editors Henry J. Raymond and Charles A. Dana, both of whom were to quarrel with their employer and to go forth, the one to create the *New York Times* and the other to revive the *New York Sun*.[18] But these were only partial explanations of his success. Greeley's experience had given him that indefinable quality called "news sense." He knew what the people wanted to read and he knew how to satisfy their desires. In his letters to Pike, whom he had first employed as Washington correspondent, there is revealed in illuminating glimpses the full measure of the master's wisdom. Comment "on any thing spicy or interesting" and let "the readers make the right comments, rather than see that you are making them." "Everybody from Mother Eve's time down, has been especially anxious to know what ought not to be known, and we must get some of it into the *Tribune* or be voted dull, indolent, and behind the times."[19]

Greeley, moreover, possessed the knack of self-advertisement. Whatever concerned him, he made of concern and interest to his readers. Was the *Tribune* plant destroyed by fire, to the readers it was described as a personal loss to all of the family.[20] Did the editor jauntily observe Europe or admire the West, the accounts appeared in the

[18] Ingersoll, L. D.: *Op. cit.*, pp. 120-124, 127-132; Howard, Oliver; "Address," in the *Proceedings at the Unveiling of a Memorial to Horace Greeley at Chappaqua, New York*, February 3, 1914, p. 94; Rand, Chester S.: "Some Recollections of Horace Greeley," in the *Proceedings at the Unveiling of a Memorial to Horace Greeley at Chappaqua, New York*, February 3, 1918, p. 225.

[19] Pike, James S.: *Op. cit.*, pp. 41, 48-50. Greeley to Pike, April 24, 1850, May 1, 1850.

[20] *New York Tribune*, February 6, 1845.

Tribune as letters to the home-folks. Did he make a public appearance as a speaker, the *Tribune* contained details in advance of the place and time of meeting and afterwards accounts of his remarks.[21] It was this same projection of his personality that made the editorial page the force that it was. At a time when the conduct of both newspapers and politics was so much a matter of personality, Greeley's capabilities were unquestioned. He treated his opponents with a satire and ridicule that was made all the more irritating by his own ingenuity at apparently remaining consistent, or by his ability to slip out of the grasp that closed upon him and begin the attack upon a new quarter. In controversy Greeley would bend double but he would not break. To his taunts and jeers he added a dogmatic and infallible air which gave to his editorials the nature of indisputable common sense. A favorite device was to start with a generally accepted proposition and then lead by a series of specious reasonings to a very unaccepted conclusion. So imperceptible are the ellipses of writing and thought, that the reader is unaware of the transition which has been accomplished. Though they may have been ungrammatical, the pungent, biting, superficially logical editorials of Greeley of the *Tribune* were the daily gospel of an impressive subscription list.

It is now possible to trace the way in which these various personal factors determined Horace Greeley's attitude toward the Civil War, and which made him the leading

<hr/>

[21] Ingersoll, L. D.: *Op. cit.*, p. 260. The first lecture Greeley ever gave was announced in the *Tribune* of January 3, 1843, in a characteristic fashion. "Horace Greeley will lecture before the New York Lyceum at the Tabernacle, this evening. Subject 'Human Life.' The lecture will commence at half past 7, precisely. If those who care to hear it will sit near the desk, they will favour the lecturer's harsh and husky voice."

participant in the peace negotiations at Niagara Falls.
It is not surprising that the period of the Civil War was
an unhappy one for Greeley for it set at odds within his
own mind irreconcilable desires and ideals. On the one
hand he had a profound abhorrence of warfare. Tem-
peramentally he was a pacifist. Convinced as he was of
the perfectibility of man and the goodness of God, war
seemed inexplicable and unrighteous. So when the prospect of the Civil War first confronted him, Greeley
jumped to the non-resistant position. In an editorial of
November 9, 1860, he wrote: "If the cotton States shall
decide that they can do better out of the Union than in it,
we insist on letting them go in peace. The right to secede
may be a revolutionary one but it exists nevertheless. . . .
Whenever a considerable section of the Union shall deliberately resolve to go out, we shall resist all coercive measures designed to keep it in. We hope never to live in a
republic whereof one section is pinned to the residue by
bayonets." [22]

On the other hand expediency whispered to Greeley
that it would be a better policy for the *Tribune* to be a
loyal rather than a disloyal newspaper. And then there
was that line of Tennyson's, "Somehow good will be the
final goal of ill." Might not warfare be justified if
through it slavery were abolished? Greeley desired
emancipation passionately. Though he had been slow to
assume the position of the abolitionist, he had taken it
with earnestness and zeal. He progressed to the most
extreme principles. He denounced the slaveholders in no
unmeasured terms, opposed all proposals for the conservative solution of the negro problem, and became the

[22] *New York Tribune,* November 9, 1860.

enthusiastic advocate of the equality of the black and the white man.   Might not the continuance of the war be justified if it was for the purpose of universal freedom? An answer to that question was given in the list of reasons which Greeley advanced for writing his monumental history of the Rebellion.   "In fact, not till the War was placed on its true basis of a struggle for liberation, and not conquest, by President Lincoln's successive Proclamations of Freedom, would I have consented to write its history." [23]   It was this bridge of reconciliation which enabled Greeley, the peace lover, to ballyhoo with the loudest militarist.   Throughout the war the calm of the *New York Tribune* was shattered by the most violent and sudden blasts of the war trumpet.   Such was the "On to Richmond" cry in the summer of 1861.   The failure of that campaign left Greeley characteristically prostrated and "all but insane." [24]   Such were his clarion calls in 1864 for the enlistment of 500,000 men in a gigantic crusade which was to be trained in the North and then converge upon the South to annihilate all resistance.[25]   Then when he saw that his measures were not adopted and that defeat met the Federal armies, he would swing back to his pacific position.   The dark days early in 1863 filled him with foreboding and anxiety.   He looked with complacency upon the possibility of peace, the mediation of foreign powers, and expressed his willingness to submit all questions to the arbitration of Switzerland and to abide by her decision.[26]   Chancellorsville found him desperate.

[23] Greeley, Horace: *Recollections of a Busy Life,* p. 421.

[24] Conway, M. D.: *Autobiography, Memories, and Experiences,* Vol. I, p. 336, Greeley to Conway, August 17, 1861.

[25] *New York Tribune,* July 15, 1864.

[26] *Ibid.*   January 14, 22, 30, 1863; February 13, 1863.

When he heard the news of this disaster, he exclaimed, "My God! it is horrible—horrible; and to think of it, 130,000 magnificent soldiers so cut to pieces by less than 60,000 half-starved ragamuffins!" [27] Once again all was lost. Finally in 1864 the delicate equilibrium of means and end, which the editor of the *Tribune* had devised to quiet the battle of his own ideals, was completely upset by the political and military events of that year.

Greeley was fascinated by politics. Perhaps one reason for this fascination is to be found in the fact that politics usurped in his unplayful life the place which sport has taken in the modern man. They furnished him entertainment and relaxation. Greeley certainly regarded them as the greatest game on earth. Just as a baseball fan carries in his head the batting averages of the leading hitters and the standing of the various clubs, Greeley stored his memory with election figures and with detailed knowledge of obscure constituencies. Perhaps Greeley, like so many other men successful in one field of activity, craved the complement of political achievement. To be sure he always denied that political office attracted him but his actions do not always support his denials. Although he threw himself into politics with all the intensity of his emotional nature, he did not achieve political success. Perhaps this failure was a tribute to the genius of the man; it certainly caused him a great deal of unhappiness.

That unhappiness had mounted during the course of the Civil War because of the truceless warfare within the Republican party of New York State. The leader of one of the warring factions was Greeley and the leaders

<hr>

[27] Gilmore, J. R.: *Personal Recollections of Abraham Lincoln and the Civil War,* pp. 102-103.

of the other were Seward and Weed.   The differences
between them were largely personal and, therefore, all the
more bitter.   Once these three had together formed the
powerful Whig machine of New York.   Thurlow Weed,
whose career in so many ways was a duplicate of Greeley's,
had been the dominating spirit of the triumvirate.   As
the editor of the *Albany Evening Journal*, he was interested in journalism only as a means to political power,
not for himself but for others whom he could control.   As
he once wrote to his wife his ideal in life was "to promote
worthy men as the representatives of right measures." [28]
To the practice of this purpose he brought a genius for
intrigue, a flexibility of principle which allowed him to
ally himself with political opponents, a secretiveness which
concealed his machinations, and an efficient unscrupulous-
ness as to methods by which he attained his ends.   For
the second member of the triumvirate, William H. Seward,
Weed cherished one of those blind friendships which are
so often seen in American politics.   The two became
practically identical.   "Weed is Seward and Seward is
Weed." [29]   Greeley furnished the propaganda for this
political machine.   By 1854 he felt that he was a partner
on terms of inferiority.   He was tired of being lectured
to "like a school boy"; [30] and he felt that he was not
receiving a proper reward for his efforts either in printing contracts from the State or in political offices for him-

[28] Barnes, T. W.: *Op. Cit.*, p. 110, Thurlow Weed to His Wife,
September 7, 1843.
[29] Welles, Gideon: *Diary of Gideon Welles,* Vol. I, p. 231.   "I remember that Seward on one occasion remarked in Cabinet: 'Weed is
Seward, and Seward is Weed; each approves what the other says
and does.'"
[30] Barnes, T. W.: *Op. cit.,* pp. 97-98, Greeley to Weed, September
10, 1842.

self. In 1854 the famous partnership was consequently dissolved [31] and Greeley spent the next ten years of his life in an endeavor to bring political retribution upon his perfidious friends.

The requirements of party harmony during the Civil War did nothing to still this quarrel. Since neither combatant could obliterate the other, the battle between them was waged without quarter. Greeley asserted that Weed's patriotism had been financially profitable to him.[32] Weed retaliated. Upon Greeley's friends he showered charges of bargaining with political offices, of robbing the government through fraudulent claims, and of equipping Northern armies with shoddy blankets. Greeley himself he accused of making money through illicit trading in Southern cotton [33] and characterized him as a "fanatic, dazed, muddle-headed aspirant for office." [34] It would have been fortunate if this barnyard squabble could have been confined to New York State but that was impossible. Both sides rushed to Washington to air their grievances and to secure the support of the national administration. The President, annoyed by the frequency with which such complaints were referred to him, tried his best to remain aloof, and, if action was forced upon him, to compromise. Three years of this executive impartiality had filled Greeley with a fundamental distrust of Lincoln. Seward,

[31] Barnes, T. W.: *Op. cit.*, pp. 225-227; Greeley, Horace: *Recollections of a Busy Life*, pp. 311-320.

[32] *New York Tribune*, February 16, 1863.

[33] *New York Tribune*, June 23, 1864, letter of Weed to the *Herald*, June 21, 1864; *Ibid.*, June 24, 1864, Letter of Greeley; *Ibid.*, June 25, 1864; *Ibid.*, July 2, 1864, Letter of Opdyke; Weed, T. W.: *Autobiography*, pp. 528-529.

[34] Brummer, S. D.: *Op. cit.*, p. 294, a quotation from Weed's letter to the *Albany Evening Journal*.

Greeley's irritating enemy, was Secretary of State and confidential advisor of the President. Rumor, quite justly, attributed to him the most influence of all the cabinet members. This distrust, originating from the obscure roots of personal politics, was increased by Lincoln's conservative war and peace policy. Since Greeley was as ardent an abolitionist as Wade, Chandler, and Stevens, he was distressed by the President's milk-and-water attitude toward slavery and reconstruction. Every influence combined to persuade the editor of the *Tribune* that Lincoln should not be the Republican nominee for president in the year 1864. In the early part of February, there were preliminary editorials to test out the wind; [35] and when the call for the National Convention was issued in the latter part of the month, Greeley was forced into open and definite opposition to the President's renomination.[36]

June itself reduced Greeley to desperation. Two blows shattered his hopes and stimulated his fears. In spite of his pontifical advice, the National Convention had met in Baltimore early in the month and renominated Lincoln. The effect of this popular mandate upon the editor of the *Tribune* can be detected in the bewilderment of his editorial page. Greeley at first accepted the unwelcome news with regret; [37] ten days later he admits the uncertainty of his own action but advises the anxious that it will be the direct opposite of what any ten malignant Copper-

[35] *New York Tribune*, February 7, 1864. An editorial in this issue blandly discusses the formation of Lincoln Clubs and declares their organization is unwise.

[36] *Ibid.*, February 23, 1864.

[37] *Ibid.*, June 9, 1864.

heads may desire.[38]   The end of June then uncovered
another disquieting development.   A trivial dispute over
the personnel in the New York custom house had gath-
ered such momentum that the President, in making an
appointment, had to choose between the New York factions.   In spite of the advice of Secretary Chase, whose
Department had jurisdiction of the matter, Lincoln made
his selection from the conservative faction; Chase resigned
his position, Weed was jubilant at this "gleam of sun-
shine," [39] and Greeley was in despair.[40]   The national
administration was now in open alignment with his foes.
Is it any wonder that Greeley in July considered Lincoln
wholly incompetent and unsafe?   Is it strange that
Greeley considered a war, conducted by such a leader,
destined to fail?

As if to deepen his gloom, the military situation at that
precise moment took a turn for the worse.   At the beginning of the year, Greeley, in one of his impetuous bursts
of optimism, had envisaged the Confederacy "tottering to
its downfall" [41] and had prophesied the conclusion of the
war by the first of July.   By that day of prophecy the
situation was different.   The rapid advances of Grant had
changed to a slower progress; the number of casualties
was horrifying; and Cold Harbor and Petersburg promised an indeterminate stalemate.   Then a brilliant and
showy maneuvre on the part of the Confederacy seemed
actually to overturn the proper relation of the armies.
General Early spilled suddenly out of the Shenandoah

[38] *New York Tribune,* June 20, 1864.
[39] Brummer, S. D.: *Op. cit.,* p. 393, a quotation from the *Albany Evening Journal,* June 30.
[40] *New York Tribune,* July 1, 864.
[41] *Ibid.,* January 21, 27, 1864.

valley, wiped away the inferior forces before him, and
for a moment thrust a wedge between Washington and
the North. To the detached observer of to-day, the military situation of the Union seems secure; but to nerves
wrought up by the hopes and fears of three years of war,
another disaster was threatening to overwhelm the Federal armies. Losses had been enormous, Richmond had
not fallen, the Federal capital was in danger, gold was at
a premium of 270, and the *New York Tribune* was con-
templating a rise in the subscription price to cover the
expenses of printing the paper in war time. Thus one disaster after another was undermining Greeley's conditional
allegiance to the Union. Publicly he was still for war.
Through June the *Tribune* glows with praise of Grant
and hope of Sherman. There are vigorous attacks upon
Fernando Wood and his allied Copperheads. The possibility of peace is spurned. In a controversy with the
Daily News, Greeley denies the President the constitutional power to treat with envoys from the Confederacy;
asserts that definite proposals for peace on satisfactory
terms have never been advanced by Jefferson Davis; and
calls for the continuance of the war until "they (or we)
have been beaten into a willingness to concede the vital
matter in dispute [independence]." [42]

But in the secret places of the man's heart, these sentiments did not ring true. Once more Greeley was emotion-
ally adrift. Any impulse was likely to push him in the
direction which he had taken after previous disasters of
the war—the direction of peace. As a matter of fact,
when he was penning the pro-war editorials in the
Tribune, he was already in correspondence with an old

[42] *New York Tribune*, June 8, 10, 17, 1864.

friend of his, William Cornell Jewett. On July 5, 1864,
the latter wrote to Greeley from Niagara Falls: "In reply
to your note, I have to advise having just left Hon.
George N. Sanders, of Kentucky, on the Canada side. I
am authorized to state to you, for our use only, not the
public, that two ambassadors of Davis & Co. are now in
Canada, with full and complete powers for a peace, and
Mr. Sanders requests that you come on immediately to
me, at Cataract House, to have a private interview, or if
you will send the President's protection for him and two
friends, they will come on and meet you. He says the
whole matter can be consummated by me, you, them, and
President Lincoln. . . ." [43]

The author of this ungrammatical epistle, "Wm. Cornell Jewett, of Colorado Territory, U. S. of America,"
was the son of Joseph Jewett, one of the many branches
of the prominent Jewett family of Portland, Maine.[44]
The exact nature of his connection with Colorado was a
matter of dispute between himself and other citizens of
that territory. He had gold mining interests there and
in their development had done much for the region.[45] His
opponents asserted that he was the holder of worthless
and disputed claims, a procurer of money under false pretences, and a fit person to be hailed into a police court.[46]

[43] Severance, F. H.: "The Peace Conference at Niagara Falls in 1864,"
Buffalo Historical Society Publications, Vol. XVIII, p. 83, Jewett to
Greeley, July 5, 1864.
[44] Jewett, W. C.: *The Friendly American Mediation Move, etc.*
Editorial from the *Portland Daily Advertiser*, December 20, 1862.
[45] *New York Tribune*, July 29, 1864. A letter from Jewett "To the
Citizens Now in Colorado," written from the Continental Hotel, Phila-
delphia, July 28, 1864.
[46] *Ibid.*, July 30, 1864. A letter from Edward Bliss, Commissioner of
Emigration for Colorado, reprinted from the *World* of July 29, 1864.

However that may be, the war found him sympathetic to peace and perhaps to the Confederacy. He applied to the Peace Convention in 1861 for admission as a delegate from Pike's Peak, he drew up a plan for reconciliation, and then tried to initiate peace negotiations through ex-President Fillmore.[47] Since these efforts were unappreciated at home, he departed in 1862 on his first peace mission to Europe. The autumn saw him busy in England and on the Continent trying to obtain mediation on the basis of slavery and the Union. He issued appeals to various potentates, ministers, and governments. When these failed, he left a prayer at the top of Milan Cathedral for Napoleon's "mediation fidelity," and then set sail for America after he had issued; a "National adieu to Europe—for a prison or for freedom, to battle for the re-establishment of American Liberty, through a restored Union, with Constitutional guarantees to the entire people—North and South"—an "adieu" which sought to explain "the complicated yet plain state of affairs." [48]

Canada seemed a congenial refuge for this independent negotiator, and from that haven he tried to get in touch with the leaders of the peace movement in America—Greeley, Wood, and Seymour. All of them held aloof. Greeley was especially displeased, for Jewett's letters to him were unkindly published in the *Herald* and the *Times*.[49] Back again to Europe fled Jewett and assailed in turn Napoleon III, M. Rogier, Minister of Belgian Foreign Affairs, Count Rechberg, Minister of Austro-

[47] Jewett, W. C.: *Mediation Position of France,* pp. 28-30.
[48] Jewett, W. C.: *The Friendly American Mediation Move,* pp. 4-7.
[49] Jewett, W. C.: *Mediation Position of France in Connection with a Congress of Nations,* pp. 18-20; *Mediation in America,* pp. 6-10.

Hungarian Foreign Affairs, Alexander II of Russia, Jefferson Davis, Disraeli, Queen Isabella of Spain, Palmerston, Earl Russell, and finally "His Excellency President A. Lincoln, the Hon. W. H. Seward, Secretary of State, and Cabinet of the United States of America." There is always an obstacle in the way of this imbecile optimist. At the conclusion of his travels and correspondence he came to the determination that it was England and the North; [50] by August it was only the North, and Jewett in a document which characterizes Lincoln as a "serpent tempter" whom "Satan must control" or from whom "reason has departed," determined to appeal to Vallandigham to "inaugurate an Independent, State Move." [51] On August 31, he called upon the governors to rally "under the gallant, brave, true hearted statesman Vallandigham, as Governor of Ohio." [52]   In furtherance of this design, he sailed to Canada where he met Vallandigham "nationally" with apparently unsatisfactory results.   Back again to Europe he went to encourage a Congress of Nations to settle the Civil War—a Congress favored by "God eternal and all powerful and Napoleon temporal and all powerful"; [53] and then suddenly back to the United States.   From New York City he issued an appeal on January 5, 1864, to the "American People and the Church Universal."   After passing in review "the progress of nations from the Creation," Jewett abandons his idea of European mediation and lends his support to

[50] Jewett, W. C.: *Mediation in America*, pp. 4, 12-15.

[51] Jewett, W. C.: *Mediation Address to England*, p. 5.

[52] Jewett, W. C.: *An Appeal to the Governors and People of the Northern States of America, and Representative Vallandigham.*

[53] Jewett, W. C.: *Mediation Position of France in Connection with a Congress of Nations*, pp. 5-8.

a national convention to settle the issues of the war.[54]
Colorado Jewett's activities now drift in and out of Greeley's notice. One week the indulgent editor commends
"his old acquaintance" and his efforts for Union;[55] the
next week he advises him to "go about his mining and keep
out of the newspapers";[56] on March 19 he chronicles a
visit of Jewett, "ambassador from Colorado to mankind
in general," to Buchanan.[57] Jewett seems to have wan-
dered to and from Canada to the United States, and
finally to have become associated with an equally fascinating and slightly saner adventurer, George N. Sanders
of Kentucky.

George N. Sanders, the second member of this precious
pair, was a dreamer whose illusions combined the practical and the bizarre. Long before the war, through an
ingenious intrigue, he had made his way into politics and
eventually secured an appointment as consul to London.
In that city he became famous for his lavish hospitality
and his "rabid Republicanism" which led him into a gran-
diose alliance with Victor Hugo, Ledrou Rollin, Garibaldi
and Mazzini to overthrow monarchical governments wherever found and to establish Republican principles.[58] The
Civil War enlisted the talents of this visionary in the Confederate cause. His imagination busied itself with the
invention of means for outwitting the Federal blockade of
the Southern states either "by a perfect self-protecting
freight transport and war vessel," or by a few fast mail

[54] Jewett, W. C.: *A National Appeal to the American People and the Church Universal.*
[55] *New York Tribune,* January 15, 1864.
[56] *Ibid.,* January 22, 1864.
[57] *Ibid.,* March 19, 1864.
[58] Castleman, John B.: *Active Service,* pp. 135-136.

schooners.[59] When these plans were failures, Sanders sank out of sight until he suddenly reappeared by June, 1864, in Canada. No motive for his presence there can be determined. His son, Major Reed Sanders, was a prisoner at Fort Warren and all efforts to secure his release through exchange had failed.[60] Possibly the unhappy father fancied that the "ambassadors of Davis & Co." might in their mission effect the release of his son. In such a cause he would be eager to volunteer.

With an inaccuracy to be expected from him, Colorado Jewett had misstated the number of Confederate ambassadors in Canada. There were three rather than two. The first of these to arrive was James Philemon Holcombe, sometime Professor at the University of Virginia and a Representative in the Confederate Congress. On March 14, 1864, he had been despatched from the Confederacy by way of the blockade runners and Bermuda to serve as a legal aid to various pirates, Confederates so-called, imprisoned by Great Britain at Halifax, and then to assemble Confederate prisoners, who had escaped from Northern prisons, for shipment back to their mother land. A month later, Jefferson Davis sent away two other envoys, Clement Claiborne Clay, Jr., and Jacob or "Jake" Thompson. Thompson had been given drafts for $600,000, and the two, thus liberally supplied with funds, had run the blockade to Bermuda and then had

[59] *Official Records of the Union and Confederate Navies,* Series II, Vol. II, pp. 220-222; *Ibid.,* Series II, Vol. III, pp. 579-580.

[60] *Ibid.,* Series II, Vol. VII, pp. 679-680; *New York Tribune,* September 6, 1864. Major Reed Sanders died at Fort Warren on September 5, 1864.

made their way by more peaceful means to Canada.[61] Exactly what the two men were expected to accomplish is a matter of doubt. Their instructions were verbal for written papers would be embarrassing if they were captured by the Federals and if the Canadian government was so discourteous as to investigate carefully their activities. In general they were told to harass the Northern government in every possible way. Individuals could be recruited from the Confederates in Canada or from the ranks of their unemployed sympathizers and sent into the United States to destroy military and naval stores, to fire Northern cities, to release Confederates from military prisons, and to manipulate the gold market. But it was realized that this policy of terrorism could be only spasmodic in execution and partial in success. More hope was placed upon the creation of peace sentiments in the North. To accomplish this purpose the support of newspapers was to be purchased, funds and encouragement were to be given to the peace Democrats, especially Vallandigham, in order to aid "the disruption between the Eastern and Western States in the approaching election." [62] Evidently the Davis government had hoped that propaganda in the decisive year of 1864 might create another Confederacy, embracing the states of the Ohio valley; and that the preservation of the Union and the extinction of slavery would be impossible in the face of this new defection. The human instruments chosen to carry out these

[61] *Official Records of the Union and Confederate Navies,* Series II, Vol. III, pp. 174, 1111, 1117; *Official Records of the Union and Confederate Armies,* Series I, Vol. XLIII, Part II, p. 935.

[62] *Official Records of the Union and Confederate Armies,* Series I, Vol. XLIII, Part II, pp. 930-931; *Official Records of the Union and Confederate Navies,* Series II, Vol. III, p. 1105.

extensive designs seemed rather inadequate. Clay was an inconspicuous politician, a Confederate Senator from Alabama. Thompson had never exhibited large abilities either in peace or in war. Perhaps he had emotional qualifications. His rancor against the North must have been increased by the realization that in Northern eyes the part he had played in Buchanan's cabinet made him one of the most detestable traitors in all Secessia; and his temper had not been sweetened by the memory of the destruction of his beautiful Mississippi home at the hands of Federal troops.[63] Whatever his capacities, Thompson was a fit agent of retribution.

From the first there was a lack of unity in the activities of the three agents. Holcombe had always been independent. A temperamental incompatibility between Clay and Thompson was increased by the peevishness caused by the former's ill health, and the two separated. Thompson employed his energies in the more violent aspects of his program. He talked with Vallandigham and other leaders of the Sons of Liberty, laid plans for various uprisings,[64] devised a method for rigging the gold market in New York City,[65] and elaborated means for delivering Northern jails and setting Northern cities on fire.[66] The sick Mr. Clay had meanwhile sought out the salubrious environment of Niagara Falls. Thither also came Mr. Holcombe, at leisure after the discharge of his duties and

[63] *Official Records of the Union and Confederate Armies*, Series I, Vol. XXXIX, Part I, p. 400.

[64] *Ibid.*, Series I, Vol. XLIII, Part II, p. 931; Castleman, John B.: *Active Service*, p. 145.

[65] *Ibid.*, Series I, Vol. XLIII, Part II, p. 933. He hoped to be able to export $5,000,000 through the expenditure of $25,000.

[66] *Ibid.*, p. 934.

ready to be of service. There, too, was Mr. Sanders, who
proved very congenial. These three friends now became
involved in an intrigue of their own. Politicians from
the "States" were frequent callers at their hotel, the
Clifton House, and the academic Holcombe and the specu-
lative Clay would talk over with them the possibilities
of peace, the need of an armistice, the evils of war, and
the distracted condition of the country. Sanders did little talking; rather he acted as a go-between. From his
wide range of political acquaintance in the North he sup-
plied a constant stream of visitors and in arranging interviews with them he utilized the services of the unusual
Mr. Jewett. Suddenly in the month of June, Sanders informed the commissioners that Greeley would come to
see them if they desired. Clay and Holcombe determined to let their assistants continue their efforts to arrange such a meeting and the letter from Jewett to
Greeley on July 5 was the result of this decision. Next
day a telegram to Greeley was dispatched. It read, "Will
you come here?" [67]

The insistence of this second communication from
Jewett revealed to Greeley the necessity of action. He
had before him the choice of meeting the Confederate
commissioners in Canada or of interviewing them, under
sufficient protection, somewhere in the United States.
Either alternative placed a burden of irksome responsibility upon the editor of the *Tribune;* either seemed likely
to thrust him into the foreground as a conspicuous advocate of peace. Although he longed intensely for peace, he

[67] Severance, F. H.: "The Peace Conference at Niagara Falls in 1864,"
Buffalo Historical Society Publication, Vol. XVIII, p. 84, Jewett
to Greeley.

was not willing to be its avowed protagonist. Such publicity would involve explanations and explanations are embarrassing to journalists. Perhaps the dim echo of the "On to Richmond" cry sounded in his ears and reminded him how disastrous had been his previous interference in the conduct of the war. That cry had nearly wrecked the *Tribune* and made its editor ridiculous. The result of his present dilemma was an appeal to Abraham Lincoln. On July 7, Greeley dispatched to the President Jewett's note of July 5, and accompanied it with a statement of the policy which he thought ought to be pursued. He began with a plea for the necessity of negotiations. "I venture to remind you that our bleeding, bankrupt, almost dying country also longs for peace; shudders at the prospect of fresh conscriptions, of further wholesale devastations, and of new rivers of human blood. And a widespread conviction that the government and its prominent supporters are not anxious for peace and do not improve proffered opportunities to achieve it, is doing great harm now, and is morally certain, unless removed, to do far greater in the approaching election." But these hysterical words did not mean that Greeley was scurrying to the covert of unconditional surrender. Rather the terms which he thought the President should offer were, although lenient, far from craven. Peace should be based upon the reconstruction of the Union; the abolition of slavery with $400,000,000 compensation to the slaveholders; a complete amnesty for all political offenses; the representation of the slave states to be in proportion to population; and the summons of a national convention to settle other outstanding disputes. Greeley then concludes with an expression of belief in the possibility of now obtaining a "just peace" and says, "That a frank offer by you to the insurgents of terms which the impartial will say ought to be accepted, will, at the worst, prove an immense and sorely needed advantage to the national cause; it may save us from a northern insurrection." [68] Although this remarkable letter contained some common sense, the spirit and the language were those of desperation. On the next day the *Tribune* saw fit to deny editorially the charge of the *Commercial Advertiser* that the *Tribune* was "clamoring" for peace.

The eulogists of Lincoln have their own conception of Lincoln's reaction to Greeley's letter. They picture him in·a stiff, heroic pose, convinced that to treat with an enemy, whose armies were still unconquered, was futile. There must not be a peace without victory. Such an interpretation does an injustice to the subtle and experimental wisdom of the President's policy. Lincoln was not committed in his own mind to warfare as the sole means of achieving his purpose; he was not willing to ignore the methods of diplomacy. As long as he obtained the ends to which he devoted his own character and the resources of the nation, he was indifferent to the means he utilized. On July 9, therefore, he replied to Greeley that he would issue a safe conduct for any person from the Confederacy who bore terms offering the unconditional restoration of the Union and the abandonment of slavery. Thus Greeley's multiple bases for peace were stripped away to reveal the fundamentals of the President's war and peace policy. But Lincoln's reply

[68] Nicolay, J. G., and Hay, John: *Abraham Lincoln, a History,* Vol. IX, pp. 185-187, Greeley to Lincoln, July 7, 1864 (MS.).

gave still further evidence of his sagacity. He was aware
of the resurgence of the peace movement; he was now
confronted with the disquieting disclosure that the editor
of the *Tribune* had allied himself in spirit with the peace
party. At the same time, he must have been aware of
the fictions which underlay the whole peace reasoning.
Perhaps these peace negotiations might bring to others
a similar comprehension. With these considerations in
mind, Lincoln very neatly delegated Greeley as the person to meet these commissioners and to bring them to
Washington.[69]

The correspondence which followed between the President and Greeley saw the progressive disintegration of the
latter's morale. Undoubtedly he was embarrassed by the
choice of himself as an intermediary. It made certain
the publicity which he had dreaded. This discomfort
heightened his suspicions of Lincoln's motives. He recalled other times when he felt that the President had
tricked him. "He thinks me a d——d fool," Greeley
spluttered on one such occasion, "but I am never fooled
twice by the same individual." [70] Yet his desire for peace
must have been increased by the unrolling tide of disasters.
Early was developing the preliminary success of his rebel
raid into a fuller victory. Peace was even more essential
than when Greeley appealed in the name of "our bleeding, bankrupt, almost dying country." In the face of
his confusion, Greeley's letters became constrained, full
of strange sentences. On July 10, he wrote that he did
not think the commissioners would give him their best

    [69] *Official Records of the Union and Confederate Armies,* Series III,
Vol. IV, p. 486, Lincoln to Greeley, July 9, 1864.
    [70] Gilmore, J. R.: *Personal Recollections of Abraham Lincoln and
the Civil War,* p. 98.

terms or show him their credentials. The task seemed hopeless.[71] After three days another letter gave the names of the commissioners and said they were empowered to treat for peace.[72] Lincoln, irritated by this dallying, wrote a sharp note which expressed his disappointment that nothing had been done, reiterated his terms of July 9, and closed with the statement, "I not only intend a sincere effort for peace, but I intend that you shall be a personal witness that it is made." [73] This letter he gave to John Hay, his personal secretary, who delivered it to Greeley in New York on July 16. Greeley was still nervous and intractable. He dreaded the publicity; he shrank from the ordeal of explaining everything to army officers who might happen to stop them; he disliked Lincoln's insistence upon the restoration of the Union and the abolition of slavery. To be sure these conditions were no different than the ones which Greeley himself had proposed hardly a week previous. But now they seemed annoying barriers in the path of peace. Greeley demanded a safe conduct for the commissioners which specified no preliminaries as essential for negotiation. Such was the burden of his conversation with Hay. New communications were then opened with Lincoln and, as a result, a safe conduct was finally issued which said nothing about the conditions which Lincoln had first laid down in his note of July 9, and which he had reiterated in that of July 15.[74] Although the written word was silent, Hay

[71] Nicolay, John G., and Hay, John: *Abraham Lincoln, a History,* Vol. IX, p. 188, Greeley to Lincoln, July 10, 1864 (MS.).

[72] *Ibid.,* pp. 188-189, Greeley to Lincoln, July 13, 1864 (MS.).

[73] *Official Records of the Union and Confederate Armies,* Series III, Vol. IV, p. 496.

[74] *Ibid.,* pp. 500-501.

asserts dogmatically that this final safe-conduct was in no
way intended to modify the conditions previously prescribed.[75] There was a verbal understanding to that
effect. There can be no serious doubt of the correctness
of Hay's assertion.

Greeley, at last forced into action, journeyed to Niagara Falls, engaged rooms on the American side at the
International Hotel, and then opened communications
with the Continental diplomat, William Cornell Jewett,
lodged in Canada at the Cataract House. Through him
on July 17 Greeley apprises the commissioners of his arrival. He had a safe-conduct for them if they were duly
accredited and had propositions for peace; if they wished
to go to Washington, he would accompany them at the
earliest time of their convenience. There was no mention of the terms which Lincoln and he had discussed.[76]
This note caused embarrassment to Clay and Holcombe,
for neither of them was an accredited representative.
They were at a loss to discover how they had acquired
this character, but finally decided that it was due either
to the fertile imagination of Jewett or else to Dame
Rumor. To admit their unofficial character, however,
would have consequences damaging to their "delicate mission." If Greeley's note was to be trusted, Lincoln was
willing to accept a negotiated peace. His proffer of the
olive branch would thus quiet disaffection in the North
and weaken the peace party. Holcombe, Clay, and
Thompson had been sent to Canada to bring about an
entirely different result. Even more harassing was the

[75] Nicolay, John G., and Hay, John: *Abraham Lincoln, a History,*
Vol. IX, p. 190.
[76] *Ibid.,* pp. 190-191, Greeley to the Commissioners, July 17, 1864.

certainty that news of Lincoln's willingness to make peace
would reach the South and incite the malcontents there
to demand the inauguration of a peace movement. Some
action was clearly necessary to avert both eventualities.
Holcombe and Clay telegraphed to Thompson to meet
them at St. Catherines for united deliberations. At this
meeting the three decided that negotiations must somehow be continued in order to uncover the real terms of
President Lincoln. Greeley was accordingly informd that
the commissioners had no credentials but that, if they
were given a safe-conduct to Washington and thence to
Richmond, they could secure the requisite official authority.[77] Greeley in his turn telegraphed this new development to Lincoln. The President's reply was his
famous letter "To Whom It May Concern." Dated July
18, 1864, it read: "TO WHOM IT MAY CONCERN:
Any proposition which embraces the restoration of peace,
the integrity of the whole Union, and the abandonment of
slavery, and which comes by and with an authority that
can control the armies now at War against the United
States, will be received and considered by the Executive
Government of the United States, and will be met by
liberal terms on other substantial and collateral points,
and the bearer or bearers thereof shall have safe-conduct
both ways. ABRAHAM LINCOLN." [78] This rescript
he entrusted to John Hay for delivery to Greeley and on
June 20, the President's secretary had a second encounter
with the editorial peacemaker. Characterized by inde-

[77] Report of J. P. Holcombe to J. P. Benjamin, November 16, 1864;
Report of C. C. Clay to J. P. Benjamin, August 11, 1864; *New York
Tribune*, July 22, 1864, Reply of the commissioners, July 18, 1864.
[78] *Official Records of the Union and Confederate Armies*, Series III,
Vol. IV, pp. 503-504.

cision and obstinacy, like the first, it finally resulted in an agreement that the two should cross the river together and transmit the letter to the commissioners.[79]

The slightly melodramatic patriotism of the President's secretary at once detected the bogus nature of the Confederate commissioners. George N. Sanders met them at the door of the Cataract House. He was a "seedy looking Rebel" with grizzled whiskers and a "flavor of old clo'." As they talked with him for a few moments a crowd filled up the bar-room and halls to gaze at the American negotiators, especially the editor of the *Tribune*. Then came an interview with Holcombe in his room while he had tea and toast. "He was a tall, spare, false looking man with false teeth, false eyes, and false hair." Greeley said that Hay had messages for him from the President; Hay delivered them; and Holcombe promised a reply on the following day after he had communicated with Clay who had gone to St. Catherines. The interview was then terminated, all walked downstairs to the veranda, and then Greeley and Hay rode away in the carriage. As they left the scene, Greeley, whose temper had been sullen and petulant all morning, became ebullient. He was glad that he had come and he "was very chatty and agreeable on the way back and at dinner." [80] If anyone should have been cheerful after the interview, it should have been the Confederates. They had obtained what they were after, a statement of peace terms. It was now necessary to draw up a reply and to disclose the whole negotiation to

[79] Nicolay, John G., and Hay, John: *Abraham Lincoln, a History*, Vol. IX, pp. 192-193.

[80] Thayer, W. R.: *The Life and Letters of John Hay*, Vol. I, pp. 179-181, a quotation from Hay's diary.

the sensitive Northerners. Accordingly John Hay, who had remained at Niagara Falls for the answer to the message which he had transmitted, was informed by Holcombe that the Confederate reply had been sent to the originator of the negotiations, Horace Greeley. Since the editor of the *Tribune* had departed posthaste for New York City on the afternoon of the day of negotiations, he had delegated Jewett to receive any communication which the Confederates desired to make. In this fashion it had come about that on July 21, Jewett had received the Confederate reply and, with genuine thoughtfulness, had at once given a duplicate to the Associated Press.[81]

The statement which found its public in this indirect manner was an ingenious one. The Confederate commissioners seized first of all upon the inconsistencies of Lincoln's various proposals. In the light of their first impression that Lincoln had proposed peace with reservations, the letter "To Whom It May Concern" was certainly a breach of faith. "We feel confident," they wrote, "that you must share our profound regret that the spirit which dictated the first step toward peace had not continued to animate the councils of your President." "To Whom It May Concern" is then attacked as precluding all negotiations since it prescribed in advance the terms of peace. The commissioners do not understand "this rude withdrawal of a courteous overture for negotiation," its interpretation is left to those who have the means and inclination "to penetrate the mysteries of his Cabinet or

[81] Nicolay, John G., and Hay, John: *Abraham Lincoln, a History*, Vol. IX, p. 193; *New York Tribune*, July 22, 1864, J. P. Holcombe to Hay, July 21, 1864.

fathom the caprice of his imperial will." The South cannot accept the terms which he offers. "And if there be any patriots or christians in your land who shrink appalled from the illimitable vistas of private misery and public calamity which stretches before them, we pray that in their bosoms a resolution may be quickened to recall the abused authority and vindicate the outraged civilization of their country." [82] This letter is not a reply to Mr. Greeley; neither is it the final note in a series of diplomatic exchanges. Rather it is a campaign document skillfully addressed to the disaffected elements in the North. It is as much an aspect of the Confederate intrigues to secure the defeat of Lincoln and the collapse of the Union cause as their attempts to fire St. Louis and Cincinnati, bribe Northern newspapers and foment insurrection with the "gallant, brave, true hearted statesman, Vallandigham."

Thus it had happened that the Niagara conference had failed to fulfill Lincoln's expectations. It had not resulted in peace; Lincoln probably never cherished that anticipation. Nor had it stilled the peace clamor. Instead of uncovering the realities of the situation, it had created a new fiction. Lincoln stood revealed either as inept or vacillating or else positively dishonest. That was the picture which the Confederate commissioners had wished to draw. That was the impression which Greeley through a conspiracy of silence left the country to infer as true. On July 22, the *Tribune* published on its first page, "The Sanders Correspondence," dated at Buffalo, Thursday, July 21, 1864. The correspondence which

[82] *New York Tribune,* July 22, 1864. Reply of the commissioners to Greeley, July 21, 1864.

was printed "explains itself" but it did not include for the purposes of that explanation any letter dated previous to July 12. Nor were the early letters which laid down Lincoln's indispensable conditions for negotiations included. The public was furnished with no evidence to dispute the charge of the Confederates that the President had, in bad faith, changed his policy in the course of negotiations. It is as difficult to forgive Greeley for his part in creating this misconception as it is for ignoring the President's unmistakable wishes as to the course of the negotiation. But it must be recalled, in all charity, that Greeley was not guilty of a petty deceit. He was too large hearted. It is more just to believe that his intense desire for peace, mounting as day after day brought its new disaster, became an hysteria which swept him beyond the narrow boundaries of balance and consistency.

While the Greeley negotiations in Canada were coming to this unfortunate issue, Lincoln was planning to exploit the more felicitous outcome of a peace mission which had on July 21 opportunely returned from Richmond. Although this commission contained no personages as notable as the editor of the *Tribune* and the private secretary of the President, and although the negotiation in which it participated attracted at the moment less public attention, the results of the conversation between Jefferson Davis and two Northerners, John R. Gilmore and Colonel James Jaquess, were more far-reaching. Neither of the two Northern emissaries seemed a fit instrument for the conduct of weighty affairs. James R. Gilmore was a rather uninteresting representative of the self-made business man, a type common to the era. After some years spent in the cotton business, he possessed a knowledge of the South, derived from his frequent trips to that region, and a competence which enabled him to live in leisurely retirement.[83] But the man's energies sought expression; and the Civil War fortunately provided an outlet for them. Developing some literary facility, he assumed the pen name, Edmund Kirke, and became a co-editor of the *Continental*, a monthly devoted to anti-slavery propaganda. He was also the author of several books which professed to give a true picture of Southern conditions and the contributor of an irregular series of pertinent sketches and essays to the *New York Tribune*. The *Tribune*, in addition, published his larger works. This loose editorial arrangement brought him into occasional contact with Greeley and by 1863 this relationship seems to have resulted in a similarity of feeling in regard to the Lincoln administration, a pervasive distrust of the President and his policy. At least Gilmore was associated in the spring of that year in one of Greeley's political maneuvers. The latter was beating the political bush to see what birds would fly forth as acceptable presidential candidates. General Rosecrans had apparently appealed to the editorial imagination; he was energetic; he could command the Roman Catholic vote; but "Was he sound on the goose?" This was the Greeley colloquialism for the proper position on slavery. To answer the question, Gilmore was dispatched on a personal mission to Tennessee to interview Rosecrans.[84]

[83] Gilmore, J. R.: "World Biographies," in the *Literary World*, Vol. XVI, p. 406-407.

[84] Gilmore, J. R.: *Personal Recollections of Abraham Lincoln and the Civil War*, pp. 66, 72, 90, 100-102. His first book on the South was *Among the Pines*.

Although the political purpose of this visit never bore fruit, it resulted in the crossing of the ways of James R. Gilmore and Colonel James Jaquess. In peace times the Colonel had been president of a small college in Quincy, Illinois. At the outbreak of the war he was commissioned by Governor Yates to raise a three-year regiment and this regiment, the Seventy-Third Illinois, had served with distinction at Fort Donelson, Pittsburg Landing, and Perryville.[85] Jaquess added a patriotic and military ardor to an intense and primitive religious fervor. The result of this blending was a man who would have seemed less incongruous praying with Cromwell's Ironsides at Marston Moor than endeavoring to bring Jefferson Davis to terms in the name of the Lord. Stirred by the spectacle of fellow Christians, especially Methodists, engaged in killing one another, he became convinced that he could go *"into the Southern Confederacy and return within NINETY DAYS with terms of peace that the Government will accept. N.B.—I propose no compromise with traitors*—but their immediate return to allegiance to God and their country."[86] Rosecrans, slightly perplexed by the request of Jaquess for a furlough for such an original mission, asked Gilmore for advice and brought the two men together.

Gilmore did not carry away from his first meeting with the Colonel a very favorable impression. Some repulsion was inevitable between characters so antithetical as a religious fanatic and a literary journeyman. But so strong were the illusions of Jaquess that others were con-

[85] *New York Tribune*, July 25, 1864.

[86] Nicolay, John G., and Hay, John: *Abraham Lincoln, a History*, Vol. IX, pp. 201-202, Jaquess to Garfield, May 19, 1863. Garfield was then Chief-of-Staff to General Rosecrans.

strained to abrogate their common sense and half believe
in the impossible. First of all General Rosecrans had
been induced to commend the Colonel's request for a furlough during which he would journey to Richmond and
summon Jefferson Davis to repentance. In turn Rosecrans prevailed upon Gilmore to serve as a personal messenger to Abraham Lincoln in the business. Two letters
were to be delivered to the President. One from Jaquess
outlined his hopes and requested an opportunity to try
them out; a second from Rosecrans urged the President's
compliance.[87] These letters, reinforced by the importuni-
ties of Gilmore himself, converted the hesitant Lincoln.
Although the administration was to have no official connection with the mission, Jaquess in an unofficial way
was to be allowed to go forth on his adventure.[88] Thus
dispatched, the Colonel made his way to Baltimore, induced General Schenk to allow him to go to Fortress Monroe, and thence he actually entered the Confederate lines
in a truce boat.[89] But here the peace crusader was
halted. President Davis refused to interview him because he was unaccredited by the Northern government.[90]
Disappointed at his failure, Jaquess wrote Lincoln that
he had offers of peace from men of character and influence in the South; but this letter Lincoln never answered.
Either it was never presented to him by the person who

[87] Gilmore, J. R.: *Personal Recollections of Abraham Lincoln and
the Civil War*, pp. 140-141, 148-149.

[88] *Ibid.*, pp. 156-164.

[89] Nicolay, John G., and Hay, John: *Abraham Lincoln, a History*,
Vol. IX, p. 203, Lincoln to Rosecrans, May 28, 1863 (MS.).

[90] Nicolay, John G., and Hay, John: *Abraham Lincoln, a History*,
Vol. IX, p. 203, Schenk to Lincoln, July 13, 1863 (MS.), Lincoln
to Schenk, July 14, 1863 (MS.); Gilmore, J. R.: *Personal Recollections
of Abraham Lincoln and the Civil War*, pp. 165-166.

received it; or else its vague character convinced him of the hopelessness of any further missions.[91]   The Colonel, meanwhile, returned to his regiment to distinguish himself at Chattanooga and Missionary Ridge and to write a military report closing with the words "We are ready to do or suffer." [92]

In the spring of 1864, Gilmore displaced Jaquess as the chief sponsor of the peace efforts which the latter had originated.   To be sure he was so busy with a lecture tour that he found it inconvenient to become an active negotiator of peace, but in April he found time to be in Washington and to interview President Lincoln.   He was disgusted with the publicity which the Jaquess mission of the previous summer had gained and convinced of the incapacity of the Colonel.   The prospect for a renewal of the negotiation was not promising.   Gilmore, according to his own account, was an able dialectician.   He told the President that there were indications that Jefferson Davis would not refuse to see Jaquess if he were sent a second time on a peace mission.   He had established on his first visit to the South a friendship with a Confederate "who desired peace even at the cost of slavery." This friend had, at Jaquess' request, interviewed Davis and secured from him the expression of a wish to see the Yankee Colonel.   Accessibility to the Confederate President was also assured through the intervention of a woman, "a near relative of Mr. Davis, now residing in the North,"

[91] Nicolay, John G., and Hay, John: *Op. cit.*, Vol. IX, pp. 203-204; Gilmore, J. R.: *Op. cit.*, p. 235. Gilmore gives the former explanation in the words of Lincoln; Nicolay and Hay assert that the letter was ignored by the President because he saw the futility of the negotiation.

[92] *Official Records of the Union and Confederate Armies*, Series I, Vol. XXI, Part II, pp. 192, 196, 200.

who had written Davis advising him to grant the commissioner an interview.[93] With such backing, it seemed
more than likely that, if a commissioner were sent, he
would be received by the President. These were the considerations which assured the success of this specific peace
mission.

The reasons for the dispatch of any peace mission at
all are partially concealed by the inconsistencies and in-
credibilities of the various narratives which Gilmore has
given. The earlier ones, published during the Civil War,
are *ex parte* documents, since they were written in journalistic controversies or to create a desired impression.
They are sheer propaganda. The later accounts have
the defects of "recollections." Their chronology is confused and the citation of documents is often inaccurate.
As a result, the details of the mission are sadly blurred.
The first full report, published in the *Atlantic Monthly*
of September, 1864, professes to give considerable space
to the reasons for the undertaking. There is a half
humorous mention of various minor motives and then the
article closes with the words "enough of mystification."
"We went to Richmond because we hoped to pave the way
for negotiations that would result in peace." [94] In view
of his later admissions, this explanation is blatantly disingenuous. In December of the same year, goaded by
"the remarks of the Copperhead press," Gilmore asserted
that the true reason for the peace commission was the
activity of the peace men in the North who thought that
peace could be obtained without dishonor and who be-

[93] *New York Tribune*, September 5, 1864.
[94] Gilmore, J. R.: "Our Visit to Richmond," in the *Atlantic Monthly*,
Vol. XIV, pp. 372-373.

lieved that the war would cease if the slavery issue were removed from the war program of the North. This possibility Jaquess, for one, knew to be untrue. After he had been brought East on leave in May for contingent use by Gilmore and Lincoln, he had had another one of his interviews, this time with a Southern clergyman whom he met in Maryland. The clergyman reported a conversation which he had had with Davis. On that occasion the Confederate President had stated that peace could be obtained only by the complete recognition of Southern independence. If this rumor could be definitely verified as a Southern ultimatum to the proffer of reasonable terms by the North, it would do much to silence the clamor of the Northern peace men and to dispel the clouds of misinformation and delusion which were casting a darkly threatening shadow over the policy of the administration and the cause of the Union. The appetite for peace which had created from falsehood the means for its own satisfaction, ought to disappear in the face of realities.[95] By these later considerations Gilmore believes that he won the President's assent to the mission. Although his vanity certainly has enlarged the rôle he played, Gilmore's reasoning, as we have seen earlier, in part motivated the President's willingness to experiment with peace negotiations. In this instance, unlike the later case of Greeley, there was no necessity for silencing the outcries of individual peace seekers. Jaquess and Gilmore were not influential people. But they might, nevertheless, bring back political material of value for use upon others, and they might aid in its diffusion.

[95] Gilmore, J. R.: "Our Last Day in Dixie," in the *Atlantic Monthly,* Vol. XIV, p. 725; Gilmore, J. R.: *Personal Recollections of Abraham Lincoln and the Civil War,* pp. 239-240.

Only the task of perfecting arrangements for this ostensible peace mission remained. Lincoln had determined to entrust Gilmore with the responsibility for the Richmond expedition; Jaquess was taken along as a ticket of admission to the Confederacy. The wholly informal character of the negotiations made it impossible for these two men to act as bearers of definite conditions from the North, but it was advisable that they have some basis for a conversation with the Southerners. This was furnished by a conference with Chase, who had just left the Cabinet, and Gilmore, in which the President drew up his statement of the terms of peace. They were: (1) "The immediate dissolution of the Southern Government," the disbandment of its armies, and the recognition of the supremacy of the Union; (2) the total, absolute, and perpetual abolition of all slavery; (3) a complete amnesty to all engaged in the rebellion; (4) the restoration of the States to the Union "as if they had never attempted to secede from the Union"; and (5) compensation to the slave owners on the basis of one-half the value of their slaves in 1860; and to secure this compensation, the issuance of $500,000,000 in stock. Passes were then issued under date of July 6, for Gilmore and Jaquess.[96]   On July 7, the same day on which Greeley saw fit to inform the President for the first time of the presence of the Canadian commissioners and their peace terms, Gilmore and Jaquess set sail for City Point. It was not until the 16th that they finally crossed the Confederate lines. The delay was caused in part by the arrangements with the Confederates which involved the forwarding to Richmond

[96] Gilmore, J. R.: *Personal Recollections of Abraham Lincoln and the Civil War*, pp. 242-247.

of their request for a conference with Jefferson Davis; [97] it was caused also by the unwillingness of the commissioners to explain the purpose of their mission to General Grant, a difficulty which was resolved by a communication with Washington.[98] Finally the two adventurers from the North were met by Colonel Ould, Commissioner for Exchange of Prisoners, at Mrs. Grover's, and then they were bumped over the rough roads to the Spottswood Hotel in Richmond, where they masqueraded as agents from Governor Brown of Georgia.[99]

The prelude to the conference which the commissioners wished to hold with Jefferson Davis was not free from guile, the use of which is necessary to obtain preliminary advantages for a basis of recrimination and accusation in the event of later public argument. In this case probably no one was deceived. The Confederate government was naturally not eager to indulge in fruitless negotiations with unaccredited agents. If it did so, the inevitable publicity would be a matter of political embarrassment. Gilmore and Jaquess, on the other hand, determined upon securing an interview and a statement of the Confederate terms, were not eager to make disclosures which would negative the objects of their mission. Upon their arrival, therefore, they dispatched a note to Judah P. Benjamin, Secretary of State, whom Gilmore later described as that "short, plump, oily little man in black . . . in the northwest room of the old United States Cus-

[97] *Official Records of the Union and Confederate Armies*, Series I, Vol. XL, Part III, pp. 74, 168-169, 201.

[98] Gilmore, J. R.: *Op. cit.*, p. 252.

[99] *Official Records of the Union and Confederate Armies*, Series I, Vol. XL, Part III, p. 202; Gilmore, J. R.: *Op. cit.*, pp. 252-258.

tom-house" in Richmond.[100]   At that time he was more
discreet.   In requesting an interview with Davis, they
professed to be "acquainted with the views of the United
States Government, and with the sentiments of the Northern people, relative to an adjustment of the differences existing between the North and South, and earnestly hope
that a free interchange of views between President Davis
and themselves may open the way to such official negotiations as will result in restoring PEACE to the two
sections of our distracted country."   Benjamin was impressed by the fact that the word official was underscored and the word peace doubly underscored.   He arranged a personal interview from which he got the impression that, although they came unofficially, they knew
Lincoln's wishes.[101]   He decided to arrange for them an
interview with the President.

On the evening of the same day, July 17, that interview was held in the Secretary's office.   The personal
charm of Davis at once put the commissioners at their
ease.   Although Davis expressed a desire for peace, he delivered at the outset an ultimatum which was the keynote
of the conference.   "We will go on unless you acknowledge our right to self-government.   We are not fighting
for slavery.   We are fighting for independence, and that,

[100] Gilmore, J. R.: *Op. cit.,* p. 259.

[101] *Ibid.,* pp. 238-259; *Official Records of the Union and Confederate
Navies,* Series II, Vol. III, p. 1191.   There are two interesting variants
of this note.   The quotations in the text are taken from Gilmore's
version printed in his *Recollections.*   Benjamin's version of the note is
quoted in the circular sent by him to consular agents on August 23,
1864.   It is in Benjamin's version that the underscoring of the words
took place.   The variation between the two notes is one of the bases
of Benjamin's accusation of bad faith and inaccuracy on the part of
Gilmore and Jaquess.   This charge is denied by Gilmore in the *New
York Tribune,* September 5, 1864.

or extermination, we will have." With this as an object he expressed a belief in the health of the Confederate cause. The military situation was favorable; the supplies of food and munitions were plentiful; and the currency of the Confederacy was soundly based upon the cotton crop. Gilmore then introduced Lincoln's terms in the guise of an expedient. There should be a universal plebiscite upon the question of peace with disunion and Southern independence; or peace with Union, compensated emancipation, no confiscation, and universal amnesty. To these considerations Davis had two objections. One was based upon the fact that here was but a new tyranny of the majority over the minority. Such a plebiscite would have to be taken by states, for each state had the inalienable right to be free from coercion. Over the terms themselves, Davis was either irritated or indifferent. As to the slaves, "You may emancipate the rest, you may emancipate every negro in the Confederacy . . . but we will be free! We will govern ourselves! We will do it, if we have to see every Southern plantation sacked, and every Southern city in flames." [102] This statement practically terminated the interview and soon after the commissioners withdrew. Now that their mission was accomplished, they were apprehensive lest they should not be allowed to return. The continual presence of Mr. Jervis of the Richmond Provost Guard seemed significant; slight delays on the following day aroused their every suspicion. But later,

[102] Gilmore, J. R.: *Op. cit.*, pp. 261-273; Davis, Jefferson: *The Rise and Fall of the Confederate Government*, Vol. II, pp. 610-611; *Official Records of the Union and Confederate Navies*, Series II, Vol. III, pp. 1193-1194.

on the 18th, they left Richmond and on July 19 Grant was informed of their safe return.[103]

Gilmore took the first boat to Washington and two days later read his written report of the proceedings at Richmond to Lincoln and to Sumner, who happened to be present. There was a short discussion as to how the news was to be placed before the public. Gilmore advocated the *Tribune*, Lincoln suggested the *Atlantic Monthly* as less partisan. Sumner suggested, as a solution, a card in one of the Boston papers, stating Davis' separation declaration, and later a full report in the *Atlantic Monthly*. On July 22, 1864, the same day on which Greeley published his account of the Niagara Conference in the *Tribune*, a "card from Edmund Kirke" appeared in the *Boston Evening Transcript*.[104] It gave a brief account of the expedition to Richmond and quoted with italics and capitals, "This war must go on till the last of the generation falls in his tracks and his children seize his musket and fight our battle *unless you acknowledge our right to self-government*. We are not fighting for slavery. We are fighting for INDEPENDENCE, and that, or extermination, we *will* have." [105]

[103] Gilmore, J. R.: *Op. cit.,* pp. 287-288; *Official Records of the Union and Confederate Armies,* Series I, Vol. XL, Part III, p. 340.
[104] Gilmore, J. R.: *Op. cit.,* pp. 288-290.
[105] *Boston Evening Transcript,* July 22, 1864.

CHAPTER III

The Collapse of the Peace Movement

"The President," wrote Fessenden in August, 1864, "is too busy looking after the elections to think of anything else." [1] Indeed, if Lincoln was to be elected and the policies of the administration were to be continued, it certainly seemed as if only the effort, the steadfastness, and the faith of the President could accomplish that result. For the situation of August was no improvement over that of July. Petersburg was a monotonous and costly stalemate; the financial condition of the country was still unstable; and the political outlook had not been improved by the events of the previous month. The bases of the President's support appeared to be crumbling away. Friends and enemies were in despair or in exaltation; both agreed that the reëlection of the President appeared improbable. For this dark political outlook, the peace negotiations of July had furnished little antidote.

It is obvious that the President's coöperation in these efforts for peace would be peculiarly distasteful to the extremists in the President's own party. For those warriors, who shouted of subjugation and military extermination, there was no place in warfare for a combination of military and diplomatic methods. For them it was not

[1] Fessenden, Francis: *Life and Public Services of William Pitt Fessenden,* Vol. I, p. 343.

a question of the olive branch but of the sword. If they, in any case, could have been induced to approve of peace negotiations as a method of ending the war, they would still have condemned the terms laid down in "To Whom It May Concern" as too lenient and too merciful. To insist only on the restoration of the Union and the abolition of slavery was to throw away the opportunity for reconstructing the Southern states on more theoretic and more extreme lines. Finally, the President—largely due to the mental evasion of Greeley—appeared to be possessed of a vacillating and uncertain temperament. The worst fears of the extremists as to the President's character were confirmed by the Niagara negotiations. The President's participation in the July negotiation blew into a flame the passions which the June convention had effectively smothered.

On August 5, 1864, the opposition of the Republican extremists was announced. On that day the press published the famous Wade-Davis manifesto, an unsparing attack upon the presidential pocket veto of the congressional plans of reconstruction. These plans had been embodied in a bill, sponsored in Congress by Wade and Davis and passed in July at the very close of the congressional session. The bill had assumed for Congress the powers which the executive had exercised in freeing the slaves as a military measure and it had gone far beyond the President's amnesty proclamation and message of December, 1863, in depriving Confederate civil and military officials of the right of United States citizenship and in demanding more stringent regulations for the actual governmental reconstruction of the states then in rebellion. It reflected, as the debate showed, the extremists' con-

tention that the states were not members of the Union
and were without rights under the Constitution. The
President, if he were to maintain any semblance of consistency, could not accept such a proposal.

The Wade-Davis manifesto knew no restraint or dignity. Its authors ascribed as reasons for Lincoln's veto
his desire to hold the "electoral votes of the rebel States
at the dictation of his personal ambition." It then re-
viewed the President's position in detail, and closed with
a declamatory statement that his act was: "A blow at the
friends of his Administration, at the rights of humanity,
and at the principles of republican government," and
with a threat that: "If he wishes our support he must
confine himself to his executive duties—to obey and to
execute, not make the laws—to suppress by arms armed
Rebellion, and leave political reörganization to Congress.
If the supporters of the Government fail to insist on this,
they become responsible for the usurpations which they
fail to rebuke, and are justly liable to the indignation of
the people whose rights and security, committed to their
keeping, they sacrifice. Let them consider the remedy of
these usurpations, and, having found it, fearlessly execute
it." [2]

The extremists had grudgingly accepted the nomination of Lincoln in June. They had been forced to approve the unescapable. Now there seemed to be an opportunity to capitalize the rising discontent of the North
and to call a new convention for the purpose of securing
the withdrawal of former candidates and the nomination
of new ones. The Wade-Davis manifesto had been the

[2] *New York Tribune,* August 5, 1864.

first blast of the trumpet in this campaign. The next was
the meeting of the disaffected at the home of David Dudley Field in New York. As a result of this gathering
there was a call for a new convention. This call, which
was to be endorsed by all the prominent politicians who
could be induced to sign it, set the date as September 28
and the place as Cincinnati. The purpose of this convention was to rally all Union supporters to Lincoln or
some other candidate.[3] On the next day the *New York
Tribune* discussed editorially the presidential possibilities. The editor ingeniously proposed that the people
who did not like Lincoln should hold their convention in
September, nominate a separate candidate for the presidency, but support the Lincoln electoral ticket. The
voters at the election would express a presidential preference and the electoral college would be bound by this
preference and vote for the choice of the majority. Thus
all friends of the Union would be united in supporting.
the same electors and squabbling over presidential nominees would be obviated. To the uninformed reader, this
innovation in the method of conducting a presidential
election might seem only an expression of Greeley's
naiveté. But such was not the case; Greeley had been
present at the meeting of August 14; [4] he had definitely
aligned himself with the extremists. The explanation of
this incongruous alliance between the foremost protagonist of peace in the North and the leaders of the bitter-
enders who desired a vigorous prosecution of the war, is
to be found in the events which followed the Niagara
Conference. They unconsciously led Greeley to con-

  [3] *New York Sun*, June 30, 1889.
  [4] *New York Tribune*, August 15, 1864.

tribute the prestige of his personality and his editorial support to the cause of the extremists.

Greeley's fear that his appointment by Lincoln as a peace negotiator would result in notoriety for himself was justified. In those days an editor was public property. His actions and his opinions were discussed, not with formality or with restraint, but in the language and in the manner of a rough-and-tumble personal encounter. On July 22, Greeley devoted on the editorial page of the *Tribune* three short paragraphs to a statement of the nature of the peace negotiations and of his participation in them. This statement, from its apparent candor and brevity, the editor evidently hoped would be final.[5] But his editorial and political rivals were not thus to be silenced. A newspaper controversy began which attacked the editor's position from every angle. He was attacked by the *New York Evening Post* for even considering negotiations with rebels and slaveholders. The sly genius of Bennett of the *Herald* delighted in tormenting and teasing the editor of the *Tribune* and took a malevolent pleasure in watching the struggling of its victim. The *Times*, Seward's organ, ably edited by the renegade Raymond, was merciless and relentless in the exposure of the impolicy of Greeley's negotiations.

Under these attacks, Greeley shifted in bewildered confusion from one position to another. On July 25, he had approved the President's "To Whom It May Concern" as "just right," [6] and he denied categorically that at the Niagara Conference he uttered to George N. Sanders any remarks reflecting on the President.[7] Yet only two days

[5] *New York Tribune,* July 22, 1864.
[6] *Ibid.,* July 25, 1864.
[7] *Ibid.,* July 26, 1864.

later he had to admit that he had said: "This is not the end of this affair. You must not think that all the Republican party are blackguards!"

But he still denied that this utterance involved any censure of the President or of his course of action! [8] This curious contradiction was but an illustration of the many which crowded the subsequent days of misty tergiversation. At one time Greeley, the proponent of abolition, can write: "We do not contend . . . that reunion is possible or endurable only on the basis of Universal Freedom," [9] and a week later, implying that the South should be allowed to go in peace, he asserted that: if emancipation came the Union would be reconstituted "even if our armies were withdrawn. We are only urging that the best possible peace for all sections, for all deserving interests, the truest and finest Peace, is one based on Universal Freedom." [10]

These quotations are only typical of others which Greeley wrote during the journalistic controversy which raged for over a month. To read the editorials of the *Tribune* during this period presents the editor in a most unfavorable light. Even when judged with pity and with charity, he must be condemned for uncertainty, vagueness, evasion, and deceit. To call that deceit willful or deliberate, is to ignore the temper of the man and the situation in which he found himself. Subject to profound emotional stress, which in moments of excitement bordered on mental instability, he now found himself involved in a web of contradictions and inconsistencies from

[8] *New York Tribune,* July 27, 1864.
[9] *Ibid.,* July 28, 1864.
[10] *Ibid.,* August 4, 1864.

which he could not gracefully escape. His mind, a battle-ground of conflicting desires, ceased to be logical and became simply inchoate. But behind this tragic confusion lay the intensity of Greeley's fixed desire for peace. That passion was as strong now as it had been in July. On August 3, he comments on the President's proclamation for a day of fasting and of prayer: "Our public burdens are fearful: our Taxes are enormous; our Public Debt, already frightful, is steadily augmenting; we are freshly summoned to send Half a Million more men to the battle-field: Never since the discovery of Arnold's treason have blacker clouds hung over us: our trust is in God alone." [11]

It was in this temper that Greeley entered into a correspondence with Lincoln. Driven to exasperation by the situation in which he found himself, he accepts, in a signed editorial of August 5, the suggestion of the *Times* to publish the whole correspondence which led up to the Niagara Falls Conference. This same editorial accuses Lincoln of having suddenly formulated new peace terms by the letter "To Whom It May Concern"—a step which was a "very grave mistake"—and for it sarcastically blames not the President but someone in the War Department. The campaign against Early and Breckinridge and "To Whom It May Concern" must have been devised by the same man, as: "There can hardly be two different men living contemporaneously who are equal to the two exhibitions of genius. Nature is not so lavish of her grand achievements." [12]

The President was willing to accept Greeley's suggestion for a publication of their correspondence, but de-

[11] *New York Tribune*, August 3, 1864.
[12] *Ibid.*, August 5, 1864.

sired to omit some of Greeley's remarks about the state
of the country. Their influence would have a depressing
political effect. He also invited Greeley to Washington.[13]
The letters which followed are simply a renewed evidence
of Greeley's passionate desire for peace and his conviction that the administration did not desire it. He
threatens and he scolds. The President is surrounded by
his bitterest enemies (Greeley never forgot Seward); the
War Department censors his telegraphic despatches. His
letter of August 9 is a shriek of despair. The election of
November is already lost; the policy of the administration
in rejecting all offers for peace: "*Must* result in disaster, or all experience is delusive. . . . I beg you, implore
you, to inaugurate or invite proposals for peace forth-
with. And in case peace cannot now be made, consent to
an *armistice for one year*, each party to retain, un-
molested, all it now holds, but the rebel ports to be
opened. Meantime, let a national convention be held, and
there will surely be no more war at all events." [14] In a
letter of August 11, Greeley refused to permit the
publication of the correspondence unless it were published undeleted. More than ever did he distrust the administration. Convinced that once again he was deceived,
he cursed all fools in high places.[15]

This frantic aftermath of the Niagara negotiations
made Greeley the willing accomplice of any group of
politicians who desired the defeat of the President. Come
war or peace, that was now the sole object of his desire.

[13] Welles, Gideon: *Diary of Gideon Welles*, Vol. II.

[14] Nicolay, John H., and Hay, John: *Abraham Lincoln, a History*,
Vol. IX, pp. 196-197, Greeley to Lincoln, August 9, 1864 (MS.).

[15] Report of C. C. Clay to J. P. Benjamin, August 11, 1864.

Other factors helped, for he found it congenial to unite with men who shared his distrust of Seward and disliked the Secretary's prominence in national politics; and who were now advocating the calling of a new convention in September—a policy which Greeley for eight months had been consistently supporting. So it was that Greeley met with the extremists at David Dudley Field's to see how they might secure a new president.

The effect of the controversy at Washington was to widen the breach between the administration and the editor of the *Tribune*. Welles read into the situation a political intrigue in which Seward had been the victor over Greeley and had through Lincoln administered to the editor of the *Tribune* a severe rebuke.[16] Lincoln became completely convinced of Greeley's uselessness. He described the process of repairing shoes in the West and added: "Sometimes, when far gone, we found the leather so rotten the stitches would not hold. Greeley is so rotten that nothing can be done with him. He is not truthful; the stitches all tear out." [17]

The peace negotiations of July, 1864, had simply increased the extremists' distrust of Lincoln and had given them the unexpected support of Horace Greeley. But what had been the result of these same negotiations upon the more conservative members of the President's party whose support was now doubly vital? The Confederate commissioners in Canada were seeking to answer that question and the answer they found satisfied them. Hol-

[16] Welles, Gideon: *Diary of Gideon Welles*, Vol. II, pp. 109-110. Before Lincoln's despatch of Greeley to Canada, he discussed the desirability of that action with Seward and Fessenden. Fessenden, however, just "came in accidentally."

[17] Welles, Gideon: *Diary of Gideon Welles*, Vol. II, pp. 111-112.

combe asserted that "To Whom It May Concern" had caused a "tremendous revolution" and Clay jubilantly announced that it had "eliminated the President's support." This unexpected result had been brought about by uniting, as indispensable, two conditions of peace— the restoration of the Union and the abolition of slavery. The statement that these were the conditions of peace of the administration should not have been surprising to those who had followed the course of events. But it must be admitted that "To Whom It May Concern" had gone beyond the President message of the previous December. Without resorting to the ambiguities of congressional acts or of his own emancipation proclamation, he stood now for abolition. But such clarification was apparently not consonant with winning the election. The insistence upon abolition would alienate, in this time of distress, that outer margin of voters—largely conservative, in part Democratic,—who had wished the war only as a war for national reunion. The moderate Republicans thought the President had indeed seriously imperiled his chances of reëlection by his statements of war and peace aims. They tried to save him from this self-created disaster.

Raymond, the editor of the *Times* and chairman of the Republican National Committee, asserted that "To Whom It May Concern" did not preclude the favorable consideration of other terms tendered by other parties.[18] Welles gloomily confided to his diary that the terms which the President had offered were "inadmissible" and that, even if the President would be willing to offer other terms, the world would receive those he had given as an "ulti-

[18] *New York Times,* August 18, 1864.

matum." [19] There is the hint here that "To Whom It May Concern" might not be the final form of Lincoln's peace policy. The President's own correspondence during the month of August lends confirmation to the statements of Raymond and Welles. Charles D. Robinson had written the President on August 7, 1864, asserting that the sudden emphasis upon the abandonment of slavery as a peace term of the administration had deprived the war Democrats of their reasons for supporting the administration.[20] To him, Lincoln replied: "That saying reunion and abandonment of slavery would be considered, if offered, is not saying that nothing *else* or *less* would be considered, if offered."

With this statement finished, Lincoln adroitly discusses the question of slavery. The steps for emancipation which he had taken were military measures. Without the support of the black men, thus added to the Northern army, the cause of the Union could not be won. Naturally, Lincoln could not reënslave those who had thus staked their lives for the "promise of freedom." The letter closes with a significant statement that no leader of the rebels: "Has offered, or intimated, a willingness to a restoration of the Union in any event, or on any condition whatever. . . . If Jefferson Davis wishes for himself or for the benefit of his friends at the North, to know what I would do if he were to offer peace and reunion, saying nothing about slavery, let him try me." [21]

[19] Welles, Gideon: *Diary of Gideon Welles*, Vol. II, pp. 109-110.

[20] Nicolay, John G., and Hay, John: *Abraham Lincoln, a History*, Vol. IX, p. 214, Charles D. Robinson to Lincoln, August 7, 1864 (MS.).

[21] Lincoln, Abraham: *Complete Works of Abraham Lincoln*, Edited by John G. Nicolay and John Hay (1905 edition), Vol. IX, pp. 193-197, Unfinished Draft of Letter to Charles D. Robinson, August 17, 1864.

But the adroitness of the President could not abate the
fever of the Republican moderates. The virus of despair
had infected them. Thurlow Weed, to whose conservative anti-Greeley sentiments the letter "To Whom It May
Concern" was not congenial, wrote Seward that "Lincoln's reëlection was an impossibility" and "the people
were wild for peace." Finally, on August 22, Raymond
called a meeting of the National Executive Committee
at New York; and, as the sense of that meeting, he wrote
that defeat seemed imminent in Illinois, Pennsylvania, and
Indiana. The reasons were the want of military success and the feeling that: "We are not to have peace in
any event under this Administration until slavery is
abandoned." To silence this criticism, he suggests a proffer of peace to the South on the one condition of the
supremacy of the constitution. Whatever answer might
be given to such an offer would redound to the advantage
of the Union cause. Thus had a month brought one of
Greeley's ardent critics to a position where he could at
least adopt some of Greeley's political arguments.

Lincoln might adopt either of two courses. In the
first place, he might yield to the wishes of his supporters.
That he debated this possibility, a draft of instructions
for a commissioner to Richmond is evidence. The commissioner was to propose that the war cease upon "the
restoration of the Union and national authority." If this
condition was not accepted, the delegate would ask for a
statement of terms embracing this restoration which would
be acceptable. Finally if this maneuver failed, the delegate was to ask what terms would be possible. The other
course open to Lincoln was the rejection of all idea of
further peace overtures. A few days after he had drawn

up his proposed draft for a commissioner to Richmond, Lincoln met the National Executive Committee which had journeyed down to Washington to reinforce by personal conference the request of their letter; and, strengthened by the advice of Seward, Stanton, and Fessenden, he convinced his callers of the unwisdom of their policy. On the next day, the *Tribune* published an item denying that the President intended to send peace commissioners to the South.

It is no depreciation of Lincoln's spiritual devotion to the Union cause to say that his policy was characterized by his usual grasp of the realities of the situation. His problem was to secure his reëlection in November and reelection involved the support of a diverse constituency. To retain that support, the policy which he had devised earlier had to be maintained in time of discouragement and despair. Even when a "peace simoon" was blowing dust in the eyes of Northern voters, he had to remain firm and unshaken. To his war and peace policy, Lincoln remained true. His terms were stated in their briefest form in "To Whom It May Concern," the reply to the Confederate commissioners. About details, he was willing to negotiate, as his outline for the Jaquess-Gilmore mission shows. With a visitor to the White House, in August, he talks of compensation for the slaves. But on the fundamental conditions—reunion and freedom— he really did not waver. It may be said that his letter to Robinson and the instructions for a commission to Richmond, which he proposed as an answer to the Republican Executive Committee, indicate a modification of his policy. In answering this assertion, the peace negotiations of July, 1864, must be taken into account. If Lincoln had

needed understanding of the issues of the war, the adven-
tures of Greeley and Jaquess and Gilmore would have
given it to him.   The results of their missions had furnished renewed evidence of the fact that the Confederacy
was fighting for independence and for independence alone.
Strengthened by this reassurance, Lincoln could afford
to be disingenuous in his letter to Robinson and could
omit from his unused instructions of August 24 all reference to slavery.   Since the President saw the situation
with unflinching clarity, he was justified in exploiting it
for political purposes.   But would the negotiations of
July, 1864, impress in the same way a public which was
blinded by visions and illusions?   The last of July had
given the news of the Greeley and the Jaquess-Gilmore
commissions to the world.   August had witnessed the
newspaper controversy over the Niagara episode, and
the first full account of the Jaquess-Gilmore mission in the
press.   In September came the complete report in the *Atlantic Monthly*.   Sooner or later the true import of the
peace negotiation would penetrate the public mind.   That
import, even if unaided by the confusion and timidity of
Lincoln's political opponents and the military success of
Northern arms, would have eventually brought about the
collapse of the peace movement.

Meanwhile the policy which Lincoln was consistently
following had already begun to dissolve the misfit aggre-
gation of Republicans who had planned earlier in August
to overthrow him.   Its only cohesive force was a common
distrust of the President and a diverse fear of his policy.
It included people who wanted war and people who wanted
abolition and people who did not know what they wanted.
For its success it required the united support of all these

factions; the secession of one of its important components meant failure. That secession took place. The abolitionists, who had been enlisted earlier to the President's cause by the emancipation proclamation, decided to continue their support of him. The sincerity of "To Whom It May Concern," the resolution with which the President refused the proposal of the Republican Executive Committee for new peace overtures, and the dawning realization of the true objects of the war—a realization to which Jaquess and Gilmore contributed by their visits upon Northern politicians—were now bearing fruit. On August 30, there was a second meeting at the home of David Dudley Field. Although the response to their idea of a new convention had been favorable, the meeting witnessed the defeat of the hopes of the extremists. Andrew, war-governor of Massachusetts, was present. He represented the abolitionist sentiment of his own state—perhaps of New England—a sentiment generally based not upon purely factional opposition to the President or upon personal reasons, but upon principle. These abolitionists distrusted him, they had attacked his deficiencies of leadership and of policy; but now they refused to co-operate with the extremists. They preferred rather to work within the machine and gain control of it. They chose to risk the chance of Lincoln's reëlection in the hope that, in return for their support, they might influence his policy. Forbes was busy writing letters to further the new movement. There were to be meetings of war supporters. Letters and delegations were to be sent to the President. The purpose was: "To infuse life and vigor, and plan, and true democracy into our campaign, and to tone up the administration to a square issue; fight off the *'Times'* tinkering about negotiation." The first fruits of Lincoln's moderation and firmness were now apparent. In spite of the intransigeance of Greeley of the *Tribune*, Godwin, of the *Evening Post*, and Tilton of the *Independent*, all of whom on September 2 sent out a last circular to the loyal governors in the hope of salvaging their cause, the opposition to the President within his own party began to collapse.

Meanwhile each Democratic faction was developing its organization, and selecting its candidates in the hope of capturing the machinery of the party. The conservative group had early chosen General George Brinton McClellan as the proper embodiment of its policy and its principles. Now he was gradually brought into the open. At first glance a discredited general would seem to be a poor standard bearer. As a matter of fact, however, McClellan possessed all the qualities which make for "availability." He had an extraordinary personal charm, enhanced by his comparative youth, his gracious manner, and his cultural background.[22]

Such characteristics inherently appealed to the upper classes. When he visited Boston in 1863, he was entertained by the more exclusive families on Beacon Hill and

[22] At the time when he was called to the command of the forces about Washington, McClellan was not quite thirty-five years of age. His life, up to that time, had been a peculiarly fortunate and happy one. He was the son of a prominent Philadelphia surgeon, Dr. George McClellan, he had been educated at the University of Pennsylvania and West Point; he had traveled abroad as a military observer; and finally, he had resigned from the army to enter the rapidly expanding railroad business. Here his promotion was rapid. (Campbell, J. H.: *McClellan, a Vindication of the Military Career of General George B. McClellan, A Lawyer's Brief*, pp. 10, 15-16, 18, 19.)

by them presented with a sword.[23]   In New York, his supporters were "the rich men" and the "young men of fashion." [24]   In particular, he enlisted upon his side the important railroad interests of the country.   McClellan had been "made" by his appointment as president of the Ohio and Mississippi Railroad Company.[25]   In New York the powerful New York Democratic machine directed by Dean Richmond, vice-president of the New York Central Railroad and chairman of the Democratic state committee, and Erastus Corning, president of the New York Central, was determined upon McClellan.[26]   In New Jersey, the Camden and Amboy monopoly, which, if the charges of its opponents are to be believed, owned and operated that state, was a bulwark of McClellan feeling.[27]

McClellan also had an undoubted appeal to the generality of voters.   From all sides, evidence poured in to substantiate this common observation.   His enormous popularity with the army had never been questioned even by his opponents.   The bases for the devotion of his men were numerous.   His dashing personal appearance be-

[23] Robinson, W. S.: *"Warington" Pen-Portrait: a Collection of Personal and Political Reminiscences from 1848 to 1876,* pp. 280-291.

[24] Forbes, John M.: *Letters (Supplementary) to John Murray Forbes,* edited by Sarah F. Hughes, Vol. II, pp. 287-288, Forbes to F. P. Blair, September 18, 1864.

[25] Campbell, J. H.: *Op. cit.,* p. 19.

[26] Brummer, S. D.: "Political History of New York State during the Period of the Civil War," *Columbia University Studies in History, Economics, and Public Law,* Vol. XXXIX, No. 2, pp. 24-26; *New York Herald,* August 28, 29, 1864; *New York Tribune,* August 31, 1864.

[27] *New York Tribune,* August 29, 1864.   John P. Stockton of New Jersey—the Stocktons were heavily involved in the Camden-Amboy monopoly—nominated McClellan at Chicago.   *Official Proceedings of the Democratic National Convention held in 1864 at Chicago,* p. 29.

fitted a military leader; his caution and prudence in strategics convinced the ordinary soldier that his own life would not be squandered in reckless or useless engagements; his care for the well-being and comfort of the private had made more easy the harsh transition from civilian to army life. Nor was testimony lacking of McClellan's popularity with the commonalty behind the lines. The spring of 1864 witnessed a series of fairs held for the benefit of the Sanitary Commission—the Red Cross of the Civil War—and patrons of these fairs for the price of a dollar had the privilege of voting as to which union commander should be the recipient of a handsome sword.

At the New York fair in April, McClellan led the balloting until the last moment, only to be defeated when sealed envelopes were opened and Grant was declared winner by virtue of votes contained in them. This announcement was followed by fighting on the floor and the gas had to be turned out.[28]   At a similar fair in St. Louis, McClellan again led until a Republican in Boston sent a check for five hundred dollars to be used in the purchase of votes for his most serious contender.[29]

It might be argued that General McClellan's career as Commander in Chief of the Army of the Potomac was a liability rather than an asset. The quality of his military genius was then, as it is now, a matter of great dispute. In any case, his career in the army made him exceedingly valuable politically to the Democrats. They laid the blame for his military failures upon a political conspiracy by his opponents. It must be admitted that

---

[28] *New York Tribune,* April 23, 1864.
[29] Forbes, John M.: *Reminiscences of John Murray Forbes,* edited by Sarah F. Hughes, Vol. II, pp. 279-280, Forbes to James E. Yeatman, May 30, 1864.

this theory of conspiracy was often justified by the circumstances. The extremists, especially Stanton, were early convinced of McClellan's utter ineptitude and of his hostility to the proper aims of the war. They accused him of sympathizing with the Confederate cause, of a desire to prolong the war without victory, of cowardice and timidity. With suspicion thus feverishly inflamed, they denied him proper support during the Peninsular Campaign, and even seemed deliberately to hamper his operations. His final dismissal from the army in November, 1862, after he had saved the Union cause at Antietam, could well be attributed not to his personal and military defects, but to the malevolence of his enemies. McClellan wore the fascinating aura of the martyr.[30]

As the conservative candidate, McClellan was anathema to the peace men of the party. The *Chicago Tribune* declared he was favored by the "bloated aristocrats" within the Democratic party, by the railroads of the East, and by the "great unwashed of the Celtic persuasion." [31] In New York, Fernando Wood's organization had declared in January: "That the National Democracy are unquali-

[30] Cochrane, John C.: *Memories of incidents connected with the origin and culmination of the rebellion that threatened the existence of the National Government*, pp. 26-28; McClellan, G. B.: *McClellan's Own Story, The War for the Union, the Soldiers who fought it, the Civilians who directed it, and his relation to it and them*, p. 650; Welles, Gideon: *Diary of Gideon Welles*, Vol. I, pp. 93-98; Hitchcock, E. A.: *Fifty Years in Camp and Field. Diary of Major-General Ethan Allen Hitchcock, U.S.A.*, edited by W. A. Croffut, pp. 438-440. Instances of the extremists' opposition to McClellan and of their efforts to hamper him are numerous. The citations given above are only illustrations of these instances. The last two citations deal with the efforts of the extremists to hamper McClellan's Peninsular Campaign by establishing a supervision over his movements and by withholding needed army corps for the defense of Washington.

[31] Cole, Arthur, C.: *The Era of the Civil War, 1848-1870; The Centennial History of Illinois*, Vol. III, p. 232.

fiedly opposed to the further prosecution of the war of emancipation and extermination now being waged against the seceded States, and demand and will continue to demand negotiation, reconciliation, and peace." [32]   In Ohio, Vallandigham and his followers, in spite of the handicap incurred by the defeat of 1863, were determined to control the party.   But the conservative Democrats ironed out all intra-party opposition.   The up-state Democratic machine in New York excluded the peace men from the delegation at large to the National Convention and carried a unit rule to control its vote.   In the Democratic State Convention of Ohio on March 23, the conservatives gained control by four votes and by four votes excluded Vallandigham as a delegate at large to the National Convention.   This victory was not complete, however.   Vallandigham, opportunely engineering a triumphant return from Canada, secured the nomination as delegate from his own county.   Finally, the conservatives, content with their preliminary victory and determined to wait, postponed the National Convention until the last of August.

The events of the summer months seemed likely to justify this policy of opportunism to radicals as well as to conservatives.   Suddenly there had blown up a "peace simoon" and the Democratic party was treated to the enjoyable spectacle of a prominent Republican, Horace Greeley, first suing for peace and then repudiating the administration.   The sardonic humor of this spectacle, moreover, was heightened by the recognition that as a result Republican disaffection was growing.   Finally, there had emerged from the peace negotiations at Niagara

[32] *New York Herald*, February 25, 26, 1864.

Falls Lincoln's rescript "To Whom It May Concern." In the effect upon the Democrats, this letter should be compared to the emancipation proclamation. Both gave clarity and sharpness to the issue of the war; angered the Democrats by insistence upon abolition; and convinced them that the perfidious injection of this issue into the conflict was the only barrier to peace. With a cause thus redefined on favorable terms, and with new hope well based upon the despair of their opponents, the Democrats looked forward to regaining political power.

In their campaign for control of the government, it would be desirable to be acquainted with the views of the Confederate commissioners as to the proper terms of peace and perhaps to utilize for political purposes the financial resources which they apparently possessed in such abundant quantity. It is these motives which directed a vari-hued stream of Democratic politicians into Canada. There they talked with Holcombe, Clay and Thompson. The Clifton House at Niagara Falls, because of its convenient and attractive location, was a delightful place for pleasant conversation. The commissioners saw Governor Hunt, Leigh Richmond, and Benjamin Wood from New York; McClean from Cincinnati; Buckalew, Black and Van Dyke of Pennsylvania; Weller of California; Judge Bullit of Kentucky; Colonel Walker of Indiana, and Clement L. Vallandigham of Ohio.[33] This was a motley crew to be labelled with one party designation, and the commissioners, with discreetness and guile, varied their conversation and their disclosures to suit

[33] *New York Tribune,* July 22, 1864; Report of J. P. Holcombe to J. P. Benjamin, November 16, 1864; Report of C. C. Clay to J. P. Benjamin, August 11, 1864.

the circumstances. Although they never for a moment compromised the idea of Southern independence, Clay writes: "We have not dispelled the fond delusion of most of those with whom we have conversed—that some kind of common government might at some time hereafter be established." [34]

What the impression carried away by each of these visitors and what the resulting decision may have been, is not certain. But at least one of the more conservative emissaries was convinced that the difficulties in the way of peace were not insuperable. The "mission" of Jeremiah Sullivan Black to Jacob Thompson is symptomatic of the aspirations of the conservative wing of the Democratic Party and of the extent of the concessions which they were willing to make for peace. In this connection alone, is the Black Mission valuable. The statement of terms which Thompson offered Black, in view of the utterances of Jefferson Davis, and the confessions of Clay, is vague and disingenuous.

Jeremiah Sullivan Black was a Pennsylvanian, a Democrat, and a lawyer—a trio of attributes which had finally resulted in his selection as Attorney-General in Buchanan's cabinet. Exhibiting adequate but not brilliant capacities, he retained this office until the prelude of the Civil War made frequent and hurried cabinet reorganizations necessary. As various secretaries resigned, the attorney-generalship was transferred to a newcomer, Edwin M. Stanton, and Black became Secretary of State and a person of great influence in shaping the administration's attitude toward the threatened war. His own position is difficult to define, for, when he had to formulate policies

[34] Report of C. C. Clay to J. P. Benjamin, August 11, 1864.

for his chief, men were changing their minds every day and advocating new measures with every new event.   To demand consistency of Black under such circumstances is impossible.   In general, he belonged to the group in the cabinet which refused to recognize the right of secession. Whether he was willing to coerce a state which refused to remain in the Union was a doubtful matter.   On January 17, he wrote: "I am not in favor of war, but I cannot resist the conviction that when war is made against us a moderate self-defense is righteous and proper.   Coercion —well, I would not care about coercing South Carolina, if she would agree not to coerce us.   But she kicks, cuffs, abuses, spits upon us, commits all kinds of outrages upon our rights, and then cries out that she is coerced if we propose to hide our diminished heads under a shelter which may protect us a little better for the future." [35] When the war came on, he assumed the conventional position of the moderate Democrat—the Union must be restored; slavery was a "right" of the South; and the methods by which the administration conducted the war were despotic and unjustified.

To live as a cabinet officer through the turbulent last months of Buchanan's administration would not naturally be an experience to increase one's belief in the goodness of human nature.   Those were days of abuse, irritation, inconsistency, suspicion, and duplicity.   Through it all, Black maintained a child-like serenity.   The motives of the Southerners, Thompson and Floyd, were unimpeachable and unquestionable; so were the motives of their op-

[35] Black, Jeremiah S.: *Essays and Speeches of Jeremiah S. Black with a biographical sketch,* edited by Chauncey F. L. Black, p. 22, Black to A. V. Parsons, January 17, 1861.

ponents.   Black trusted all his associates implicitly—in spite of contradiction.   There is something pathetic in the post war controversy which he had with Senator Henry Wilson over the part that Stanton had played in Buchanan's cabinet.   Wilson's story of Stanton's attitude toward slavery, of his clandestine relationship with prominent abolitionists and Republicans, of his secret disclosures of cabinet meetings and political plans shocked Black.   He would not believe in the perfidy of his friend; he rallied to the defence of what he thought Stanton's integrity ought to be.   Then as Wilson piles up evidence, Black gives way grudgingly.   To the very end he refuses to be disillusioned.   A nature like his, which believes in the rectitude of all men, is apt to be naïve and credulous.

Black, in the summer of 1864, saw an opportunity to utilize his experience with the righteous men of Buchanan's cabinet for initiating authoritative peace negotiations.   On the one side, he knew Jacob Thompson, who as Secretary of Interior had been a former colleague and who was now Confederate Commissioner in Canada.   On the other side, he was peculiarly intimate with Stanton. To Stanton, a fellow Pennsylvanian, Democrat and lawyer, Black as Attorney-General had given many cases, and he had been influential likewise in securing Stanton's appointment to the Buchanan cabinet.[36]   Now Stanton

---

[36] Black, Jeremiah S.: *Op. cit.*, p. 269. Black claims that "he struggled long . . . to remove the prejudices of Mr. Buchanan and others against him (Stanton)." As a result of Black's efforts, Stanton was brought into presidential favor and eventually received office. Flower, on the other hand, asserts that Stanton was a personal friend of Buchanan at the time of the latter's nomination. If such were the case, there might well have been other reasons for Stanton's appointment than Black's influence. (Flower, Frank A.: *Edwin McMasters Stanton, The Autocrat of Rebellion, Emancipation, and Reconstruction*, p. 67.)

was Secretary of War of Abraham Lincoln. Might not Black act as intermediary between his two former friends? He was in a personal position well suited for undertaking peace negotiations. The actual relation which Stanton bore to this mission is a matter of dispute between Black and himself. Before he departed, Black called upon Stanton, and on returning from Canada wrote to him that: [37] "Agreeably to the wishes expressed by you in our last conversation . . . I saw Mr. Thompson of Mississippi," and also confessed that he had assured Thompson that the results of the interview would be reported "to some member of the administration at Washington." Perhaps the former Secretary of State was understating the extent of his communicativeness to the Confederate commissioners in Canada; they were under the impression that Black was very much Stanton's envoy. Black confided to them that Stanton condemned "To Whom It May Concern" as a grave blunder, and would give Thompson safe-conduct to Washington to discuss terms of peace.[38]

Stanton, on the other hand, had quite a different conception of the whole proceeding. In reply to Black's letter, he wrote a short note, denying all complicity in the negotiations. This note has a decisive, almost brutal, tone

[37] This mission is very briefly treated in Flower, Frank A.: *Edwin McMasters Stanton, the Autocrat of Rebellion, Emancipation, and Reconstruction*, p. 359; and more fully in Gorham, George C.: *Life and Public Services of Edwin M. Stanton*, Vol. II, pp. 148-153. The account in this chapter is based upon Black's letter to Stanton, dated York, Pennsylvania, August 24, 1864, and Stanton's letter to Black, dated Washington, August 31, 1864. These letters are in the Library of Congress.

[38] Report of Clement C. Clay to J. P. Benjamin, September 12, 1864; Gorham, George C.: *Op. cit.*, pp. 148-149, a portion of a letter from Jacob Thompson to Mason and Slidell, August 23, 1864, reprinted from the *Southern Bivouac*, January, 1887.

which carries sincerity. He did not suppose that in
Black's friendly visit the latter was "making out credentials as an agent of my *wishes*, or a seeker of my *'approbation.'* " Black's desire to see Thompson: "May have
helped you (Black) to the belief that I wished what was
to me a matter of perfect indifference, and approved what
I did not care about one way or the other."

In any event, Black brought away from Canada a distinct impression of what the Confederates desired on the
two main points at issue—abolition and independence.
As to the first point, they were very decided. Abolition
is a violation of the federal constitution and an abroga-
tion of the rights of the states. The South, moreover,
could not surrender into the hands of the abolitionists the
power of determining the methods of emancipation. To
the Southern mind, this thought was a nightmare. At
the worst, the abolitionists who were "so many fiends from
the bottomless pit" would arouse and incite the negroes
into the indiscriminate slaughter of the white population;
and at the best, the regulation of the vital relationship
between white and black would be entrusted to for-
eigners, unacquainted with the needs of the Southerners'
country. The Confederates finally have a solemn duty
"to protect the negroes against the pitiless cruelty of
the Abolitionists."

On the matter of self-government—"the administration
of their domestic affairs"—Black writes a little vaguely.
Probably Thompson was not quite frank. On one point,
he was decisive; they would have this self-government even
if it involved their annihilation. As to what self-government meant, there arises ambiguity: It: "does not mean
the separate nationality of the South. They are not

opposed to the federal *Government* (using the word government in the sense of the Constitution and laws) . . . They struck for independence because it was the simplest and readiest means of saving the rights of the States from violation. . . . If they could now have some absolutely certain guarantee that the same end might be accomplished in the federal Union they are not so perverse as to fight an army of half a million and expose their country to desolation for a punctilio."

When it came to the details of this guarantee, Black had to use his imagination. The South will demand: "some means of enforcing the execution of the stipulations made in their favor," and they will insist upon the power and the right to pay their debts and to honor and reward their defenders. As to the procedure for bringing about the reconstruction the South will enter at once into a commercial and military alliance with the North; and then there will be an armistice during which angry passions will subside and arrangements for reunion will be made. Still there is doubt if the elaboration of all this machinery will be effective. "You are not to suppose that Mr. Thompson gave any direct assurance that the Confederate Government would dissolve and the States return into the Union upon the terms mentioned or upon any specific terms."

Black closes with the suggestion that Stanton ask the President for an armistice of three to six months. Negotiation can then be initiated by the dispatch of a safe-conduct for Holcombe, with whom might be coupled Clay and Thompson, which would enable him to go to Richmond and find out what terms the authorities there would grant. "If it be probable that the attitude of the Govern-

ment as taken in the letter '*To Whom It May Concern*'
will change, and the negotiations can proceed upon the
basis of a Constitutional Union I am thoroughly convinced that peace, harmony and a Union never again to
be broken are very near at hand." In a second post-
script, Black admits: "my desire to see a restoration
(of the Union) may have helped me to the conclusion."

Just as Black's peace mission exemplifies the hopes and
the ideas which the moderates cherished, so his own post-
scripted statement expresses a judgment upon their feasi-
bility. To have returned from Canada convinced that
peace could be had upon any terms of reunion, at a time
when Jaquess and Gilmore had just returned from Richmond and had published the account of their mission, was
to convict oneself of an extraordinary credulity. The
case of the conservative Democrats was not founded upon
realities, but upon delusions.

The extremists within the Democratic Party had,
meanwhile, entered into communication with the Confederate commissioners in Canada. The commissioners,
especially Thompson, had turned their particular attention to the most important object of their mission—
the creation of a Northwest Confederacy.[39] By means
of propaganda and of violence, it was hoped to detach
Ohio, Illinois, Indiana, Missouri, and Kentucky from the
Northern cause and ally them with the Southern Confederacy. In the attainment of this purpose, they were

[39] The hope of the Southerners that the Northwest would revolt found
frequent expression in the South. McPherson, James S.: *The Political
History of the United States of America during the Great Rebellion*,
pp. 303-304; *Official Records of the Union and Confederate Armies*,
Series IV, Vol. II, pp. 137-138, 489-494.

determined to utilize the secret societies which were the
centers of greatest and most vigorous disaffection in the
North. The first recourse was naturally C. L. Vallandigham. He had been exiled from the North for his opposition to the government, he was Supreme Commander of
the Sons of Liberty and he was now living conveniently
at Windsor, Ontario. Early in June, Vallandigham and
Thompson discussed the situation together. The former
gave useful information about the strength of the secret
societies and considered the possibilities of revolt promising. He, however, preferred that James A. Barrett of
St. Louis, "grand lecturer" of the order, should distribute
the funds which Thompson was willing to furnish. A
few days later Vallandigham returned to Ohio. He left
behind a Thompson convinced that everything was moving
to a "supposed successful consummation." The Northwest was certain of revolt.[40]

To accomplish this highly desirable result, July and
August were set aside for rebellions. The first was to
take place on July 20. Nothing happened. Another
meeting with Thompson was held on July 22 at St.
Catherines, Canada. At this conference the insurrection
was set for August 16, and funds were again advanced
by the wealthy Thompson. Vallandigham was not present.[41] But even before this insurrection broke out, it was

[40] Castleman, John B.: *Active Service*, pp. 144-145; Foulke, William
D.: *Life of Oliver P. Morton*, Vol. I, p. 401; *Official Records of the
Union and Confederate Armies*, Series I, Vol. XLIII, Part II, pp.
930-931, Thompson to Benjamin, December 3, 1864.

[41] Stidger, Felix: *Treason History of the Order of Sons of Liberty,
formerly Circle of Honor, succeeded by Knights of the Golden Circle,
afterward Order of American Knights*, pp. 111, 115. The most promi-

again postponed—this time until the night of the Chicago Convention—August 29. Captain Hines, who had been attached to the Canadian mission to carry out their military plans, was put in charge. But once again the insurrection failed to materialize.[42]

The reasons for the failure of the Democratic extremists and their Confederate friends successfully to effect their design of an armed insurrection in the North are many. For a small group of conspirators to succeed in overthrowing an established government, it is necessary that the attack be unexpected and decisive. Secrecy, therefore, is absolutely necessary. It was, however, an essential advantage which the Confederate commissioners and sympathizers never had. Thompson complains bitterly that two or three men cannot exchange views without the danger of being reported.[43] It is small wonder, for informers, detectives, and spies, animated by all the motives from greed to loyalty, were in continual touch with the plans of the Confederates and their Federal allies. The government had agents in the various lodges of the secret societies; and its detectives swarmed everywhere. Felix R. Stidger, one of the leading informers, was even

nent conspirators were Dodd, Bowles and Walker of Indiana; Bullitt of Kentucky; and Barrett of Missouri. Pitman, Benn: *The Trials for Treason at Indianapolis, Disclosing the Plans for Establishing a North-Western Confederacy*, p. 113.

[42] Castleman, John B.: *Active Service*, pp. 148, 157-159, Report of Captain Castleman to James C. Seddon, Secretary of War, September 7, 1864; *Official Records of the Union and Confederate Armies*, Series I, Vol. XLV, Part I, pp. 1077-1078; Bross, William: *Biographical Sketch of the Late General B. J. Severt, History of Camp Douglas*, pp. 15-20.

[43] *Official Records of the Union and Confederate Armies*, Series I, Vol. XLIII, Part II, p. 934.

a prominent office holder in the Sons of Liberty.[44] A second reason for failure was the character of the conspirators themselves. The Southerners, for instance, who were detailed to these hazardous enterprises possessed personal defects. Captain Hines, in charge of the military designs concocted in Canada and attempted in the United States, accuses his subordinates of being mere "idle talkers" or those who "had been highly connected" in Southern society.[45] If the Confederates were lacking in the qualities requisite for daring adventure, their Northern allies could not be expected to be an improvement. Recruits, attached to the Southern cause by the hope of finding profitable employment, had a constant fear of betrayal and a disconcerting readiness to confess, once they were arrested. The peace extremists whose attachment was presumed to be less pecuniary, were ineffective accomplices. By the end of the year, J. P. Holcombe was sufficiently disillusioned to admit that the revolutionary sentiment in the Northwest had been weak at best.[46] This popular weakness the peace advocates did not recoup by their efficiency, daring or decision. Hines calls their leaders visionary and impractical; describes their forces as disorganized; and says that their readiness for war was only theoretical.[47] Certainly Vallandigham's coöperation was of an equivocal variety; he was a "safe and sane" hero if there ever was one. Probably he was but typical of the whole movement.

But meanwhile the time left before the Democratic

[44] Stidger, Felix R.: *Op. cit.,* pp. 30-55.
[45] Castleman, John B.: *Active Service,* pp. 159, 193.
[46] Report of J. P. Holcombe to J. P. Benjamin, November 16, 1864.
[47] Castleman, John B.: *Active Service,* pp. 158, 161.

Convention was speeding away. If the extremists within that party did not act quickly to counteract the early victories of the conservatives, their cause and the cause of the Confederate commissioners was lost. Unfortunately, fate played a curious jest upon them both. The letter "To Whom It May Concern" had been gratifying because it had deprived Lincoln of his conservative support and had given the Democratic Party a newly defined principle to uphold. But at the same time, it diminished all enthusiasm for revolution except on the part of a few of the most turbulent extremists. It now seemed possible to defeat the administration, not by an insurrection to set up a Northwest Confederacy, or to embarrass the conduct of the war by internecine strife, but at the ballot box. This unforeseen result of the Greeley episode was not to the taste of Thompson and Holcombe.[48]   In Indiana, Dodd and Walker, bent on an aggressive revolutionary policy, were warned by the leaders of the Democratic Party to give up their plans because they would endanger the election of 1864.[49]   In other states there was a similar development. So the extremists turned with renewed zeal to the task of influencing the Democratic National Convention through a marshalled public opinion. In Illinois, for instance, two gigantic outdoor conventions were held. The first, at Peoria, demanded an armis-

[48] Report of J. P. Holcombe to J. P. Benjamin, November 16, 1864; *Official Records of the Union and Confederate Armies,* Series I, Vol. XLIII, Part I, p. 931, Jacob Thompson to J. P. Benjamin, December 3, 1864.

[49] Pitman, Benn: *Op. cit.,* pp. 101-103. In reply to the arguments of the conservatives, Dodd and Walker said that the "government could not be restored again under the old state of things without a forcible revolution. That an appeal to the ballot-box was all folly."

tice and a convention of states; the second, at Springfield, witnessed a crowd wearing white rosettes and peace
badges.[50] In New York, Wood, whose brother's paper
printed personal notices from which Thompson in Canada derived his instructions from the Confederacy, was
active for peace. A gigantic mass meeting was held at
Syracuse on August 18. After addresses by Vallandigham, ex-Governor Walker of California, and Wood himself, a resolution was adopted which condemned the letter [51] "To Whom It May Concern" because it showed
that the Northern war aims were no longer Union but the
abolition of slavery and the annihilation of states rights,
and which demanded a national convention to make peace
and an immediate armistice.[52] The fact that the open air
mass meeting was patronized by the *Argus*, the organ
of the conservative Democracy, and was attended by
delegates from other than Wood strongholds, was
disquieting.

On Monday, August 29, 1864, the Democratic National Convention assembled in the Wigwam at Chicago
where four years previous the Republican Party had
nominated Abraham Lincoln. It was apparent from the
very first that the conservatives had control of the machinery. August Belmont, chairman of the national
committee, opened the convention with a keynote speech
which stressed "devotion to the Union and Constitu-

[50] Cole, Arthur C.: *The Era of the Civil War, 1848-1870; The Centennial History of Illinois*, Vol. III, pp. 321-322.
[51] *Official Records of the Union and Confederate Armies*, Series I,
Vol. XLIII, Part II, p. 935. In August Benjamin Wood was furnished
by the Confederate Commissioners with $25,000 to "purchase arms."
(Castleman, John B.: *Active Service*, p. 146.)
[52] *New York Herald*, August 19, 1864.

tion";[53] the temporary chairman, William Bigler, was a member of the Pennsylvania delegation which supported McClellan;[54] all dangerous and inflammatory resolutions—especially one submitted by Alexander Long of Ohio, a furious advocate of peace,[55] which called upon the President to suspend the draft until the nation had decided the question of war or peace at the November election—were referred to the Committee on Resolutions.

The second day of the convention began peacefully. No quarrel arose over the nomination of Governor Seymour of New York as permanent president, for various aspects of his peculiar political position recommended him to all factions. His dislike for McClellan appealed to the ultra-peace faction in the Democratic Party, while his political orthodoxy recommended him to the moderates. He was an admirable presiding officer. Faultlessly groomed, he stepped forward to deliver the keynote address. Its statement of principles was antiquated; it was reminiscent of the days before Sumter, of the Crittenden Resolution, of Democratic opposition to the eman-

[53] Belmont, August: *Letters, Speeches and Addresses of August Belmont*, pp. 140-141.

[54] *Proceedings of the Democratic National Convention held in 1864 at Chicago*, pp. 4, 46. How the Republicans regarded this convention can be ascertained from an account of it, published by the *Congressional Union Committee* at Washington, 1864. Its title reads: "The Chicago Copperhead Convention. The Treasonable and Revolutionary Utterances of the Men who composed it. Extracts from all the Notable Speeches delivered in and out of the National 'Democratic' Convention. A surrender to the Rebels Advocated—A Disgraceful and Pusillanimous Peace Demanded—The Federal Government Shamefully Vilified, and not a Word Said against the Crime of Treason and Rebellion."

[55] McPherson, James: *The Political History of the United States of America, during the Great Rebellion*, pp. 387-388. Alexander Long had been censured by the House of Representatives for his treasonable approbation of the Confederacy.

cipation proclamation. Its reasoning was based upon the fundamental delusion of the war weary nation—that peace could be had if it were not for the reckless and extreme demands of the administration. "This administration cannot now save this Union if it would. It has, by its proclamation, by vindictive legislation, by displays of hate and passion, placed obstacles in its own pathway which it cannot overcome, and has hampered its own freedom of action by unconstitutional acts. . . . But if the administration cannot save this Union, we can. . . . There are no hindrances in our pathways to Union and to peace. We demand no conditions for the restoration of our Union; we are shackled with no hates, no prejudices, no passions. . . . We demand for them (the South) what we demand for ourselves—the full recognition of the rights of the States." [56] If he had wanted a criticism of his statements, Seymour should have confronted Davis in the custom house at Richmond.

The inevitable hostility of the extremists and conservatives had, meanwhile, developed over the question of the platform. The fight over that statement of principles was not a public one; it was confined to the Committee on Resolutions. Upon that body, as representative from Ohio, sat Vallandigham, and there he had determined to force the issue of peace and war; and to his determination he seemed to have enlisted popular support. He was the hero of the convention.[57] Crowds followed him through

[56] *Proceedings of the Democratic National Convention held in 1864, at Chicago*, pp. 22-24.

[57] Keefe, Thomas H.: "How the Northwest Was Saved. A chapter from the Secret Service Records of the Civil War," in *Everybody's Magazine*, Vol. II, p. 85; *New York Tribune*, August 31, 1864; Castleman, John B.: *Active Service*, p. 154.

the streets; when he rose to speak, the audience was hushed; at the Richmond Hotel which was the headquarters of the peace men and of the "Missouri delegation"— the picturesque disguise for the Confederate conspirators from Canada and their allies from the secret orders—he held frequent receptions. But the approval of the mob did not erase the opposition of the conservatives on the platform committee. The fight against Vallandigham was led so well by the New York delegation, the bulwark of the conservative cause, that they secured the election of their candidate, Guthrie of Kentucky, as Chairman. Thus organized, the committee struggled to reconcile the two points of view. There was delay while a subcommittee ironed out differences. At last the completed platform was read to the excited convention. It condemned military interference with the elections in border states, the usurpations of the administration, and the denial of civil rights; pledged "unswerving fidelity to the Union under the Constitution"; and then, in its second resolution, asserted: "That this convention does explicitly declare, as the sense of the American people, that after four years of failure to restore the Union by the experiment of war, . . . justice, humanity, liberty and the public welfare demand that immediate efforts be made for a cessation of hostilities, with a view to an ultimate convention of the States, or other peaceable means, to the end that at the earliest practicable moment peace may be restored on the basis of the Federal Union of the States." [58] This statement was a distinct triumph for Vallandigham; even with the modification of other resolutions, it was the

[58] *Proceedings of the Democratic National Convention held in 1864, at Chicago*, pp. 25-28.

key plank of the platform. The crowd in the Wigwam sensed its significance. Before the first reading of this resolution could be completed, the secretary's voice was drowned in the uproar; when order was restored, the resolution was read a second time in silence; and then the crowd, unchecked, "surrendered itself to the wildest enthusiasm." [59] The peace party had captured the platform.

It is a pity to spoil the dramatic purity of this moment by suggesting that the first part of a political bargain had been executed. But it is unlikely that a resolution would have been reported by a committee generally hostile to it, unless something was given in return. That something was to be the nomination of George B. McClellan. That nomination, however, was not to be accomplished easily. The afternoon of the second day wore away in an unseemly wrangle over the nominees. McClellan, who had been nominated by J. C. Stockton of New Jersey and seconded by Cox of Ohio, was attacked by B. G. Harris of Maryland who claimed that the convention really asked him "to support the man who stabbed my own mother"—an oratorical reference to McClellan's arrest of some members of the Maryland legislature and his suspension of *habeas corpus* in that state.[60] Alexander Long in a frenzied peroration accused the candidate of surpassing Lincoln in abridging civil liberties, demanded "any man" as candidate rather than McClellan, and closed with a statement that McClellan's speeches: "were directly opposed to a peace platform, and if he accepts a nomination upon it, after what he has said,

[59] *Proceedings of the Democratic National Convention held in 1864, at Chicago*, pp. 27-28.
[60] *Ibid*, pp. 30-32.

he stultifies himself, and, in my judgment, is unworthy the support of the democratic party." [61]   The convention during the remarks of these speakers resembled a bedlam; there were cries, hisses, applause, laughter, and counter-charges. The wearied delegates adjourned to the next day. During the night the uncompromising peace men worked diligently to defeat McClellan, but, in spite of the efforts of the Woods, of Harris, of Long, the nomination of McClellan was certain.[62]   On the following day, George Brinton McClellan received the nomination on the first ballot. His nearest competitor was Thomas H. Seymour, the Democratic war governor of Connecticut and the candidate of the peace men. He drew his support from the border states and from the divided States of Illinois, Indiana, and Ohio.[63]   The peerless Vallandigham now mounted the platform and, animated by the desire to have peace in the convention that there might be peace in the land, moved that the nomination be made unanimous. Then followed further compensation for the peace men. On August 31 the convention closed its session by nominating for Vice President George H. Pendleton of Ohio, a representative of the peace party in that distracted state.[64]

[61] *Proceedings of the Democratic National Convention held in 1864, at Chicago,* pp. 38-40.

[62] *New York Herald,* August 31, 1864; September 1, 1864.

[63] *Proceedings of the Democratic National Convention held in 1864, at Chicago,* pp. 43-44. Seymour's total of 38 votes was composed as follows: Maine, 3 out of a vote of 7; Vermont, 1 out of 5; Delaware, 3; Maryland, 7; Kentucky, 5½ out of 11; Ohio, 10½ out of 19; Indiana, 3½ out of 13; Wisconsin, 1 out of 8; California, 2½ out of 5; Oregon, 1 out of 3. The Illinois delegation cast all its votes for McClellan owing to the unit rule. A member claimed, however, that the vote within the delegation was 21 to 11.

[64] *Ibid.,* p. 55.

As the delegates were streaming home from Chicago, General Sherman was pressing closer and closer about Atlanta. On September 2, he was master of this important metropolis of the Confederacy. The *Tribune* retailed the "GLORIOUS NEWS" in large headlines to its readers.[65] At last there was the military victory for which the Northern cause had been waiting. Its effect was likely to be immediate, for the Northerners "were as unstable and capricious as spoiled children" and their spirit responded readily to good news.[66] It seemed as if the advent of the autumn had brought new vigor to the Union cause. The fresh winds of September had blown away the miasma of the summer months.

Atlanta gave the promise of military success to Lincoln's policy. It was, therefore, an earnest of the political success of November. But there were other factors at work which were to further the triumph of the administration. Chicago had given the country a party of opposition, reconciled only by an obvious compromise. McClellan's letter of acceptance made the obvious fatal. His own supporters had not been peace-at-any price men; his own army upbringing made any surrender of the Union unthinkable; the news from Atlanta now added expediency to these other motives. His answer on September 8 to the committee of notification ignored everything but the Union. "The re-establishment of the Union in all its integrity is, and must continue to be, the indispensable condition of any settlement. . . . If a frank,

[65] *New York Tribune,* September 3, 1864.
[66] *Official Records of the Union and Confederate Armies,* Series IV, Vol. III, p. 639, Report of Clay to M. P. Benjamin, September 12, 1864.

earnest and persistent effort to obtain these objects (peace and Union) should fail, the responsibility for ulterior consequences will fall upon those who remain in arms against the Union. But the Union must be preserved at all hazards." [67] This letter was a soldierly guarantee that the Union would not be abandoned; and it envisaged the possibility of war, as well as of peace, as a means of Union saving.

A compromise presents alternative methods of attack and requires alternative methods of defence. At once it opens up avenues of criticism and fails to enlist against critics the whole-hearted support of adherents. Such was the case of the Democratic Party after McClellan's letter of acceptance. The commissioners of the Confederacy in Canada, for instance, found it difficult to make up their minds about the northern Democratic Party. Individually their views varied according to their temperaments and to the time of their written reports. In September, Clay was enthusiastic over the convention; its platform was for peace. McClellan, whose letter of acceptance made him little better than Lincoln, would, however, be controlled by the peace factions of the Democracy. He urges that the South do nothing to make his election unlikely.[68] But by December Thompson and Holcombe were united in ascribing their defeat to McClel-

[67] *Proceedings of the National Democratic Convention held in 1864, at Chicago,* pp. 60-61; G. B. McClellan to Hon. Horatio Seymour and others, Committee, September 8, 1864.

[68] *Official Records of the Union and Confederate Armies,* Series IV, Vol. III, pp. 637-638. Clay says that McClellan's cabinet will include Horatio or T. H. Seymour as Secretary of State and Vallandigham as Secretary of War.

lan's nomination.[69] He had pandered to the military element in the Democratic Party and alienated the peace men.

McClellan's letter of acceptance undoubtedly disgusted the Democratic extremists. Vallandigham felt compelled to deny through the columns of the *New York News* the lukewarmness of his support.[70] The *News* itself considered that the peace democracy had been dealt a treacherous blow, and, in the first rush of disillusionment, announced that McClellan had no claim to the allegiance of loyal Democrats.[71] On September 14, fifty peace delegates met at the St. Nicholas Hotel in New York to select a candidate to succeed McClellan. Wood of the *News*, McMaster of the *Freeman's Journal*, Singleton and Green of Illinois, Long of Ohio,—all were either present or sent a promise of their support.[72] A month later a similar convention met in Ohio under the leadership of Long and Cory. Delegates assembled from the middle West and passed resolutions for peace and states rights, but failed to make nominations because of the lateness of the campaign. The extreme peace men, although restless, had no choice but the support of McClellan.[73]

[69] *Official Records of the Union and Confederate Armies*, Series I, Vol. XLIII, Part II, p. 931; Report of Jacob Thompson to J. P. Benjamin, December 3, 1864; Report of J. P. Holcombe to J. P. Benjamin, November 16, 1864.

[70] *New York Tribune*, October 26, 1864; Porter, George H.: "Ohio Politics during the Civil War Period," *Columbia University Studies in History, Economics and Public Law*, Vol. XL., No. 2, pp. 196-197.

[71] *New York Tribune*, September 13, 1864.

[72] *Ibid.*, September 15, 1864; October 10, 1864.

[73] Porter, George H.: "Ohio Politics during the Civil War Period," *Columbia University Studies in History, Economics, and Public Law*, Vol. XL, No. 2, pp. 197-198.

The failure of the party of national opposition to outline a definite policy not only increased disaffection within
its own ranks, it solidified its opponents and gave them
an opportunity to attack from both front and rear. Chicago and Atlanta had helped to convince the extremists in
the Republican Party that their salvation was the support
of the President. Early in September the abolitionists
had so decided; by October the radical factionalists pla-
cated in part by Lincoln's sacrifice of Montgomery Blair,
were busy administration supporters. They resolved to
impose their terms of peace upon the President; to convert
the election into an endorsement of their extreme position.
Speaking at Philadelphia on October 4, Cochrane promised the South not the Union as it was, but as it should
be,[74] and a month later Henry Winter Davis gave free
rein to his gift of rhapsodic prophecy: conservatives "will
be drowned in the thunders of the coming majority."
Those who voted against the Wade-Davis bill will be
defeated. "Trembling and doubting conservatives with
their swollen feet will cease to stand in the way of the
march of the nation to universal freedom." [75] Following
the policy of Andrew, the Republican extremists were
determined to save the machine in order to run it. They
would postpone their efforts to force their war and peace
policy upon the President until after the election.

But, meanwhile, the summer, ending as it did in Chicago and Atlanta, had drawn to the President's support
the leading peace advocate of the Republican Party,
Horace Greeley. The editor of the *Tribune* had decided
to accept the situation. A political victory in the state

[74] *New York Tribune*, October 5, 1864.
[75] *Ibid.*, November 4, 1864.

convention over his arch rival, Weed, may have made the
transition easier. On September 7, in spite of the latter's
best efforts, Greeley had received the nomination of presidential elector at large.[76] He had at last gained office.
The *Tribune* now turned its unmatched powers of vitu-
peration upon McClellan. It reported conversations in
which Confederate officers were overheard to say: "Never
fear anything from McClellan; we *know* he is all right." [77]
It asserted that the initials of the Democratic presidential
candidate, *G.B.*, stood properly for "Gun Boat" McClellan, since he had spent his time on a gunboat during the
battle of Malvern Hill and was quite uninformed of hostilities; [78] it composed doggerel about "the obliging young
man from Antietam"; [79] declared "the only effective
Peace Commissioners" to be "Grant, Sherman, Farragut,
and Sheridan"; [80] and it claimed that the idea of an
armistice "springs from folly or treason." [81]

All those statements must have been very reassuring to
those whose memories stretched back as far as July, 1864,
and whose hopes were bent upon the success of the administration's war and peace policy. If Lincoln's supporters
wanted more reassurance, they should have scanned the
columns of the *Tribune* for September 25. Two items
were in juxtaposition. The first quoted the *Buffalo
Courier* of the 24th to the effect that: "William Cornell
Jewett was in town yesterday and, we believe, moves off on
his mysterious way today. . . . He considers 'peace' as

[76] *New York Tribune*, September 8, 1864.
[77] *Ibid.*, September 7, 1864.
[78] *Ibid.*, September 19, 1864.
[79] *Ibid.*, November 9, 1864.
[80] *Ibid.*, September 24, 1864.
[81] *Ibid.*, September 27, 1864.

dead." The second read: "HORACE GREELEY will speak for the cause of the country at *Newburgh*, N. Y., *this* evening." "Also, in *Brooklyn*, N. Y., on *Wednesday* evening. Also, at *Winsted*, Conn., on *Thursday* evening." [82] After these two items, the election returns of November were a superfluous demonstration that the peace movement of July and August had collapsed.

[83] *New York Tribune,* September 25, 1864.

CHAPTER IV

A Politician's Dream of Peace

To most observers the election of 1864 meant that the war would now run its logical course to a dictated peace. The military stalemate had been broken; the pre-election uncertainty of public opinion had disappeared, and the peace movement of July and August had collapsed. But before the end of November there were rumors of a new peace overture, initiated and conducted by a great politician, Francis Preston Blair, father of Montgomery Blair, recently Postmaster-General in Lincoln's cabinet, and of Francis Preston Blair, Jr., a general in the Federal army. The mere recital of these three names was enough to mark a distinction between this and previous negotiations. The Blairs, so intimately connected with the Civil War, could not have been pacifists animated by a horror of warfare and a desire for its cessation; other motives must have governed men such as they. The solution of this dilemma can be given in a word—politics. The Blairs were primarily politicians—great politicians. As members of that profession, they have not become historically famous but the partial accounts of their activities suggest a fascinating area of such wide influence that they ought to be remembered. Perhaps the reason for their comparative obscurity lies in the methods which they employed. They worked in secret, behind the scenes of great events. And in that shadowy domain, they influenced the course of

national politics for over half a century. It is a unique
record, important not only for its influence upon the peace
negotiations but also for itself.

The patriarch of the family was Francis Preston Blair.
According to actuarial statistics he should have been
dead or in senile retirement at the time of the Civil War
for he was then over seventy years old. Born in Virginia
in 1791, he began the long span of his political career over
the mountains in Kentucky. And he began it inauspi-
ciously. After the election of 1824, he intemperately
quarreled with Henry Clay and thus incurred the hostility
of the man who was to dominate Kentucky politics for
nearly thirty years; and then he became involved on the
losing side of a bitter political war over the State's financial policy. Out of favor and out of office, he began con-
tributing to a political journal, the *Frankfort Argus*.[1]
With the inexorability of a syllogism, a revolution in the
prospects of the young politician now took place. The
editor of the *Argus* was Amos Kendall; Amos Kendall
was one of the talented schemers manipulating the presidential ambitions of Andrew Jackson; Andrew Jackson
was triumphantly elected in 1828; and Amos Kendall was
transported to Washington as unofficial adviser to his successful protegé. The precise opportunity for the employment of Blair's talents eventually occurred. It was a
question of the press. In those days Presidents did not
rely upon unofficial spokesmen and party machines did
not depend upon newspapers ostensibly divorced from
politics; both required a partisan journal which would

---

[1] Baber, George: "The Blairs." *The Register of the Kentucky State
Historical Society*, Vol. XIV, No. 2, pp. 28-29, 38-39; Shaler, N. S.:
Kentucky, A Pioneer Commonwealth, pp. 177-184.

speak definitely and authoritatively for the administration. This function had been fulfilled for the Democracy at Washington by the *Telegraph*, edited by Duff Green, but the usefulness of paper and editor to Jackson had disappeared when both showed sympathy for Calhoun and his faction of the Southern Democracy. A feud had broken out between Jackson and the South Carolinian and, in the general proscription, the *Telegraph* had to go. In its place the administration needed a journal of undoubted and undivided loyalty. The thought that Blair should be its editor was a natural one. He was a friend of Kendall and he was heavily in debt to the United States Bank, an institution which Jacksonites did not regard with favor. So Blair was summoned to Washington and the *Washington Globe* was created for the exercise of his editorial talents.[2]

Thus began the heyday of Blair's political fortunes. He became a member of the Kitchen Cabinet,[3] a group of Jackson's trusted and influential advisers. His daughter, Elizabeth, spent an entire winter at the White House,[4] and to his wife, Jackson, on retiring from the presidency, sent a "heifer raised by me since my second election."[5] This close personal and political relationship continued even after "Old Hickory" left the presidency. When Jackson was old and dying in poverty, it was Blair who helped finance a loan of $10,000 which was never expected to be repaid.[6] And at Jackson's death Blair

---

[2] Kendall, Amos: *Autobiography of Amos Kendall,* Edited by his son-in-law, William Stickney, pp. 370-374.

[3] Bassett, John S.: *The Life of Andrew Jackson,* Vol. II, pp. 513-540.

[4] Blair, Gist: "Annals of Silver Spring," *Records of the Columbia Historical Society,* Vol. XXI, p. 167.

[5] Bassett, John S.: *Op. cit.,* Vol. II, p. 706.

[6] *Ibid.,* Vol. II, p. 745.

became the inheritor of the former's papers and political mantle. Meanwhile the impetus given to the Blair fortunes by the favor of Jackson continued. Under the Crown Prince, Martin Van Buren, the *Globe* was still the spokesman of the administration, and when the Whigs came in after the hurdy-gurdy campaign of 1840, it assumed the task of partisan opposition and looked forward to the next presidential contest as the time for party reward and personal success. It was not to be. Although 1844 returned the Democracy to power, it was a party under the domination of Calhoun and the Southerners. To a Jacksonian, like Blair, this transformation was unendurable; to the Southern faction, the continuance of Blair in his editorial capacity was unthinkable. The editor of the *Globe* saw his paper superseded by the *Washington Union* and saw his own place taken by Ritchie, a Virginian and a representative of the Southern Democrats.[7] Blair's political career was apparently at an end. In fact the editor of the *Democratic Review* sang a requiem for him. In an article, accompanied by a mezzotint of its subject and written in the manner of an obituary, Blair is pictured as living "at a farm known as the 'Silver Spring,' which it is his insatiable delight to adorn and improve. . . . No cause is likely ever to bring him forward before the country as an active political writer." [8]

The retirement of F. P. Blair to this bucolic retreat might well have induced other reflections. A more jaundiced observer might have mused upon the conversion of

---

[7] *Niles National Register,* May 10, 1845, Vol. LXVII, pp. 153-154.
[8] "Blair of the Globe," in the *United States Magazine and Democratic Review,* New Series, Vol. XVII, p. 14.

a poor country editor, who came to Washington so penniless that he could contribute nothing to the establishment of the paper which he was to edit, into a retired gentleman-proprietor of an extensive estate near Washington. Evidently the perquisites which Blair and his associate, Rives, had enjoyed in the way of government printing, had brought their material reward. One hostile critic asserts that their profit on the publication of the sixth census was 622 per cent.[9] But personal aggrandizement and financial gain were not the dominating motives of the Blairs. They were rescued from selfishness by an intense devotion to their friends and they were saved from a mere cold calculation by their hot tempers. F. P. Blair, then, was not the man to retire willingly under pressure. Fifteen years of party warfare had wedded him to the cause of "Old Hickory." Jackson's friends were Blair's friends; Jackson's enemies were Blair's enemies. To Van Buren, as a part of the Jackson tradition, Blair always gave his able and unwavering support. As for Calhoun, Polk, and later Buchanan, the representatives of the anti-Jackson Democracy, they were "conspirators," "traitors," and "nullifiers." Blair had no intention of allowing Silver Spring to mellow his political bitterness or soften his implacable hatred for such men. To overthrow the corrupt crew which now ran the Democracy was his duty. Although the struggle was likely to be merciless—"The Blairs when they go in for a fight, go in for a funeral," was a family boast [10]—the old man was not above adroitness. Through the years he kept in touch closely but

---

[9] Grouard, George M.: *A Practical Printer's Answer to Mr. Kendall's Tract No. 5, on the public printing. Addressed to himself,* p. 4.

[10] Riddle, A. G.: *The Life of Benjamin F. Wade,* p. 287, a remark of Montgomery Blair to Riddle.

unobtrusively with the current of affairs. Silver Spring was not so remote from Washington but what he could drive into the city and be at the center of activity.[11] Correspondence and visits were also useful. But the long effort of Blair and Van Buren and other Democrats of the proper school to manipulate nominations and secure control of the party was unsuccessful.[12] Perhaps some consolation for his own failure could be derived from the political careers of his two sons.

The older, Montgomery Blair, in spite of his early training at West Point, elected to follow the law and to take the first steps in the practice of that profession at St. Louis. There he would naturally enjoy the favor of Thomas Hart Benton, "Old Bullion," picturesque overlord of the State of Missouri, for Benton was related to the Blairs through the extensive Preston connection.[13] The career of the young lawyer included a decade of minor political positions—United States District Attor-

[11] Polk, James K.: *The Diary of James K. Polk during his Presidency, 1843-1849,* Edited by Milo Menton Quaife, Vol. IV, pp. 39-40; Bigelow, John: *Retrospections of an Active Life,* Vol. I, p. 166.

[12] Polk, James K.: *Op. cit.,* Vol. IV, pp. 51-52. The convention of 1848 was a tremendous disappointment to F. P. Blair since it so shamelessly betrayed Van Buren. Blair asserted that he would vote for Cass because of a "point of *punctilio*" but his "heart was with Van Buren." Buchanan, James: *The Works of James Buchanan comprising his Speeches, State Papers, and Private Correspondence,* Edited by John B. Moore, Vols. VIII and IX, *passim.*

[13] Andrews, Henry P., and Wiggins, P. Porter: *The Descendants of John Porter, of Windsor, Conn., in the line of his great, great Grandson, Col. Joshua Porter, M.D., of Salisbury, Litchfield County, Conn., with some account of the Families into which They Married,* p. 21; Green, Thomas M.: *Historic Families of Kentucky, with special reference to Stocks immediately derived from the Valley of Virginia; tracing in detail their various genealogical connexions and illustrating from historic sources their influence upon the political and social development of Kentucky and the States of the South and West,* pp. 28-29.

ney, Mayor of St. Louis, and Judge of the Court of Common Pleas; and then he returned to Maryland in 1852.
Since the compromise measures of 1850 had temporarily
closed the breach in the Democratic Party, he may have
anticipated political preferment.   At any rate, in 1855
President Pierce appointed him Solicitor in the Court of
Claims.[14]   Francis Preston Blair, Jr., however, was the
center of the family's admiration and ambition.   Lincoln,
realizing the situation with his customary shrewdness,
remarked that "Frank is their hope and pride." [15]   Montgomery was devoted to his brother and thought him "the
greatest man in the country." [16]   Like his father and
brother, "Frank" started out as a lawyer.   After obtaining an education at Princeton, he went West, first to Kentucky and then to St. Louis, where he might benefit from
the Benton relationship.   Then came the Mexican War.[17]
It carried "Frank" into the army and then sent him back
to St. Louis, not as a mere lawyer but as an active
politician.

Difficult as they are to understand, Missouri politics
offered a wide opportunity for a restless and daring spirit.
A border state, delicately balanced between the North
and South, it was only natural that there should be an
intense divergence of opinion on the question of slave and
free labor.   A western state, as well, the clear issue of
slavery was obscured through modifications incident to

[14] Appleton's *Cyclopædia of American Biography*, Edited by James
Grant Wilson and John Fiske, Vol. I, p. 282.
[15] Nicolay, John G., and Hay, John: *Abraham Lincoln, a History*,
Vol. IV, pp. 414-415, a quotation from John Hay's Diary (MS.).
[16] Welles, Gideon: *Diary of Gideon Welles*, Vol. III, p. 408.
[17] Croly, David G.: *Seymour and Blair.   Their Lives and Services with
an appendix containing a History of Reconstruction*, pp. 235-240.

the desire for westward expansion and to the allegiance to American nationalism. Finally there were the politicians who, in Missouri as elsewhere, were willing to manipulate causes and create principles for their own self-advancement. By 1848 this array of crossed purposes and incompatible interests had torn apart the Democratic Party. In part this dissension reflected the division in the national party where Martin Van Buren failed to secure the presidential nomination because of the hostility of the Southern faction. But the quarrel in Missouri had a particularly local tinge. There was a feud between Benton, who decried slavery agitation as a threat against the Union, and a rival faction which thought that the interests of the State were best served by the adoption of the extreme Southern position. In these rough tides, Frank Blair sailed his own course. Although a slaveholder, as was his father,[18] he did not ally himself with the pro-Southern Democracy. That faction, wherever located, was distasteful to all the Blair clan. On the other hand, he was not in complete accord with Benton on the question of slavery. In 1848, following Van Buren out of the Democratic Party, he became a mainstay in Missouri of the resultant Free Soil Party and a coeditor of its paper, the *Barnburner*.[19] Three years later, however, he was wholeheartedly in the Benton camp. For some time the power of "Old Bullion" had been waning and at last it

[18] Blair, Gist: *Op. cit.*, pp. 179-180; Stevens, Walter B.: "Lincoln and Missouri," in the *Missouri Historical Review*, Vol. X, No. 2, p. 67. Montgomery Blair never owned a slave. Frank freed the last of his slaves in 1859; when the elder Blair freed his is uncertain.

[19] Johnson, C. P.: "Remarks of Charles P. Johnson on the occasion of the Presentation of the Portrait of Oliver D. Filley to the Missouri Historical Society, Thursday, May 21, 1903," *Missouri Historical Society Collections*, Vol. II, No. 6, p. 6.

had been successfully called in question. In 1850, he was defeated in his campaign for reëlection to the United States Senate. Among the younger men who rallied around him were Frank Blair and his cousin, B. Gratz Brown. It is not certain just how precisely these recruits accepted the views of their aged leader, they at least determined to capitalize his splendid tradition. As his supporters,they purchased the *Morning Signal* and renamed it the *Missouri Democrat*. This paper became the organ of the Benton faction and of the "free Democracy." In 1852 the efforts of this newly organized bloc, accomplished a political overturn. Benton was elected to the national House of Representatives and Blair and Brown became members of the Missouri Legislature.[20]

During the next four years of Missouri politics the Democratic factional quarrel grew so important that it intruded upon the course of national history. The four years started out with a tremendous effort on the part of the Benton group to undo the work of their enemies. The object of attack was the Jackson resolutions which the State Legislature of 1849 had enacted as a proper creed on the question of slavery and of state's rights. Blair hated both the author and the sentiments of these resolutions; he pressed to the attack. These resolutions, he said, were passed by Benton's opponents and are a reflection upon his policies; they "seek to interpolate a new dogma in the Democratic creed"—an attempt which "first brought division into our ranks, and has defeated that party which was before invincible"; and finally, in threatening to concert measures with other slave-holding states

[20] McElroy, John: *The Struggle for Missouri*, p. 19.

if the North denies the justice of these resolutions, they simple restate the pernicious Calhoun doctrine of nullification.[21] Here speaks the Blairs' personal loyalty to friends and relatives; their desire for party discipline that it may bring party success; their fundamental allegiance to the old Jacksonian tradition of American nationalism. At the same time Missouri affairs were being converted at Washington into a national issue. There several questions—the location of the proposed transcontinental railroad and the expansion of slavery into the western territories—were intertwined with the local feud of Benton and his enemies. Out of this welter of issues eventually emerged the Kansas-Nebraska Bill, which allowed the settlers of the territories in question to determine for themselves whether the existence of slavery would be permitted. Frank Blair did not bother himself about the connection of Douglas with this measure; he attributed the authorship to Atchison, Benton's arch foe and successor in the Senate. The Kansas-Nebraska Bill was simply another step in the anti-Benton strategy. Accordingly he delivered in the State Legislature a tempestuous attack upon this "odious measure" originated "by a cabal of nullifiers" of which Atchison was the leader. He then elaborated the reasons why Kansas would serve Missouri better as a free than as a slave state. The territory would be settled more rapidly and more numerously; it would provide larger and readier markets; and, as a consequence, the Pacific railroad would be built at an earlier date. In making his argument, he rejected all hint of abolitionism;

[21] Blair, F. P.: *Remarks of F. P. Blair, Jr., of St. Louis, in the House of Representatives of Missouri on the Repeal of the "Jackson Resolutions,"* pp. 5-7.

he grounded his appeal upon pure expediency.[22]   Nevertheless the Kansas-Nebraska Bill went through.   Its passage was a victory for his rivals and an ill omen for the
Benton-Blair alliance.

By the end of 1855 it must have become apparent to
the Blairs that if they were to enjoy political success, they
would have to depend upon some new alignment.   Their
hopes from the Democracy were increasingly delusive.
To the elder Blair the Republican Party suddenly offered
opportunity.   Doubtless to his great surprise, he was
asked to become the President of the "Republican Association of Washington, District of Columbia," which in
spite of its resounding title, consisted of six men, headed
by Lewis Clephane, the business manager of an anti-slavery paper.[23]   In a letter the retired farmer of Silver
Spring declined the proferred offer because of his relin-
quishment "of public employment" and his "addiction to
country life."   He went on to say, however, that he approved of the objects of the Association; that the repeal
of the Compromise of 1850 through the Kansas-Nebraska
Bill, unwise from the expedient point of view, marked the
first step toward "the destruction of the Confederacy, on
which the welfare of the whole country reposes"; and that

[22] *Remarks of Mr. F. P. Blair, Jr., of St. Louis, in Joint Session of
the General Assembly of Missouri upon the Subject of the Senatorial
Election*, pp. 1-5; *Ibid., January 10, 1855, in reply to Mr. Stewart,
Senator from Buchanan, on the motion of Mr. Gilstrop, of Macon, to
adjourn the Joint Session sine die*, pp. 9-11; Ray, P. O.: *The Repeal
of the Missouri Compromise, Its Origin and Authorship*, pp. 232-233,
note 324, a letter of F. B. Blair, Jr., to the *Missouri Democrat*, March
1, 1856.

[23] Clephane, Walter C.: "Lewis Clephane; A Pioneer Washington
Republican," *Records of the Columbia Historical Society*, Vol. XXI, p.
265. *The National Era* was the name of the paper with which Clephane
was connected.

the present administration, dominated by Atchison and
his fellows, was supporting the Calhoun doctrine of nullification.[24] The thought of Missouri apparently inflamed the old man. One holding such vigorous sentiments was almost certain to fall an easy victim to the
intrigues of the adroit Clephane. From his "Quaker
friends" the latter organized a Maryland Republican
Club, and this organization unexpectedly elected F. P.
Blair a delegate to the Pittsburg Convention, the first convention on a national scale of the Republican Party. On
his arrival there, again through the ingenious management of Clephane, Blair became President of the convention. Other delegates were bewildered by the unexpected
prominence gained in the Republican Party by a famous
Democrat, who had owned slaves and who hailed from a
border state, but the enthusiasm of the new movement was
so intense that even the abolition idealists were able to forget the conservative slavery views of the presiding officer.
It was only natural after these unsought honors, that
Blair should become a member of the Executive Committee which was to issue the call for the first National
Convention at Philadelphia.[25] Soon afterwards the allegiance of F. P. Blair to the new party was finally sealed.

[24] Clephane, Lewis: *Birth of the Republican Party with a brief history of the important part taken by the original Republican Association of the National Capital. An address delivered by Lewis Clephane,
Esq., at a reunion of the surviving members of the Republican Association of 1853 to 1861, and of the Wide-Awakes, January 26, 1889, with
accompanying documents. Appendix A, Letter of F. P. Blair, Sr., to
the Republican Association of Washington, December 1, 1855,* pp. 19-23.
[25] Clephane, Lewis: *Op. cit.,* pp. 11-12; Julian, George W.: *Political
Recollections, 1840-1872,* p. 148; Johnson, C. W.: *Proceedings of the
First Three Republican National Conventions of 1856, 1860, and 1864,
including proceedings of the antecedent national convention held at
Pittsburg, in February, 1856, as reported by Horace Greeley,* pp. 9-10.

The medium was a letter—appropriately headed in its published form as "A Voice from the Grave of Jackson!" —to a public meeting held in New York City on April 29, 1856. The writer traced with feeling the conspiracy of the South to spread slavery over the nation—a conspiracy which incidentally involved his retirement from the *Globe* —and declared that, since the Democratic Party had become one of nullifiers, "I, as a Democrat of the Jefferson, Jackson, and Van Buren school enter my protest." There were other charges of a similar nature.[26]   With the co-operation of other past masters, such as Thurlow Weed, John Bigelow, and Nathaniel Banks, the practical ambitions of this new crusader were immediately enlisted in the selection of the proper candidate for president.   Seward was laid aside because of the danger of his record, and Fremont, the Rocky Mountain "Pathfinder," was chosen because of his romantic past and his popular appeal.[27] Perhaps the availability of this picturesque figure was heightened by the fact that, through the Bentons, he was a member of the numerous Blair connection.

The election of 1856, with its defeat of Fremont, postponed the revenge which old Blair may have hoped to inflict upon the Democracy.   Instead he and his family were compelled to endure the fate of party deserters, for the victorious Buchanan had no occasion to treat them with mercy.   The first blow of the new administration fell upon Montgomery Blair when he was allowed to resign his

[26] Blair, Francis P., Sr.: *A Voice from the Grave of Jackson! Letter from Francis P. Blair, Esq., to a public meeting in New York, held April 29, 1856 (Dated Silver Spring, April 26, 1856)*, pp. 1-11.

[27] McClure, Alexander K.: *Colonel Alexander K. McClure's Recollections of Half a Century*, pp. 213-214; Bigelow, John: *Retrospections of an Active Life*, Vol. I, pp. 141-143.

position as Solicitor General. He "had not the ability to make a respectable advocate of the Government in the Court of Claims," wrote the President.[28] The second blow fell upon the campaign which F. P. Blair, Jr., was waging for his own reëlection to the national House of Representatives. In 1856 the younger son had not impetuously followed his father into the Republican Party. There was something still to be gained in Missouri within the Democratic Party. Frank's caution had been rewarded by an election to the lower house of the National Congress. This honor gained, he began to turn toward the Republicans. He had conferences with Lincoln and determined to align himself eventually with the new party.[29] For the present he thought it better to avoid all taint of abolition and during the campaign of 1858 he was ostensibly a Democrat. But the administration and its local allies, the anti-Bentonites, were determined to bring about his defeat. To the bed of the dying Benton both factions rushed for a final blessing. Each came away satisfied. For Buchanan, Benton expressed his friendship. To F. P. Blair, Sr., who wanted aid for "my son and his Missouri Canvas," Benton called the adminis-

[28] King, Horatio: *Turning on the Light, a dispassionate survey of President Buchanan's Administration, from 1860 to its close*, pp. 203-204, Buchanan to Horatio King, October 5, 1865. Montgomery Blair had not endeared himself to Southern hearts or hearts in sympathy with the South by his connection with the Dred Scott case. He was the counsel for Scott and delivered the argument in his behalf before the Supreme Court of the United States at its December Term, 1856. (Blair, Montgomery: *Argument of Montgomery Blair, Counsel for the Plaintiff in Error, Supreme Court of the United States, No. 7—December Term, 1856. Dred Scott (a Coloured Man) vs. John T. A. Sandford*, Washington, 1856.)

[29] Stevens, Walter B.: "Lincoln and Missouri," *Missouri Historical Review*, Vol. X, No. 2, p. 65.

tration "corrupt and deluded." [30]   Whatever may have
been the effect of these contradictory benedictions, young
Blair was defeated.   The time had now come for him
openly to join his father and brother in the Republican
ranks.

If the Republican Party was to have any existence in
the border states, it would have to be the protagonist of
a conservative policy in dealing with the slave.   If the
Blairs, representatives of the border states, were to be
successful, they would have to force such a policy upon
Republican leaders.   The experiences of F. P. Blair, Jr.,
in Missouri, had served as a school to try out principles
which would appeal to their "own meridian."   As slaveholders and residents of states where slaves were held in
considerable numbers, they had worked out a practical
solution of the relationship between black and white.
They opposed slavery, not on theoretical or moral
grounds, but on the plea that it was an inferior and disastrous economic organization.   Slavery should be abolished because free and slave labor cannot exist side by
side without the degradation of the former.   Although
slavery should, therefore, be abandoned, the freed black
cannot live in the same community with the white man.
Such a possibility is repugnant to the latter and retards
the progress of manumission in the South.   The only
remedy is the emigration of the blacks to some climate
suited to their nature and their temperament.   For all
practical purposes, some place in Central or South America will answer.   These regions are near at hand; we
could acquire land there by purchase or make other
arrangements by treaty.   The incidental advantages of

[30] King, Horatio: *Op. cit.,* pp. 244-251.

this policy of colonization are numerous. The newly settled lands will furnish us markets; they will be successful but peaceful rivals of Great Britain's colonizing
system; filibustering will cease; the South, relieved of
the fear of the freed black will rush to emancipation.[31]
This plan the three Blairs endeavored to impress upon
public attention. They sought to have Northern governors approve it in their messages; they strove to convert
state legislatures; they secured the endorsement of negroes
and of white men such as Lyman Trumbull, Governor
Bissell of Illinois, Theodore Parker, and others.[32] Armed
with this conciliatory policy as to slavery and with a
strong insistence as to the integrity of the Union, they
hoped to carry their own states in 1860 for the Republican party and themselves.

The Blairs then turned to the pleasant task of selecting
a presidential nominee who should embody their principles. For this purpose they resurrected from obscurity
Edward Bates of St. Louis, an old line Whig, who had
been partially associated with the Know-Nothing movement. His chief qualifications were the facts that he came

[31] Blair, Francis P., Jr.: *Speech of Hon. Frank P. Blair, Jr., of
Missouri, on the acquisition of territory in Central and South America
to be colonized with free blacks, and held as a dependency by the
United States, Delivered in the House of Representatives on the 14th
day of January, 1858;* Blair, Francis P., Jr.: *The Destiny of the Races
of this Continent, an address delivered before the Mercantile Library
Association of Boston, Massachusetts, on the 26th day of January,
1859.*

[33] Mowry, Duane (Editor): "Negro Colonization," *Publications of the
Southern History Association,* Vol. X, pp. 283-288, F. P. Blair to J. R.
Doolittle, October 18, 1859, November 3, 1859, Montgomery Blair to
J. R. Doolittle, November 11, 1859; Blair, Francis P., Jr.: *The Destiny
of the Races of this Continent, an address delivered before the Mercantile Library Association of Boston, Massachusetts, on the 26th day
of January, 1859,* pp. 29-31, 33-34, 37-38.

from a border state and that he was a "practical emanci-
pationist" who had freed his own slaves.[33]   Around his
candidacy the Blairs tried to rally the border states and
their friends, the politicians. In this purpose they met
with both failure and success. The border state phalanx
was ruined by the defection of Kentucky. Cassius M.
Clay, a prominent Republican leader of that state, had
been invited to Silver Spring and promised the office of
Secretary of War in the new cabinet if he would lend his
support to the Bates candidacy. But the memory of the
old Clay hostility to the Blairs was too strong to be for-
gotten and besides there was some uncertainty as to Bates'
exact principles.[34] From other quarters there were acces-
sions of strength. Horace Greeley, casting about for a
good opponent to work off his grudge against Seward,
hit upon Bates.[35] The Blairs also obtained a good share
of the Indiana and Pennsylvania delegations. It was
rumored that Weed consented, if Seward were not nominated, to turn over New York's votes to Bates.[36] In
advance this was a fairly safe promise. At the Convention itself the Blairs formed a family party. F. P. Blair,
Sr., was a delegate-at-large from Maryland, Montgomery
represented his own district in that state, and F. P. Blair,
Jr., came as a delegate-at-large from Missouri. On the
surface their experiences at Chicago were difficult and

[33] Greeley, Horace: *Recollections of a Busy Life*, p. 389; Hollister,
O. J.: *Life of Schuyler Colfax*, p. 142, note p. 144.

[34] Clay, Cassius M.: *The Life of Cassius Marcellus Clay, Memoirs,
Writing, and Speeches, showing his conduct in the overthrow of Ameri-
can Slavery, the Salvation of the Union, and the Restoration of the
Autonomy of the States*, Vol. I, pp. 244-246.

[35] Greeley, Horace: *Op. cit.*, p. 389.

[36] Gibson, Charles: "Edward Bates," *Missouri Historical Society Collections*, Vol. II, No. 1, p. 55; Hollister, O. J.: *Op. cit.*, pp. 147-148.

often humiliating.   An element in the Convention de-
murred at granting recognition to the Maryland delegation.   Its representatives, so the assertion ran, were
backed by no constituency and had been selected by a
state convention of only thirty men.   Even when the
delegation was seated, the Blairs found it impossible to
hold it in line for their candidates.   A recalcitrant minority insisted upon voting independently and in making the
most unpleasant disclosures.   Then Bates was defeated.
On the first ballot he had received forty-eight votes
largely from Connecticut, Maryland, Delaware, Missouri,
and Oregon; on the second ballot, his support began to
melt away; and on the third ballot, although Missouri
remained fast, Maryland and Oregon swung away to
Lincoln.[37]

In truth the candidacy of Bates possessed fundamental
weaknesses.   While he might enlist the support of the
border states, he did not possess a policy, definite or vigorous enough to elicit enthusiasm from the North which
was the real center of Republican strength.[38]   Bolles, the
editor of the *Springfield Republican*, had withheld his
support on this ground.[39]   One of Pike's correspondents

[37] Johnson, C. W.: *Op. cit.*, pp. 148-149, 152-153. On the first ballot
the Bates strength was distributed as follows: Rhode Island 1 out of
8; Connecticut 7 out of 12; Maryland 8 out of 11; Delaware 8; Missouri
18; Texas 2 out of 6; Iowa 1 out of 8; Oregon 5. Greeley was a member
of the Oregon delegation. The Maryland split vote was a great
annoyance to the Blairs. On the second ballot, Bates received 35 votes.
Delaware and the scattering votes were the chief defections. The
former state swung to Lincoln and so did a portion of the Connecticut
vote for Bates. On the last ballot in addition to the Missouri vote,
Bates obtained 4 votes from Connecticut.

[38] Gordon, J. W.: *The Hon. Edward Bates, of Missouri, Is He Fit
. . . Is He Available, as the Republican Candidate for the Presidency?*

[39] Hollester, O. J.: *Op. cit.*, pp. 146-147.

writes, "Why go into the bowels of Niggerdom for a candidate?   If you can carry Missouri for Bates, you can
carry Arkansas for him; and you can lift yourself up by
the waistband daily for ten years before you can do
either.[40]   The Bates candidacy, moreover, was not a genuine one.   He was simply a rallying point for the opposition to Seward.   The Indiana Bates men deserted to Lincoln when it became clear that he was to be the more
successful center of this opposition.[41]   Some one questioned whether the true orthography was *"Bates* or
Baits." [42]   It is probable that the Blairs did not take
Bates seriously.   Frank had been in close relationship
with Lincoln.   The *Missouri Democrat* had supported
Lincoln against Douglas in 1858, and John Hay, who
worked in Lincoln's law office, was its special correspondent.   The ideas of Blair and of Lincoln as to the needs
of the national crisis were identical; they had planned
together the political development of the Republican
party.[43]   Under such circumstances Lincoln would have
been as natural a candidate for the Blairs to support as
Bates.   Probably the latter was only their temporary
choice.   Events immediately after the election of 1860
reinforced this view.   It was at once plain that the Blair
family would exercise a great deal of influence in the new
administration.   In the stream of visitors which rushed
to and from Springfield, Illinois, both the senior and
junior F. P. Blair were prominent.   The latter carried

[40] Pike, James S.: *First Blows of the Civil War,* p. 484, Fitz-Henry
to Pike, February 2, 1860.
    [41] Hollester, O. J.: *Op. cit.,* pp. 147-148.
    [42] Pike, James S.: *Op. cit.,* p. 496, Fitz-Henry to Pike, February
23, 1860.
    [43] Stevens, Walter B.: *Op. cit.,* pp. 65-69.

the news to Bates, a Blair creation, that he was to be
Attorney General.[44] But more important still was the
news that Montgomery Blair, a representative of the
border states, was to have a seat in the new cabinet as
Postmaster General, a position which carried with it the
dispensation of an extensive patronage. Intrenched in
the cabinet, favored by the administration because of
political gratitude, personal association, and identity of
outlook, the Blairs were in a position to make their
influence felt.

But what was the nature of that influence? To the
Blairs' eyes the election marked the end of "nullifiers"
and "national demagogues" and opened anew for themselves the inviting vistas of political activity, patronage,
and preferment. Not one of these anticipations could be
adequately realized if the Union were to be dissolved.
There were many reasons, therefore, in addition to the
Jacksonian tradition, why secession could not be tolerated.
The way to deal with such a movement had already been
devised. Four years earlier, the author of "A Voice from
the Grave of Jackson" declared that nullification will "be
paralyzed by the frown of an indignant nation, made
potent by an honest and firm Executive." [45] In the vigorous mind of F. P. Blair, Sr.,—and his sons were of the
same temperament—there was no doubt as to the course
which should be pursued by an "honest and firm Executive." By the end of January, 1861, Montgomery Blair
was writing to Gustavus Vasa Fox, "It needs but determination in the rulers of the people to maintain and save it

---

[44] Gibson, Charles: *Op. cit.,* pp. 55-56.
[45] Clephane, Lewis: *Op. cit.,* p. 23, F. P. Blair, Sr. to the Republican
Association of Washington, December 10, 1855.

[the Union] from all its enemies, and with less of blood and treasure than any alarmist will believe. I am for the Union, now and forever, and against all its enemies, whether fire-eaters or abolitionists." [46] And Gustavus Vasa Fox, who had married a sister of Montgomery Blair's wife,[47] went busily ahead on the plans which he had devised for the relief of Fort Sumter. The preservation of the Union, with all its material advantages for the victorious political party, was a Blair obsession. So it was that in the uncertain days of March, 1861, Montgomery Blair was an uncompromising adherent of the view that Sumter should be relieved; [48] that F. P. Blair Sr., wrote to Lincoln that the South believed the North deficient in courage and that the evacuation of Sumter would convince the former that the administration was one of great weakness.[49] Finally a Blair tradition asserts that it was only the interposition of the elder Blair himself, who rushed into the President's presence and called upon him to remember his oath of office, which prevented Lincoln from taking steps toward pacification.[50] Whether this story is true or not, the policy of the administration had at least followed along the lines which the Blairs had advocated.

[46] Fox, Gustavus Vasa: *Op. cit.*, Vol. I, p. 5, Montgomery Blair to Gustavus Vasa Fox, January 31, 1861.

[47] Woodbury, Charles L.: "Memoirs of Hon. Levi Woodbury, LL.D.," *New England Historical and Genealogical Register,* Vol. XLVIII, p. 16. Mary Elizabeth, one daughter of Levi Woodbury married Montgomery Blair, and Virginia L., another daughter, married Gustavus Vasa Fox.

[48] Nicolay, John G., and Hay, John: *Abraham Lincoln, a History,* Vol. III, pp. 394-395.

[49] *Ibid.,* Vol. III, p. 386, F. P. Blair, Sr. to Lincoln, March 15, 1861 (MS.).

[50] Welles, Gideon: *Diary of Gideon Welles,* Vol. I, pp. 13-14.

Although the edifice of the Blairs' political success possessed no visible fault, under the surface there were latent possibilities of misfortune. In Washington their policies and their personalities were arousing criticism. Conservative men, who believed in compromise, winced at the thought of the Blairs' determination to incite a civil war, abolish slavery by force, and "expel the whole negro race from the continent." [51] Such views were distasteful in the President's cabinet. In particular there was Seward who, working for conciliation, disliked their extreme policies. He also nourished a grudge against them for more personal reasons. It is likely that his hostility dated back to the early days of New York politics when Seward and Weed were Whigs and Van Buren and the Blairs were Democrats. Good feeling between the two parties was not increased by the action of "Old Blair of the Globe" and his two sons at Chicago where they had contributed, along with Greeley, to the defeat of Seward's aspirations for the presidential nomination.[52] Thurlow Weed was pained when Lincoln told him that Montgomery Blair was to be a member of the cabinet. "Blair blood," he protested, was "troublesome," [53] and the Blairs really represented nobody.[54] As for the Blairs' opinion of Seward, the latter's conciliatory policy toward the South confirmed their worst suspicions. Several years later Montgomery Blair drew up an indictment against this Polonius, "who by

[51] "The Diary of a Public Man," in the *North American Review*, Vol. CXXIX, pp. 260-261.

[52] Barnes, Thurlow: *Memoirs of Thurlow Weed*, p. 274, a letter of H. J. Raymond.

[53] *Ibid.*, p. 294.

[54] Weed, Thurlow: *Autobiography of Thurlow Weed*. Edited by Harriet A. Weed, pp. 607-608.

indirection found direction out," which included assertions that Seward intrigued to surrender the Southern forts and allow secession its course; that he persuaded Scott to advise the surrender of Fort Pickens and Fort Sumter; and that he secured the detachment of the *Powhatan* from the Fort Sumter relief expedition in order to ruin it.[55]   On the last count, the Blairs spoke with feeling.   Gustavus Vasa Fox, practically one of the family, in charge of the relief expedition off Charleston, was mad with disappointment when he heard the Confederate bombardment and saw the smoke rising from stricken Fort Sumter.   The relief, which he had tried to give, was now impossible, and his efforts had failed because of the absence of the *Powhatan,* which Seward had malevolently detached in order "to utterly extinguish the expedition." [56]   So he writes angrily to Montgomery Blair.   At times it seems a little difficult to determine whether the irritation of the Blairs' protégé at the Secretary of State was not greater because the failure of the Sumter relief made remote the possibility of promotion or office for himself.   He need not have been so despondent.   In May he was eased into the Navy Department by an appointment as Chief Clerk, and in August he became the Assistant Secretary of the Navy.[57]

Already in the middle of 1861 there was a difference, sensed rather than developed, between the Blairs and the

[55] Welles, Gideon: "Mr. Lincoln and Mr. Seward.   Remarks upon the Memorial Address of Charles Francis Adams on the Late William H. Seward," *The Galaxy,* Vol. XVI, pp. 691-692, Montgomery Blair to Gideon Welles, May 17, 1873.

[56] Fox, Gustavus Vasa: *Op. cit.,* Vol. I, pp. 33, 40-41, Gustavus V. Fox to Montgomery Blair, April 17, 1861, Result of G. V. Fox's plan for reinforcing Fort Sumpter [sic] in his own writing.

[57] *Ibid.,* p. 2.

conservatives.   At the same time the Blairs could not
count upon the support of the radicals or bitter-enders.
To be sure Montgomery and his father had been influential in supporting a policy of coercion and resistance
rather than compromise.   F. P. Blair, Jr., was a devoted
admirer of Wade, consorted with the radicals, and voted,
alone among border states' representatives, for the first
Confiscation Act.   By their adoption of a vigorous war
policy the Blairs were certainly allied with the extremists; but, while the intensity of their devotion to American nationalism and their choice of means to preserve it
allied them with the radical faction, there was a hint that
the accord of the Blairs and the radicals was not complete.   In their scheme for the control of the government,
Frank Blair, who had been reëlected to the national
House of Representatives from his Missouri district, was
to run for the Speakership of that body.   The balloting,
which resulted in the defeat of Blair, showed the latent
hostility of Thaddeus Stevens, already marked as a leader
in the House and destined for the chairmanship of its important Committee on Ways and Means.   Blair had to be
content with the chairmanship of the Committee on Military Affairs.   Questions inevitably intruded themselves.
Was it possible that the Blairs were soon to be out of
touch with all the groups in the Republican Party?   Was
it possible that their early triumph was a mere façade
concealing failure?

Developments in the states, for which the Blairs were
self-constituted representatives, were vital in shaping an
answer to these questions.   As in the case of all politicians, the basis of the Blairs' power in their own party
and in the nation was the control of their own constitu-

encies. If the voters of their own "meridian" failed them,
they were ruined. Decisive then was the course of affairs
in Missouri and Maryland. Maryland was important;
but Missouri was the state of destiny for the Blairs. For
twelve years or more, Francis Preston Blair, Jr., had
been either a member or a leader of the minority party in
its truceless politics. His political existence during that
period had been possible only because his early anti-
slavery sentiments had built around him in his St. Louis
district an unshakable bloc of support, a bloc composed
largely of the German elements which were from the first
radical and anti-slavery.[58] Blair had arrayed against
him the older and wealthier families of St. Louis, and the
majority opinion of the state outside of the city.[59] Then
came the election of 1860. The state cast its vote for
Douglas, the candidate of compromise. Still conservative, in the time of gathering crisis which ensued, a state
convention was summoned to consider the policy which
Missouri should follow toward the other states and the
Union. These events, although they did not materially
alter the Missouri situation, changed Frank Blair's relation to it. The advent of the Republican Party, of which
the Blairs were charter members and in which they exercised a subtle and pervasive control, to national power
gave to Frank an unmeasured opportunity for action in
Missouri. Intoxicated by the prospect of success, the
suppressed recklessness of the man burst forth. The cautious policy which the state was pursuing irked him.
There was a depressing absence of disciplined Republican

[58] Rombauer, Robert J.: *The Union Cause in St. Louis in 1861, An
Historical Sketch*, p. 105.
[59] *Ibid.*, p. 345.

voters; there were Union men who favored the preservation of the Union on terms of compromise; and finally
there was the state government, headed by no less a vil-
lain than Claiborne F. Jackson, arch anti-Bentonite and
author of the notorious Jackson resolutions of 1849.[60]
The inaugural address of this nullifier gave color to
Blair's worst fears and suspicions. It traced the natural
dependence of Missouri upon the South and stated that,
"Missouri will in my opinion best consult her own interests, and the interests of the whole country, by a timely
declaration of her determination to stand by her sister
slave-holding states, in whose wrongs she participates,
and with whose institutions and people she sympa-
thizes." After such words Blair was certain that
the situation called for action, action, and then more
action. He must save St. Louis and Missouri for the
Union.

Since the state government was controlled by Jackson
and the national government by Buchanan, the saviour of
Missouri found difficulty in securing governmental assistance. Over Jackson and Buchanan, Frank possessed the
slightest influence imaginable. He apparently decided
that it was safe to defy the state government. The
"Wide-Awakes," political clubs formed during the campaign of the previous year, were transformed into military organizations; secret organizations met for drill; a
committee of public safety, headed by Blair and composed
of leading Republicans—large merchants and manufacturers—was formed; funds for military equipment were
solicited in the North; and Governor Yates of Illinois sent

[60] Snead, Thomas L.: *The Fight for Missouri from the Election of
Lincoln to the Death of Lyon*, pp. 17-18, 55-57.

muskets.[61] To complete their unofficial military preparations, however, they had to control the Federal arsenal
at St. Louis, commanded by Major William H. Bell, who
had the misfortune to be a North Carolinian and hence a
suspicious person. Blair resolved upon his removal. Accordingly I. H. Sturgeon, Assistant Treasurer at St.
Louis and a political time-server with influence over
Buchanan, was induced to write the President and General Scott to the effect that the arsenal was in danger of
capture. By the end of January, Major Bell had been
succeeded in command by Major Peter V. Hagner. This
new appointee, to the Blair mind, was as bad as his predecessor; for Hagner, whose wife was the daughter of a
slaveholder, was suspected of Southern sympathies.[62] A
week or two later, however, Captain Nathaniel Lyon,
Second Infantry, arrived at the St. Louis arsenal with
a company of soldiers as reinforcement—an event so
happy in its results as to suggest the probability of Blair
manipulation.[63] Lyon was a Connecticut man by birth,

[61] Rombauer, Robert J.: *Op. cit.,* pp. 109, 188-193; Snead, Thomas L.:
Op. cit., pp. 65-66, 104-106; Evans, General Clement A. (Editor): *Con-
federate Military History. A Library of Confederate State History,*
Vol. IX, Part II, Missouri by Colonel John C. Moore, pp. 23-24.

[62] Snead, Thomas L.: *Op. cit.,* pp. 117-118, 125; Evans, C. A. (Editor):
Op. cit., Vol. IX, Part II, pp. 26-27.

[63] Rombauer, Robert J.: *Op. cit.,* p. 150; Evans, C. A. (Editor):
Op. cit., Vol. IX, Part II, p. 27. Rombauer claims that while Lyon
was stationed in the territory of Kansas, he called at the office of the
Missouri Democrat to pay his subscription. In a conversation with
Daniel M. Houser, one of the proprietors, Lyon made a favorable impression because of his radical views. When a successor for the arsenal
command was sought, Houser suggested Lyon's name to a committee
of Union men and the appointment was obtained. If this story is true,
the committee to which Rombauer refers, was probably the one of
which Blair was the chairman. Moore evidently considers Lyon's appointment a stroke of luck, although he asserts that Blair knew Lyon's
temper through a letter written by the latter to a friend in Missouri.

a West Pointer by training, and a professional soldier by occupation. These details give no idea of his vigor and his impatience. Holding the conviction that slavery was threatening the life of the Union, he felt that the "aggressions of the pro-slavery men will not be checked till the lesson has been taught them in letters of fire and blood" and he did not care to delay the inevitable sectional strife.[64] The temper in which this fanatic approached the delicate situation in St. Louis can best be gauged by a letter which he wrought a short while before his arrival. "I do not see how war is to be avoided. Under quack management it may be long and bloody; yet I have no apprehension about the final triumph of Almighty Truth, though at the cost of many unnecessary sacrifices. I would rather see the country lighted up with flames, from its center to the remotest borders, than that the great rights and hopes of the human race should expire before the arrogance of the Secessionists." [65] These sentiments were heartily acceptable to the younger Blair. The subordinate officer at the arsenal and the saviour of Missouri were soon working in perfect harmony.

The general situation in Missouri had meanwhile developed in a manner very satisfactory to the great majority of the loyal men of that State. The elections to the state convention had been held and, much to the surprise of the Southern sympathizers who had promoted it, resulted in the choice of a majority of Union delegates.[66] The

[64] Snead, Thomas L.: *Op. cit.*, pp. 122-123, letters of Lyon, March, 1855, December 1855.

[65] Rombauer, Robert J.: *Op. cit.*, p. 152.

[66] Snead, Thomas L.: *Op. cit.*, pp. 58-59, 66; Rombauer, Robert J.: *Op. cit.*, pp. 145-149; Evans, C. A. (Editor): *Op. cit.*, Vol. IX, Part II, p. 19. The last account claims that this anti-secession majority

cause of secession had received its first severe blow. Another followed in March when the convention Committee on Federal Relations reported that no adequate reason for secession existed; that the Union should be preserved; but that the use of military measures for coercive purposes should be stayed.[67] This second mishap to Governor Jackson's design for an alliance between Missouri and her sister slave states, was ignored by Blair. He had only contempt for the conservative Union men who would save the Union by compromise and concession. Too impetuous and too reckless to follow a middle course he continued his extra-legal military preparations to save Missouri. Lyon was with him. When this resolute pair undertook to execute their plans, there was always someone in the way. First there had been Major Bell, North Carolinian. After his adroit removal had been accomplished, Major Hagner, another tainted Southerner, ranked Lyon in command of the arsenal. The latter complained bitterly of his inferior position and of his difficulties in carrying out the proper measures for the defence of government property.[68] At last, in March, Blair succeeded in having Hagner's activities restricted solely to the Ordnance Department and in placing Lyon

was obtained by violence and fraud. In St. Louis, Blair's Wide-Awakes terrorized the Confederate vote. On the contrary, it would seem that the election was carried largely by the conservative element—the Douglas and the Bell-Everett men, which had cast 71 per cent of the vote in 1860. In St. Louis, Blair had coöperated with this conservative element, in spite of his divergence from them, and a joint ticket of 7 Douglas Democrats, 4 Lincoln Republicans, 3 Bell-Everett men, and 1 unclassified was put into the field and elected by a 5,000 majority.

[67] Rombauer, Robert J.: *Op. cit.,* pp. 171-172.

[68] Peckham, James: *General Nathaniel Lyon and Missouri in 1861. A Monograph of the Great Rebellion,* pp. 66-68, Captain Nathaniel Lyon to F. P. Blair, Jr., February 25, 1861.

in command of the arsenal.[69]   The Connecticut captain
now collided with a third obstacle, General William Selby
Harney, Commander of the Department of the West, with
headquarters at St. Louis.   Against his fitness for the
position were several damaging relationships.   His ante-
cedents were Southern: he was an intimate friend of
Jefferson Davis; he had married into one of St. Louis'
old, wealthy and distinguished families; and he owned
slaves.[70]   He was, moreover, an ally of the conservative
Union men and did not think the secessionist movement
considerable enough to justify desperate measures for its
suppression.[71]   Even during the first days of the war,
when Sumter was fired upon and when the country was
stricken with confusion and uncertainty, he preserved his
calmness and his balance.   He refused to authorize the
arming of the extra-legal military groups which Lyon
and Blair had created.[72]   It was apparent that he was
determined to run the Department in his own way—con-
servatively.   A month later, there is new and damaging
evidence of the General's ineptitude.   Benjamin Farrar,
the Assistant Treasurer of St. Louis, wrote to Montgomery Blair that the Department was run for the benefit of Harney's friends—"the secessionists."   Traitors are
patronized at the expense of patriots and merchants with
Confederate sympathies are favored in the purchase of

[69] *Official Records of the Union and Confederate Armies*, Series I,
Vol. I, pp. 636-639.

[70] Reavis, L. U.: *The Life and Military Services of Gen. William
Selby Harney*, pp. 39-40, 351, 355-356; Snead, Thomas L.: *Op. cit.*, pp.
99-100.

[71] Rombauer, Robert J.: *Op. cit.*, p. 291; *Official Records of the Union
and Confederate Armies*, Series I, Vol. I, p. 654.

[72] *Official Records of the Union and Confederate Armies*, Series I,
Vol. I, p. 668.

supplies. Farrar closes with the suggestion that a good
command for Harney could be made "embracing Utah
and the Indians." [73]

If Harney had been governed by expediency he would
have been slow to defy the Blairs. They had now an
exceedingly workable organization for the control of Missouri affairs. Frank P. Blair had by his sheer energy
become an authoritative spokesman for Missouri; and he
was seconded at Washington by his brother, Montgomery, "the Pisistratus of his race, the man of madness,
sedition, and intrigue," who had become by some legerde-
main the self-appointed guardian of Missouri.[74] Behind
the two sons lurked the sinister shadow of "father."
Frank was not slow in utilizing this powerful and effective machine. On April 19 he dispatched a letter to his
brother urging him to secure the immediate removal of
Harney from his command.[75] Two days later a telegram
to Governor Curtin of Pennsylvania urged him to put
pressure upon Secretary of War Cameron, a fellow Pennsylvanian, to bring about the same end.[76] The effect of
these communications was immediate. On April 23,
Harney, in response to a peremptory telegram from
Washington, relinquished his command and departed to
the capital to report to the general-in-chief. In his
absence, Lyon and Blair had a turbulent holiday. They
accepted and armed the volunteer regiments which Blair

[73] Reavis, L. U.: *Op. cit.,* pp. 377-378, Ben Ferrar to Montgomery
Blair, May 29, 1861.
[74] *Ibid.,* p. 380.
[75] Peckham, James: *Op. cit.,* pp. 110--110, Frank P. Blair, Jr. to
Montgomery Blair, April 19, 1861.
[76] Peckham, James: *Op. cit.,* pp. 109-110, Frank P. Blair, Jr. to
Governor A. G. Curtin, April 21, 1861.

had organized, and with this army at their back attacked
Camp Jackson, which had been established as a training
camp for the regular state militia. Its occupants were
made prisoners. This act of aggression, justified only by
the suspicions of the two Union conspirators, resulted in
an all-day riot in St. Louis and the definite precipitation
of the State Legislature into the arms of the secessionists.[77] Luckily further extreme action was delayed by a
most unpleasant and unexpected event. Harney returned
from Washington, exonerated.

It took a month of the Blairs' time and energy to
reverse this miscarriage of justice. The operation was
typical of Missouri politics and Blair methods. Rival
delegations were sent by the two local factions to Washington. The conservative delegates enlisted the support
of Bates; the Blair representative was under the protection of Montgomery. In spite of difficulties, the Blair
influence was too strong to be denied. An order was written creating Lyon a Brigadier General and a second gave
Harney a leave of absence. Both were dispatched to
Blair, but the second was to be used against Harney only
in case of necessity.[78] This order Blair carried around

[77] Rombauer, Robert J.: *Op. cit.*, pp. 242-243.

[78] Peckham, James: *Op. cit.*, pp. 191-198, 209-210, 225. Two letters
from Franklin A. Dick, the Blair representative at Washington, to Ben
Farrar, May 16, 1861, May 17, 1861, Montgomery Blair to Ben Farrar
or Colonel E. P. Blair, Jr., May 17, 1861, Abraham Lincoln to F. P.
Blair, Jr., May 18, 1861, Montgomery Blair to General W. S. Harney,
May 17, 1861; *Official Records of the Union and Confederate Armies*,
Series I, Vol. III, p. 374. It is evident that the Blairs obtained the
order for Harney's removal, for such in effect it was, only on condition
that it be used with the greatest discretion and restraint. F. A. Dick
wrote Ben Farrar that F. P. Blair, Sr., and Montgomery did not think
it necessary to use the order for removal. Montgomery Blair wrote
Ben Farrar or his brother that it was to be utilized only if necessary.

until the end of the month, when Harney's endeavor to prevent civil war in the state by an agreement with Price, the commander of the state militia, convinced Frank that there was no use trifling any longer with this person of Southern connections who had fallen "into the hands of our opponents." On May 30, he delivered to General Harney the order for the later's relief from command.[79]

But the Blairs had to pay for this success with a compromise as to Harney's successor. Lyon was their logical choice; but opponents of Lyon and Blair had to be conciliated. Bates and the faction he represented were able to insist on the extension of McClellan's command over Missouri. Montgomery preferred to see the silver lining to the rebuff. McClellan will "sympathize strongly with your people" and his appointment will remove the unfortunate impression that Frank is trying to convert the Union feeling in the state into a political and personal asset. But the new appointee was finding the duties of his new and extensive command exacting. A new Western Department would have to be created. Again the Blairs urged the appointment of the ardent Lyon and

Lincoln wrote F. P. Blair, Jr., to remove Harney only if it was indispensable. At the same time, Montgomery wrote a letter to Harney, which was to be delivered to the latter if he was removed. This letter stated that Harney had been restored to command earlier in May "without my having decided the question" and stating that Harney was removed, not because of any question of loyalty on his part, but because the Union men distrusted Harney's relations.

[79] Peckham, James: *Op. cit.*, pp. 204-208, 222-227, Union Safety Committee of St. Louis to Montgomery Blair, May 22, 1861, F. P. Blair, Jr., to Abraham Lincoln, May 30, 1861, Montgomery Blair to F. P. Blair, Jr., June 4, 1861: Snead, Thomas L.: *Op. cit.*, pp. 190-191, Montgomery Blair to Secretary Cameron, May 24, 1861; *Official Records of the Union and Confederate Armies,* Series I, Vol. III, pp. 376, 381, L. Thomas, Advocate General, to General W. S. Harney, May 27, 1861.

again they were compelled to compromise with the Bates faction.[80] The result was the appointment of Major General John C. Fremont to the command of the new Western Department which consisted of Missouri, Illinois, and all Western states and territories between the Mississippi and the Rocky Mountains. The commander-in-chief of this vast military domain owed his success largely to association with the Bentons. It was rumored that Fremont's journals of western adventure which had cast about him the romantic glamor of the explorer had been written largely by Colonel Benton himself.[81] But the connection of the Bentons was even more intimate. It was the disturbing influence of Jessie, Benton's daughter and Fremont's wife, which made this reserved and retiring man uncomfortable and forced him into courses of action for which his own ambition and ability were alike inadequate. But Mrs. Fremont furnished more than an irritant; she possessed political associations, inextinguishable energy, and brains. Driven and directed by this domestic dynamo, the "Pathfinder" was destined for a stormy political career.[82] The appointment of Fremont, while less acceptable than would have been the promotion of General Nathaniel Lyon, was, nevertheless, a victory for the Blairs. Lincoln said that Fremont was appointed owing to their "earnest solicitation" and that he went to Missouri as their "pet and protégé." [83] In fact he was also

[80] Peckham, James: Op. cit., pp. 266-267, Montgomery Blair to Edward Bates, June 19, 1861.

[81] Welles, Gideon: Diary of Gideon Welles, Vol. II, p. 42.

[82] Forbes, John M.: Letters (Supplementary) of John Murray Forbes, Edited by Sarah F. Hughes, Vol. I, p. 294, Forbes to W. P. Fessenden, November 13, 1861.

[83] Nicolay, John G., and Hay, John: Abraham Lincoln, a History, Vol. IV, p. 415, John Hay's Diary, (MS.).

a member of the family—a member of the great Preston-Blair-Benton connection—and was under obligations of political gratitude to the Blairs for their support of him in the past. Under such circumstances critics of the Blairs thought they detected a gigantic conspiracy by which Frank and Fremont were to control the West, while the elder Blair and Montgomery dominated the East.[84] Such fantasies are of course incredible. But the appointment of Fremont did elevate Blair to the undisputed mastery of his state. In the light of such success he could ignore the fact that his policy there had already alienated forever the possibility of conservative support.

Then followed Fremont's spectacular "one hundred days in Missouri." At the close of that period, Fremont himself was a ruined man and the Blairs were fatally injured. The cause of both disasters was a quarrel between Fremont and his creators. Disagreement between the two began immediately for Fremont, although he received his appointment on July 3, dallied in the East until the end of the month. This delay stirred Montgomery Blair to impatience, a mood which was not softened by the General's actions on his arrival in Missouri. Just recently returned from a tour of the Continent, Fremont was still under the fascination of the pomp and gold braid and the formality of European armies. On his arrival in St. Louis, he made his headquarters in the Brant Palace, a splendid mansion owned by a relative of Mrs. Fremont, and surrounded himself with a bodyguard which contained, in addition to fifteen aides-de-camp, not only such un-American and un-Western officers as "adlatus to the

[84] Reavis, L. U.: *Op. cit.*, p. 379.

chief of staff," and "military regulator and expeditor,"
but also a few politicians of pronounced anti-slavery
views.[85]   Surrounded in splendor, Fremont drew aloof
from the common herd.   For a short time, nevertheless,
the Blairs were on confidential terms with their "pet and
protégé," but soon the letters which Frank wrote to his
brother took on a different tone—one of doubt and uncertainty.   These letters Montgomery showed to the President who was in turn influenced by their skepticism.[86]
At this delicate juncture, Fremont issued a proclamation
which established martial law through the state, asserted
that those who were found "with arms in their hands
within these lines" would be shot, and finally emancipated
the slaves of all Missourians who took up arms against the
United States.   This last clause, providing for the emancipation of slaves, was naturally most distasteful to an
administration which in 1861 was bent upon hiding the
slavery issue.   Under the circumstances, the step taken
by Fremont showed either his insubordination or his stu-
pidity.   Lincoln, after a preliminary correspondence, re-
voked certain clauses of the proclamation, among them
that on emancipation, and then sent Montgomery Blair
and M. C. Meigs, the Quartermaster-General of the army,
to investigate the affairs of the Western Department in a
friendly way.

On their journey to St. Louis the pair were passed by
Mrs. Fremont who was flying eastward.   On her arrival

[85] Koerner, Gustave: *Memoirs of Gustave Koerner, 1809-1896,* Vol.
II, pp. 172-173.   Among the politicians were Owen Lovejoy, a member
of Congress, and John A. Greeley, "one of the best known abolition
leaders."

[86] Nicolay, John G., and Hay, John: *Abraham Lincoln, a History,*
Vol. IV, p. 415, John Hay's Diary (MS.).

at Washington she obtained an interview with Lincoln
and "taxed" him "violently" for sending "their enemy,
Montgomery Blair," to Missouri.[87]   She followed this appeal by one to F. P. Blair, Sr., and then hurriedly returned home.   On her arrival, Frank was arrested by the
irate Fremont for shaking the President's confidence and,
when on his release he preferred charges against Fremont,
he was re-arrested [88]   Soon after there arrived from
Washington another mission of investigation which consisted of Simon Cameron, Secretary of War, and Lorenzo
Thomas, the Adjutant-General of the army.   The latter, determined "to rake up all the slum of St. Louis," [89]
submitted a report to Cameron, containing material, one-
tenth of which if true, would have been enough to secure
the dismissal of Fremont.[90]   Evidently Lincoln and those
who influenced him were of the same opinion.   Another
discretionary dismissal, à la Harney, was written out by
the President with the understanding that it was to be
used only if Fremont were not in the presence of the
enemy or in actual combat.   This order, despatched to
General Curtis, was served upon Fremont on November
2.[91]   Thus fell another victim of "that precious trio, General Thomas, the flying reporter, Postmaster Blair, the

[87] Nicolay, John G., and Hay, John: *Abraham Lincoln, a History,*
Vol. IX, p. 414, John Hay's Diary (MS.).
[88] *Report of the Joint Committee on the Conduct of the War, 1863,*
Part III, p. 176, Testimony of F. P. Blair, Jr.
[89] Brotherhead, William: *General Fremont; and the Injustice Done
Him by Politicians and Envious Military Men,* p. 6.
[90] Forbes, John M.: *Reminiscences of John Murray Forbes,* Edited
by Sarah F. Hughes, Vol. III, pp. 148-149, Forbes to W. H. Aspin-
wall, November 11, 1861.
[91] *Official Records of the Union and Confederate Armies,* Series I,
Vol. III, pp. 553-555, 559.

self-constituted viceroy of Missouri, and Colonel F. P. Blair who, having once smelt powder at Boonville, deserted the brave Gen. Lyon and exchanged the perils of the tented field for the less dangerous bureaus of Washington city." [92]

Whatever may have been the rôle of the "flying reporter," the powerful Blair family was the real cause for the disaster which overwhelmed the ill-fated Fremont. He had incurred their hostility because he had tried to ignore them. Sent to Missouri as a Blair creation, Fremont and his wfe determined to shove their relatives aside and set out upon an independent policy of personal aggrandizement. Their prospects were alluring. A day dream might suggest that Fremont's military command in the Western Department, if it were sufficiently glorious, might be the prelude to the presidency. He had run in 1856 and had been defeated. The time was now at hand to retrieve that forlorn hope. However much such considerations may have appealed to the Fremonts, they did not conform to the rôle which the Blairs had conceived for him. They expected him to be their instrument rather than their master. The first sign of Fremont's intractability seems to have been his masterly inactivity in military affairs. General Nathaniel Lyon, although not oversupplied with troops or equipment, had resolved upon an offensive campaign to drive the last vestiges of secession from the state and had accordingly penetrated southwest beyond the rail-head to confront a Confederate army tremendously superior to his own. Fremont, in spite of

[92] Thomas, James S.: *The Case of General Fremont, Remarks suggested by the Speech of the Hon. F. P. Blair, delivered in the House of Representatives, March 7, 1862*, p. 29.

earnest solicitations from Lyon and the Blairs, appeared
untroubled by the dangerous position of his subordinate
and advocated a retreat.   The strategic wisdom of this
latter proposal appealed to Lyon's intellect but tempera-
mentally it left him cold.   The idea of retreat distressed
him; no matter what the odds, the "final triumph of Almighty Truth" could perhaps work wonders.   On August
8, therefore, without consultation with all his officers, he
turned upon the Confederates who were pursuing him and
threw his little army against one four times its size.   In
the inevitable defeat, Lyon went to his own death.   His
demise was a fortunate one for the Blairs, since, by silencing all intelligent criticism of Lyon's military ability as
a slander on a dead hero, it strengthened their accusa-
tions of a deliberate conspiracy on the part of Fremont to
neglect him.   Fremont sacrificed a brave man (incidentally a friend of the Blairs) for the sake of his own political ambitions.[93]

More worldly matters—the manipulation of patronage, the handling of contracts, and the purchase of supplies—now increased the Blairs' suspicions.   At first,
Frank had no difficulty in securing proper consideration
for his own friends, many of whom were large merchants
and manufacturers of St. Louis; he was always given access to the General and granted every favor.[94]   But this

[93] *Report of the Joint Committee on the Conduct of the War, 1863,*
Part III, pp. 161-166, Testimony of F. P. Blair, Jr.; *Official Records
of the Union and Confederate Armies,* Series I, Vol. III, pp. 48, 59-63;
Blair, Frank P., Jr.: *Fremont's Hundred Days in Missouri. Speech of
Hon. F. P. Blair, Jr., of Missouri, on Fremont's Defense, delivered
in the House of Representatives,* March 7, 1862, pp. 5-9; Peckham,
James: *Op. cit.,* pp. 314-318, 320, 342-345; Schofield, John M.: *Forty-
Six Years in the Army,* pp. 39-41, 48-49.

[94] *Report of the Joint Committee on the Conduct of the War, 1863,*
Part III, pp. 177-180, Testimony of F. B. Blair, Jr.

era of prosperity did not endure. Fremont was surrounded by Californians and by friends of Mrs. Fremont.[95] To F. P. Blair these and other hangers-on could
be described only "as obscene birds of prey." They received privileges, patronage, and contracts. Finally by
the end of August Frank's ability at vivid characteriza-
tion was taxed anew when a contract which had been
promised to an influential friend of his suffered a strange
metamorphosis. Fremont, denying that he had previously approved the whole contract, reduced it by erasures
and cancellations. There was apparently collusion between Fremont and McKinstrey, the Quartermaster-General, whose appointment Blair regretted he had urged.[96]
Both of them by jockeying to and fro, gave color to the
impression that there was a clumsy effort to shift responsibility and avoid a breach with Blair.[97] It was after this
experience that the note of uncertainty was detected in
the letters which Frank wrote to his brother. The breach
once made was widened when Blair observed the precious
coterie of adventurers on Fremont's staff receiving lucra-
tive contracts for unnecessary fortifications and other
jobs.[98] The tone of the Blairs' feelings toward Fremont
had, therefore, changed before the latter's emancipation
proclamation. Both the Blairs and Fremont admit that

[95] Koerner, Gustave: *Op. cit.*, Vol. II, p. 180, Gustave Koerner to
his wife, October 3, 1861.
   [96] *Report of the Joint Committee on the Conduct of the War, 1863*,
Part III, p. 183, Testimony of F. P. Blair, Jr.
   [97] *Ibid.*, Part III, pp. 202-212, Testimony of I. C. Wood; pp. 75-77,
Testimony of General J. C. Fremont; pp. 178-179, Testimony of
F. P. Blair, Jr.
   [98] *Ibid.*, Part III, pp. 180-183, Testimony of F. P. Blair, Jr.; Blair,
F. P., Jr.: *Fremont's Hundred Days in Missouri. Speech of Hon.
F. P. Blair, Jr., of Missouri, on Fremont's Defense; delivered in the
House of Representatives, March 7, 1862*, pp. 13-14.

the General's slavery policy was not the primary reason for their dislike of each other.[99]   To the Blairs the proclamation seemed only one more maneuver in Fremont's game of building up an independent political machine. It would naturally appeal to the Germans of St. Louis, the basis of Blair support in Missouri, and of the West; and it would serve as an admirable campaign document in New England and other abolition centers. The Blairs needed no further evidence of the faithless designs of their "pet." They proceeded to work his undoing.

To discover justice on either side of such a political intrigue is difficult. But it must be admitted that Fremont had opened an easy path for criticism. He had to be sure a measure of extenuation. The difficulties of his task were innumerable. The Department was so large that even his wife and numerous secretaries were unable to manage the correspondence, and there was a consequent lack of adequate supervision. The Department, moreover, and the war were both young; there was a consequent confusion and delay. But Fremont's dilatory and spasmodic movements cannot be wholly justified. He seems always to have moved with an excess of caution and preparedness. As for contracts and purchases, the first year of the war was not characterized by prudence in

[99] Blair, F. P., Jr.: *Fremont's Hundred Days in Missouri. Speech of the Hon. F. P. Blair, Jr., of Missouri on Fremont's Defense; delivered in the House of Representatives, March 7, 1862*, p. 15; *Report of the Joint Committee on the Conduct of the War, 1863*, Part III, pp. 70-71, 75, Testimony of J. C. Fremont. A reading of Fremont's testimony does not give a favorable impression of his ability as a dialectician or as a talker. In fact he missed the guidance of his wife. Koerner records a meeting with Fremont in 1856 in which the General appeared "embarrassed" and Jessie Benton "bore the principal part of the conversation." (Koerner, Gustave: *Op. cit.,* Vol. II, pp. 13-14.)

that respect. Fremont deemed it necessary to purchase supplies outside the regular army channels and to erect forts with enormous dispatch. Both of these processes are risky and expensive under the best of circumstances.[100] Yet Forbes, who had a great liking for Fremont and especially for his wife, felt compelled to write, "Yet I feel it in my bones that Fremont has not the qualities for a General. Rogues have a sort of chemical affinity to his honesty." [101] Culpable or not, the Blairs had triumphed over him. But it was a costly victory for the defeated Fremont was in reality the victor. In Missouri he had by his emancipation proclamation bound to himself the support of the radical elements. The Germans were devoted to him; his dismissal from the army aroused fears of a popular outbreak; on his return to St. Louis he was given a monster reception. Throughout the nation, moreover, he became the idol of the extremists and a martyr for his championship of their favorite doctrine—abolition. All these outraged elements now turned upon Fremont's accusers. In Congress, the Hon. John P. C. Shanks of Indiana asserted that Fremont's dismissal had

[100] *Official Records of the Union and Confederate Armies*, Series I, Vol. III, pp. 463-465; *Report of the Joint Committee on the Conduct of the War, 1863*, Part III, pp. 115-116, Montgomery Blair to J. C. Fremont, August 24, 1861. The Blairs and the Washington authorities were willing enough in August for Fremont to spend money recklessly. Montgomery wrote on August 24 deprecating Chase's parsimonious ways of conducting the war; and M. C. Meigs, Quartermaster-General, remarked: "If General Fremont orders Captain Turnley to pay $1,000 for an ax, Captain Turnley will be supported by this Department in obeying. The propriety of such a payment, however, will be between General Fremont and the Government."

[101] Forbes, John M.: *Reminiscences of John Murray Forbes*, Edited by Sarah F. Hughes, Vol. III, p. 148, Forbes to C. W. Sedgwick, February 17, 1862.

been brought about by the "politician who fears his popularity; the friend to slavery, who prefers that institution even in rebel hands to the life and prosperity of free, true, and just men, at field, camp, or homestead; the military bigot, who sees West Point first, and after it, the country; and lastly speculators at the public treasury." [102] This attack was a little too dignified for William Brotherhead who described the same dismissal as due to "Blair and Co., and his political rats, and Thomas, an envious West Pointer." [103] Under this onslaught the fate of the Blairs was not a happy one. Although Frank had been victorious in Missouri, he was left without any tangible political support. Previously he had alienated the conservative group of Unionists by his recklessness; now he had driven away the radicals by his treatment of Fremont. He was, as Lincoln said, likely to be turned out of the house of his own building. And in the nation at large the reverberations of the Fremont-Blair conflict were to echo through the passing years of the Civil War. The burden of enmity which the Blairs had obtained was at last to crush them beneath its weight.

After the Fremont episode, the events in the Blair provinces—Maryland and Missouri—were in the nature of an anti-climax. But in both states the Blairs were slowly and remorselessly squeezed out of political power by the increasing control which the radicals exerted in the state governments. It was a curious outcome—that the radi-

[102] Shanks, John P. C.: *Vindication of Major General John C. Fremont against the Attacks of the Slave Power and its Allies, by Hon. John P. C. Shanks, of Indiana, in the House of Representatives, Tuesday, March 4, 1862*, p. 7.
[103] Brotherhead, William: *General Fremont and the Injustice done him by Politicians and Envious Military Men.*

cals should become dominant in border states where originally opinion had been so conservative. As a matter of
fact this reversal was due to the disappearance of opposition. For one thing the Confederate sympathizers
drifted southwards. Missouri's quota in the Southern
armies, for instance, was always full. Then restrictions
of one sort or another hampered the conservatives who
remained behind. State legislatures would impose test
oaths for the suffrage or for other purposes. The Missouri Convention in 1862 adopted an oath of stringent
nature and compelled all teachers, lawyers, preachers,
jurymen, and officers of companies incorporated by the
state to take the oath or cease work.[104] Another means
of restraint was military interference. In the Maryland
election of 1863 it is estimated that one-third of the elec-
torate was kept away from the polls through intimidation
on the part of General Schenk.[105] His successor, General Lew Wallace, of *Ben Hur* fame, glories in his interference with elections and advances suggestions of Lincoln
and of Stanton to justify his action.[106] Finally a psy-
chological factor contributed to the victory of the radicals.
The military and political struggle in the border states
was so intense that it was impossible to maintain a judi-
ciously balanced point of view. A Missourian, who saw his
home destroyed by Confederate armies or guerrillas, was

[104] McDougal, M. C.: "A Decade of Missouri Politics, 1860 to 1870,
from a Republican View Point," *Missouri Historical Review*, Vol. III,
pp. 135-139.

[105] Myers, William S.: "The Maryland Constitution of 1864," *Johns
Hopkins University Studies in Historical and Political Science*, Series
XIX, Nos. 8-9, pp. 19-24.

[106] Wallace, Lew: *Lew Wallace, An Autobiography*, Vol. II, pp. 670,
672, 678-685.

not apt to remain a "middle of the road man"; a Marylander, loyal to the Union, who lived among neighbors whom he suspected of being agents or spies of the Confederacy, did not usually support conservative principles. Since the border states were a battleground, there was no place for neutrality. By 1864 the operation of these factors had brought it about that the bitter-enders and not the Blairs actually controlled Maryland and Missouri.

Whatever power the Blairs still possessed was due to the support which the national administration gave them. The Blairs were favorites of Lincoln. They, in turn, gave him the warmhearted allegiance of which they were so capable. In the old days Jackson had borne witness to their intense personal devotion; now Lincoln had taken the place of Jackson. At first the Blairs found the championship of the President's policy congenial, for their views as to slavery were identical. They both believed in colonization and in compensation and, when occasion arose in the cabinet, Montgomery was earnestly in favor of such measures. Later, when the question of emancipation arose, Montgomery opposed it on grounds of expediency, and throughout the month-long discussion maintained his original position. But once the policy was determined upon, he accepted it so loyally that he campaigned for abolition in Maryland.[107] Then the radicals raised the issue of reconstruction. Here, like Lincoln, the Blairs would not yield. Montgomery delivered a tremendous attack against men who would attempt "amalgamation, equality and fraternity." The only way to execute such hideous possibilities would be to extinguish the rights of the Southern states—a procedure invalid and

[107] Myers, William S.: *Op. cit.*, p. 14.

illegal. Lincoln's policy of reconstruction, practical and lenient, was much better.[108]

Such loyal support of the President ought to have entitled Montgomery Blair to a position of serene superiority in the cabinet. On the contrary, he had a personal feud with most of his colleagues. First of all, there was the Blair distrust of Seward, upon whom they laid the blame for the Sumter disaster and later of the Fremont episode.[109] The elder Blair professed to believe that Seward and Fremont desired to incite an abolition "phrenzy." To make a charge so contrary to all the principles of the accused shows the extent of their obsession. Then Missouri politics separated the Blairs from Bates, another one of their protégés. Stanton's appointment as Secretary of War added one more incompatibility, for Stanton was the epitome of perfidy. As a member of Buchanan's cabinet, he had played a double rôle, for he had talked secession and the division of the Union while acting with the Republicans.[110] Perhaps Montgomery was disturbed by the fact that Stanton so often seemed a supporter of Seward and a member of the inner circle of the cabinet. Stanton's hostility equaled that of his enemies and in reprisal he had some of the Blairs' Maryland relatives arrested on the charge that

[108] Blair, Montgomery: *Speech of the Hon. Montgomery Blair (Postmaster General), on the Revolutionary Schemes of the Ultra Abolitionists, and in defence of the policy of the President delivered at the Unconditional Union Meeting, held at Rockville, Montgomery Co., Maryland, on Saturday, October 3, 1863.*

[109] Bigelow, John: *Op. cit.*, Vol. I, pp. 375-377, F. P. Blair, Sr., to John Bigelow, October 26, 1861.

[110] Welles, Gideon: *Diary of Gideon Welles*, Vol. I, pp. 355-356.

they were engaged in the clandestine supply of quinine to the Confederates.[111]   All in all, the War Department seemed much inferior to the Navy Department, where Gustavus Vasa Fox occupied the Assistant Secretaryship and where the kindly Gideon Welles believed everything the Blairs told him.   Montgomery, indeed, had need of an ally, for he was not on good terms with Chase.   The cabinet fairly smoked with his enmities.

By the end of 1863, the Blairs had become a national issue; and they had to devote nearly all their time and energy to the management of the warfare in which they were involved.   Great old warriors, they did not shrink from the combat.   The presidential year seemed a magnificent opportunity to crush their enemies.   For the battle royal, all their forces were mobilized.   Frank Blair, now an officer in the army which had fought through the Vicksburg campaign, returned to Congress to occupy the seat to which he had been elected in 1862.   Since he was a Major General, he was excluded from holding this civil office, but an arrangement was made with Lincoln by which Frank surrendered his commission temporarily, with the proviso that it was to be restored to him in case he should desire to reassume his military duties.   Once back in Congress by this very safe though slightly illegal performance, rumor centered around his name as a possible compromise candidate for the Speakership.[112]   This proved to be empty gossip.

[111] Flower, Frank: *Edwin McMasters Stanton, the Autocrat of Rebellion, Emancipation, and Reconstruction*, p. 255.

[112] Nicolay, John G., and Hay, John: *Abraham Lincoln, a History*, Vol. VII, pp. 392-393, Lincoln to Montgomery Blair, November 2, 1863 (MS.).

Then followed the day when the extremists were gathering courage to meet the challenge which the President had delivered by his message and proclamation of amnesty in December, 1863. From the shadows materialized the Chase boom for the presidency; in the open the radicals were attacking the President's war and peace policy. This situation led the Blairs to believe that there was a vast Jacobin conspiracy on the part of the extremists to defeat Lincoln's reelection, negative his policy of amnesty, and "enjoy the license of another French Revolution under some chief as malignant as themselves." These Jacobins evidently propose the complete equality of the negro with the white; they were to give him the right to vote and a rifle to protect that right. In Maryland they were headed by Henry Winter Davis; in Missouri they were aided by the actions of the Treasury Department. In the latter state, Chase, by his regulations and practices, is attempting to build up a vast political machine. He gives his "permits" to trade in cotton "to politicians and favorites from distant parts of the country," rather than to Union sympathizers in St. Louis; his trade monopolies in certain districts are dispensed in the same unprincipled manner.[113] These charges were the complete statement of a case which F. P. Blair, Jr., had been creating for over a month in the fiery controversies of the lower house. On January 26, he had introduced a resolution for the investigation of the regulations which the Treasury Department had drawn up for trade with the

---

[113] Blair, F. P., Jr.: *The Jacobins of Missouri and Maryland. Speech of Hon. F. P. Blair, of Missouri, in the House of Representatives, February 27, 1864, The Congressional Globe*, 38th Congress, 1st Session, Appendix, pp. 46-51.

states in rebellion.[114]   The running debate upon this motion was the occasion for a series of attacks upon the Blairs. Henry Blow, one of Frank's erstwhile colleagues and friends in Missouri, accused Blair's intimates of making vast sums by contracts and called for Montgomery Blair's dismissal from the cabinet.[115]   Henry Winter Davis, whose criticism of the Navy Department, the preserve of the Blairs, had indicated his perverse disposition, characterized Gustavus Vasa Fox as a "cotton spinner," [116]   This insult to the Blair connection aroused as much fury as Davis' sneers at their plans for colonization,[117] and Frank complained with bitterness that, while the Navy Department did not shrink from investigation, "the gentleman from Maryland and his friends . . . in solid phalanx, vote against an investigation leveled" at another cabinet officer.[118]

The controversy now sank to the lowest level of personalities.   Joseph W. McClurg, a Representative from

[114] *The Congressional Globe,* 38th Congress, 1st Session, Part I, p. 406.

[115] *Ibid.,* Part I, pp. 780-782. Remarks of Henry T. Blow in the House of Representatives, February 23, 1864.

[116] *Ibid.,* Part I, p. 830. Remarks of H. W. Davis in the House of Representatives, February 25, 1864.

[117] Davis, Henry W.: *Speeches and Addresses delivered in the Congress of the United States, and on several Public Occasions, by Henry Winter Davis, of Maryland,* pp. 358-367. In this speech, delivered before Congress, January 25, 1864, Davis opposes negro colonization because of its vast expense, the difficulties of transportation, the rights of the negro, and finally the necessity for the labor of the negro in the region where he now lives. F. P. Blair, Jr., paid his respects to anti-colonizers in an address of February 27, 1864. (*The Congressional Globe,* 38th Congress, 1st Session, Appendix, pp. 48-49.)

[118] *The Congressional Globe,* 38th Congress, 1st Session, Part I, pp. 833-834. Remarks of F. P. Blair, Jr., in the House of Representatives, February 27, 1864.

Missouri, accused Frank of smuggling liquors into Vicksburg during the siege. Blair, in moving for a committee of investigation, said that McClurg had aligned himself with the forger and the falsifier and pronounced him "an infamous liar and scoundrel." [119] The committee reported that the order, which was the basis of McClurg's charges, had been tampered with and mutilated.[120] But this exoneration was insufficient. On April 23 Blair rose in his place in the House and delivered a terrific tirade at Chase and all other extremists. He saw in the proposed Fremont convention at Cleveland only an intrigue of the Chase men to use Fremont as a cat's-paw for influencing the Republican convention in favor of Chase; he asserts that the McClurg attack was instigated by Chase, and finally claimed that the whole reconstruction proposal of the radicals was devised to crush the South in such a way that the returned states might not hinder the presidential aspirations of the Secretary of the Treasury.[121] This furious speech marked Frank's final appearance in the House of Representatives. The next day he left the House and resumed the military command which Lincoln had held for him. But the extremists were furious. Chase received the news of the attack as he was about to depart from Washington for Baltimore. His special car fairly "trembled with his rage" and he was later convinced that the attack had been made with the

[119] *The Congressional Globe,* 38th Congress, 1st Session, Part II, pp. 1017, 1252. Remarks of J. W. McClurg in the House of Representatives, March 9, 1864, and of F. P. Blair, Jr., in the House of Representatives, March 23, 1864.

[120] *Ibid.,* Part II, pp. 1827-1828, Report of the Special Committee of Wm. Higly, Brutus J. Clay, John V. L. Pruyn.

[121] *Ibid.,* Part II, pp. 1828-1832. Remarks of F. P. Blair in the House of Representatives, on April 26, 1864.

connivance of the President.[122]   In the House, Thaddeus
Stevens introduced a resolution calling upon the President to explain the process by which Blair had played
his dual military and civil rôle.   By the end of June Congress had passed two resolutions—one declaring that
Blair had never rightly held office as a Representative
and the second asserting that in the future any officer
of the United States whose resignation had been accepted
or who served in either house while still an officer, must
have a second appointment in the manner provided by the
Constitution before he can be restored to his position.[123]

Blair's dramatic exit was followed for the moment by
his return to Missouri.   Here the extremists had run wild.
A radical convention met and voted to send delegates to
the Baltimore Republican Convention, although there was
an element opposed to any recognition of that latter body.
The supporters of Fremont would have preferred recognition of the Cleveland Convention.[124]   In the Baltimore
Convention, this radical delegation was seated at the expense of its rival, the creation of the Blairs; it voted
against Lincoln on the first ballot; and was in part responsible for the resolution declaring for a reorganization of the cabinet.   This last accomplishment was re-
puted to be a direct blow at the Postmaster General, but
the resolution was so ambiguous that Welles was persuaded that it was really directed against Seward.[125]
The Convention of 1864, although in general a radical

[122] Riddle, A. G.: *Recollections of War Times, Reminiscences of Men
and Events in Washington, 1860-1865,* pp. 267-268.
[123] *The Congressional Globe,* 38th Congress, 1st Session, Part II, pp.
1854-1855, Part IV, pp. 3389, 3412.
[124] *New York Tribune,* May 31, 1864.
[125] Welles, Gideon: *Diary of Gideon Welles,* Vol. II, p. 174.

defeat, marked the demise of the Blair influence in Missouri. Francis Preston Blair, Jr., was now a politician without a constituency.

This defeat in Missouri was followed by another in Washington. There Montgomery Blair was still entrenched in the cabinet. The events of the summer, however, did not further happy relations between him and his fellow members. In July the Blairs had "strangely" left Washington for a fishing trip in Pennsylvania.[126] Later disclosures, incidentally, showed that the fishing was largely political, since old Blair had secretly gone to New York in an endeavor to heal the breaches within the Republican Party and to secure the withdrawal of McClellan from the Democratic canvass.[127] During this vacation of the Blairs, General Early encircled Washington and occupied their estate at Silver Spring as his headquarters. Whatever may have been the motive for the distinction, the house of Montgomery Blair was burned by the invaders while that of his father was left undamaged. Some time later, one Cutts met Montgomery on the steps of his Washington town-house and tried to express some sympathy for the loss at Silver Spring. Blair's reply exploded. "Nothing better could be expected while politicians and cowards had the management

[126] Welles, Gideon: *Diary of Gideon Welles*, Vol. II, p. 70.

[127] *New York Tribune*, October 11, 1864. This idea had long been a favorite one of the Blairs. In the winter of 1863 they tried to put McClellan in Halleck's place in order to prevent the possibility of the former being a presidential candidate. Seward frustrated this design according to the Blair idea. (Welles, Gideon: *Diary of Gideon Welles*, Vol. I, p. 345.) In the spring of 1864 Montgomery had written Barlow, a "Copperhead leader" of New York and friend of McClellan, that he would try to secure McClellan an army appointment if the latter would abandon politics. (Welles, Gideon: *Diary of Gideon Welles*, Vol. II, pp. 28-29.)

of military affairs." This remark was carried to Halleck, Chief-of-Staff, who demanded justification in a letter to Stanton; and Stanton laid this letter before the President. The whole intemperate incident did not increase cabinet good feeling. It became almost impossible for Stanton and Blair to attend the same cabinet meeting.[128]

By the middle of September, Montgomery Blair had hints of a cabinet reorganization to take place the following March. There is no sign that these rumors disquieted him; the blow of September 23 must have been a sudden and heavy one. As the President's advisors were separating after their meeting of that day, Montgomery joined Bates and Welles and said "I suppose you are both aware that my head is decapitated, that I am no longer a member of the cabinet." [129] In the first burst of anger he blamed all the Blairs' enemies. Seward and Weed were responsible; Washburne advised it in order to get the German vote; and finally, he was a peace offering to Fremont's friends. Fremont had withdrawn on the previous day from the presidential contest and he had been induced to this act of renunciation by the sacrifice of Montgomery Blair.[130] It was a new version of the old "bargain and corruption" cry. Although the exact details

[128] Welles, Gideon: *Diary of Gideon Welles,* Vol. II, pp. 80, 84, 91.
[129] *Ibid.,* Vol. II, p. 156.
[130] *Ibid.,*Vol. II, pp. 156-158; Bigelow, John: *Op. cit.,* Vol. IV, p. 57; *New York Tribune,* August 29, 1864, September 13, 16, 21, 22, 23, 1864. On August 25, 1864, Fremont wrote an equivocal letter to the supporters of the plan for a new convention which was to secure, if possible, the withdrawal of the candidates then in the field and the nomination of new ones. He expressed his willingness to coöperate in such a movement. On September 6, it was a Washington rumor that Fremont and Cochrane were to retire from the canvass and that Wade was to speak for Mr. Lincoln. These rumors persisted throughout the month. On September 17, Wade addressed a mass meeting at Meadville, Pennsyl-

of such an arrangement are difficult of verification, it is true that Montgomery was dismissed because of extremist opposition. The Chase men, for instance, felt that the machinations of the Blairs were a reason for the dismissal of their leader from the cabinet,[131] and they could not endure the sight of the Blairs enjoying continued power and influence. The same feeling animated other extremists. In fact, Montgomery had become a political liability. His influence was diminished in his own state by a factional quarrel with the extremists,[132] his presence in the cabinet was alienating support throughout the nation. Henry Wilson wrote that tens of thousands would not vote for Lincoln because of Blair.[133] Early in February Warrenton had written the Springfield Republican "It is the uncertainty which prevails among earnest and radical men as to what Lincoln will do with this family of Maryland serpents which makes the opposition movement to Lincoln so formidable." [134] If this extremist element could be conciliated and a source of undoubted irri-

vania, for Lincoln and Johnson. On September 23, the press published Fremont's and Cochrane's letters of withdrawal. The latter retired rather gracefully from the scene; the former was grudging. He retired "not to aid in the triumph of Mr. Lincoln, but to do my part toward preventing the election of a Democratic candidate." Fremont was evidently acting under some rather unpleasant pressure. In any case he had secured revenge upon his old rivals, the Blairs.

[131] *New York Tribune,* July 1, 1864.

[132] *Ibid.,* June 10, 1864. In the summer of 1864 the Maryland Republican Convention had thrown out conservative delegates from Baltimore; had chosen radical presidential electors; and had adopted a resolution condemning the course of the Blairs in that state.

[133] Nicolay, John G., and Hay, John: *Abraham Lincoln, a History,* Vol. IX, p. 339, Henry Wilson to Lincoln, September 5, 1864.

[134] Pearson, Henry G.: *Op. cit.,* Vol. II, p. 151, note 1.

tation removed from the cabinet, Lincoln was both cruel
and wise in demanding Blair's resignation.

But the Blairs were not the sort to accept political
misfortune lying down. For a month or two, there seemed
an immediate likelihood of retrieving disaster. On October 12, Chief Justice Taney died and his position had to
be filled. Montgomery Blair, by his training as a lawyer,
by his legal services to the cause of Dred Scott, and by
his political experience seemed entitled to the appointment. At least the Blairs thought so, for they moved
heaven and earth to accomplish his selection.[135] But
the radicals were insistent upon Chase. On December 7,
the Blairs had the humiliation of receiving the news that
Chase had secured the Chief Justiceship. The reaction
of this defeat upon Maryland politics was most disastrous,
for it "brought the Maryland malcontents into position,
and the trimmers . . . were looking to what they thought
the rising power. Blair fears the President is flinching
and will succumb." [136] Even before this last hope proved
delusive, the Blairs recognized the tragedy of their situation. On September 27, old Blair paid a visit to Secretary
Welles. He came to protest the detachment of his son-
in-law, Admiral S. P. Lee, from command of the North
Atlantic Squadron. "He thought himself hard used in
the blows that fell upon his children." [137] Pathetic judgment. The Blair family, indeed, had fallen sorry victims to the march of circumstances. Restored to power

[135] Forbes, John M.: *Letters (Supplementary) of John Murray
Forbes,* Edited by Sarah F. Hughes, Vol. II, pp. 312-313, Forbes to
W. C. Bryant, November 21, 1864.
[136] Welles, Gideon: *Diary of Gideon Welles,* Vol. II, p. 195.
[137] *Ibid.,* Vol. II, p. 161.

by the advent of the Civil War, the events of that conflict had swept away the last vestige of their influence.
They had, from the first, alienated the conservatives.
Then the growth of the extremist wing and its increasing
prestige had left the Blairs without the support which
they might have expected. Inflexible, they refused to
compromise with the new situation. The bitterness of
their personal dislikes, of their political animosities, made
any such conformity doubly impossible. The year of
1864 had witnessed the exit of Frank Blair from the political stage and the enforced resignation of Montgomery
Blair from the cabinet. The four years of Lincoln's administration told the story of the descent of the Blairs'
political fortunes into catastrophe.

The old man, the father of his race, was to strike one
last blow to recover the prestige which had thus dwindled
away. By making himself instrumental in bringing about
a peaceful settlement between the North and South he
could recoup his political fortunes and deal a death blow
at the extremists and their policies. By forestalling a
peace, dictated to a subjugated people, he could prevent
the imposition of extreme terms of reconstruction; by an-
ticipating a victorious conclusion to the war, he could
ease the pressure which the extremists were exerting upon
Lincoln to compel him to adopt their war and peace
policy. The time for such a movement was now, before
the radicals organized or were conscious of their power.
Other reasons made it logical for the older Blair to undertake such negotiations. A long political career, an
extensive family connection, and a position in the border
states, had given Blair a wide acquaintance among Confederate statesmen. Jefferson Davis had been a frequent

visitor at Silver Spring in the old days; [138] Mrs. Blair in 1867 thought he was one of the greatest men she ever knew or "that ever lived"; [139] and hardly was the war over when Burton M. Harrison, the private secretary of Jefferson Davis, married one of her "blood relations." Then the Blair relatives were scattered all through the Confederacy. Their connection even involved the Lees, for a third cousin of Robert E. Lee, Rear Admiral S. P. Lee, had married Elizabeth, the daughter of F. P. Blair Sr.[140] Other "cousinhoods" included General Joseph O. Shelby, Major-General William Preston, and Brigadier-General R. L. Gibson—all of the Confederate Army; and the respective wives of General Albert Sidney Johnston and of John B. Floyd.[141] It might well seem desirable to protect this vast family connection from the ravages of confiscation and racial amalgamation.

At just what time F. P. Blair, Sr., conceived the idea of a peace mission it is impossible to say. By the end of November, John Murray Forbes writes to Montgomery deprecating the talk of peace; perhaps the astute Bostonian was trying to head off such negotiations at their source.[142] It is certain that old Blair applied in De-

[138] Blair, Gist: "Annals of Silver Spring," *Records of the Columbia Historical Society,* Vol. XXI, p. 168; Davis, Jefferson: *The Rise and Fall of the Confederate Government,* Vol. II, p. 6161. F. P. Blair, Sr., had known Jefferson Davis as a school boy in Lexington, Kentucky.

[139] Bigelow, John: *Op. cit.,* Vol. IV, p. 50.

[140] Lee, Edmund, J.: *Lee of Virginia, 1864-1892, Biographical and Genealogical Sketches of the Descendants of Colonel Richard Lee,* pp. 396, 399, 412.

[141] Andrews, H. P., and Wiggins, P. P.: *Descendants of John Porter of Windsor, Connecticut,* p. 21; Hollister, Wilfred R., and Norman, Harry: *Five Famous Missourians,* p. 331.

[142] Forbes, John M.: *Letters (Supplementary) of John Murray Forbes,* Edited by Sarah F. Hughes, Vol. II, p. 311, Forbes to Montgomery Blair, November 21, 1864.

cember to Lincoln for permission to undertake such a
negotiation, but Lincoln postponed his permission until
after the fall of Savannah.   When this provision had been
met, on December 28, 1864, he issued a pass to the old
man.   Lincoln's knowledge of the plan which his peace
emissary proposed to offer the Confederates was very
slight.[143]   F. P. Blair, Sr., and Montgomery Blair then
departed for the military headquarters of the Northern
armies, whence they sent two notes to Jefferson Davis.
One, which was to be used as an explanation for the public, asserted that F. P. Blair came to Richmond in search
of papers which had been taken from his house at Silver
Spring during the raid of General Early.   The other
stated that the writer, a private citizen of the North,
wholly unaccredited, requested an interview to discuss
the "state of our country" with a view to repairing the
ruin wrought by the war.[144]   When no reply was received to these two communications, the Blairs returned
to Washington.   Hither a belated but favorable answer
of Jefferson Davis was forwarded and on January 7 the

[143] Davis, Jefferson: *Op. cit.*, Vol. II, pp. 612-613; Nicolay, John G.,
and Hay, John: *Abraham Lincoln, a History*, Vol. X, p. 94; Bigelow,
John: *Op. cit.*, Vol. IV, p. 51 (A record of a conversation between
Bigelow and F. P. Blair, Sr., on March 22, 1867).   The relationship
of various members of the cabinet to this mission is a matter of some
speculation.   Stanton is supposed to have protested the issuance of the
pass and newspaper rumor ascribed the failure of Blair's first attempt
to meet the Confederates to his influence.   (Bates, David H.: *Lincoln
in the Telegraph Office; Recollections of the United States Military
Telegraph Corps during the Civil War*, p. 324; *New York Tribune*,
January 24, 1865.)   Seward's connection with the mission was problematical.   Welles thinks he "may have been in the movement."   (Welles,
Gideon: *Diary of Gideon Welles*, Vol. II, p. 232.)

[144] Nicolay, John G., and Hay, John: *Abraham Lincoln, a History*,
Vol. X, pp. 94-95, F. P. Blair, Sr., to Jefferson Davis, December
30, 1864 (MS.).

elder Blair left Washington at once. A few days later
he was at the Spottswood Hotel in Richmond.[145] The
departures and arrivals, North and South, of F. P. Blair,
Sr., were the occasion to a buzz of comment. It was rumored that he went to sell some North Carolina stock.
At another time he was seeking to recover papers taken
in Early's raid. The degree of authority he possessed
was a matter of great speculation. The *Times* lamented
his mission; the *World* gave a prospectus of his terms
which were amnesty, abolition, and the Union as it was
and the constitution as it is; and an "old hand at peace
negotiations" declared that hostilities would cease within
ten days.[146]

On January 12, F. P. Blair, Sr., held a confidential
interview with the President of the Southern Confederacy.
Blair began the interview with a few remarks which were
prefatory to the reading of a long paper in the form of
an editorial—a form native to his genius. In these in-
troductory words Blair asserted his affection for the South
which had been the home of his family; and said that
he relied upon the frankness of the President to tell him
if the "dreams of an old man," which he was about to
submit, could be realized or not. Then followed the reading of the plan which Blair had drawn up. Its keynote
was the fear that, if the Civil War should continue any
longer, the republican and democratic institutions of this

[145] Davis, Jefferson: *Op. cit.,* Vol. II, p. 612; Welles, Gideon: *Diary
of Gideon Welles,* Vol. II, pp. 219, 221; *Official Records of the Union
and Confederate Armies,* Series I, Vol. LXVI, Part II, p. 29; *New York
Tribune,* January 10, 1865, January 16, 1865, a quotation from the
Richmond Despatch of January 13, 1865. The *Don,* a vessel under the
control of the Navy, carried Blair to and fro.

[146] *New York Tribune,* January 4, 11, 13, 14, 16, 1865.

country were in danger of overthrow by monarchy and tyranny. This danger had appeared in tangible form in Mexico. Here Louis Napoleon had set in motion his grand design to make "the Latin race supreme in the southern section of the North American Continent." This object previously had been a dream, foreshadowed by the great Napoleon "in a letter or one of his dictations at St. Helena"; it was at present in process of realization by the subjugation of Mexico and the appointment of Maximilian to rule over its shattered liberties. Now Napoleon stands ready on the flank of our nation to march northward and to create a vast Latin colony on the shores of the Gulf of Mexico. But this disaster to free institutions will occur only if the differences between the South and North continue. What are the bases of these differences? There is first of all, slavery. This institution, Blair says, is condemned by all the world and its extinction is inevitable. Even the South proposes to use its slaves in order to conquer a peace. The inescapable result of such use will be the freedom of the blacks. Slavery as a cause for the separation of the North and South has, therefore, disappeared. With diffidence Blair approaches the other issue—the question of Southern independence. With slavery gone, one object for which independence was coveted has disappeared. But in any case, independence, he insinuates, will be impossible. Either it will be bargained away in return for foreign aid and assistance, or taken away by the victorious march of Louis Napoleon. There is but one method by which to prevent this disaster, and that is Union—a natural Union. "The people are one people, speak a common language, are educated in the same common law, are brought up in one common habitude,—the growth of republican representative institutions,—all fixed in freeholds rooted in the soil of a great luxuriant continent bound as one body by backbone mountains, pervaded in every member with gigantic streams running in every direction to give animation and strength like arteries and veins in the human system. Such an embodiment, in such a country, cannot be divided."

The analysis of the situation completed, Blair endeavored to give his solution for the problem. Slavery was to be abandoned; the Northern offer of amnesty was to be enlarged to include everyone engaged in the War of the Rebellion; and the union of North and South would be brought about through an armistice. Secret preliminaries to this armistice would enable Davis to transport his army to the Mexican border. There he could secure the coöperation of Juarez, whose minister, Romero, "is intimate with my son, Montgomery, who is persuaded that he could induce Juarez to devolve all the power he can command on President Davis—a dictatorship, if necessary—to restore the rights of Mexico and her people. . . ." The North, moreover, although officially aloof, would send recruits for such an expedition. For this purpose "I think I could venture to pledge my son, General Blair, now commanding a corps against the Confederacy." To Jefferson Davis this plan ought to make an especial appeal. If he accepts it and thereby restores the Southern states without "proscription, conscription, or confiscation," as equals in the Union, he can write his name with those of Washington and Jackson, "as a defender of the liberty of the country. If in delivering Mexico, he should mould its States in form and principle to adapt them to our

Union and add a new Southern constellation to its benig-
nant sky while rounding off our possession on the continent at the Isthmus, and opening the way to blending the
waters of the Atlantic and Pacific, thus embracing our
Republic in the arms of the ocean, he would complete
the work of Jefferson, who first set one foot of our colos-
sal government on the Pacific by a stride from the Gulf
of Mexico.   Such achievement would be more highly ap-
preciated in the South, inasmuch as it would restore the
equipoise between the Northern and Southern States—
if indeed such sectional distinctions could be recognized
after the peculiar institution which created them had
ceased to exist."

When the reading of this paper was finished, the two
men discussed its provisions.   Davis expressed his desire
for reconciliation and reiterated his love for the old nation.
At the Battle of Bull Run, so near alike were the two
flags, he said, that he had mistaken the Union one hanging
limp at the staff, for his own.   And of all the plans for
reconciliation, the one Blair had proposed was the best.
There were two obstacles in the way—the feeling of vin-
dictiveness which the war had aroused and the necessity
of absolute honesty on the part of persons making such
an agreement.   Davis admitted that, in regard to the
first consideration, the union of North and South in an
aggressive war upon a foreign power, assailing the principles of government common to both sections, would be of
great assistance.   The feelings of resentment, moreover,
both Blair and Davis agreed were stronger not in the army
but in the politicians and profiteers and in the people at
home who "brooded" over its disasters.   As to the second
consideration, Davis and Blair again agreed in a fortunate

distrust of Seward who was ambitious, selfish, perfidious, and designing although "he has good social feelings." But Blair gave Davis assurance that, if the plan were carried out, it would have to be carried out by Mr. Lincoln who was absolutely responsible and capable of "great personal sacrifices . . .", capable "of sacrificing a friend when he thinks it necessary for the good of the country." Then the interview closed with Davis' assertion that, in order to bring about an understanding, he would appoint commissioners. As for his personal fame, a matter to which Blair had made allusion, he did not care for a great name; all he desired was to "restore the prosperity and happiness of his country. . . . For himself, death would end his cares, and that was very easy to be accomplished." On the following day he sent a note to Mr. Blair to be delivered to Mr. Lincoln.[147]

The spectacle of those who had been most active in provoking war, now most ready to make peace, would probably amuse the sophisticated Seward. There are laughable incongruities in the sight of old F. P. Blair, who had talked so vehemently of "nullifiers" and "rebels,"

---

[147] Nicolay, John G., and Hay, John: *Abraham Lincoln, a History,* "Blair's Mexican Project and the Hampton Roads Conference, the Thirteenth Amendment," in the *Century Magazine,* Vol. XVI, pp. 839-844. This is the complete report of the Blair mission as given in a manuscript copy. This report is not published in full in the ten volume work on Abraham Lincoln by the same authors. In an abbreviated form it can be found there in Vol. X, pp. 96-106. Davis, Jefferson: *The Rise and Fall of the Confederate Government,* Vol. II, pp. 612-615. Memorandum Dated Richmond, Virginia, January 12, 1865, of a confidential conversation held this day with F. P. Blair, of Montgomery County, Maryland. There is an endorsement of January 14, which says: "The foregoing memorandum of conversation was this day read to Mr. Blair, and altered in so far as he desired, in any respect, to change the expressions employed."

and who had urged a vigorous war as a means for restoring national harmony, now boasting of the Southern blood in his veins and urging Jefferson Davis to make peace. Even if four years of political struggle with conservatives and extremists had wrought this transformation, they had not diminished the astuteness and the subtlety of this master politician. Blair's Mexican project is a marvelously adroit appeal to the Confederacy and to the personality of her President. With delicacy Blair points out the hopelessness of the situation for the Southern states by stressing their determination to use the slaves and to secure foreign intervention. Then he eases their inevitable return into the Union by proposing a "joint crusade against foreign powers" and by arousing the hope that in the newly acquired territory the South may have an equipoise to the power of the North.[148] Then comes the appeal to Davis himself. He will protect the independence of the South no longer against the North but against Louis Napoleon, the real enemy; he may hold his

[148] Of interest in connection with the Blair Mexican project is the proposal of Lincoln, through F. P. Blair, Jr., to General J. O. Shelby, Blair's cousin, that, when the Confederacy fell, the Transmississippi Confederates might invade Mexico with such aid from Federal soldiers as would be forthcoming. Shelby received this information "long before the killing of Lincoln." At least such is Shelby's recollection of the episode in 1877. (Stevens, Walter B.: *Op. cit.,* Vol. X, pp. 115-118.) General Lew Wallace also believed that he would be able to negotiate an agreement with the Transmississippi Confederates for a joint invasion of Mexico. On January 14, 1865, he wrote Grant: "While Blair and Singleton are in Richmond, let me from Brazos, upon my own authority, invite the commandant of Brownsville to an interview on the old battle field of Palo Alto. If the man's a soldier I'll wager you a month's pay that I win and Blair and Company lose." (*Official Records of the Union and Confederate Armies,* Series I, Vol. XLVIII, Part I, p. 512.) Grant took the bet, despatched Wallace, but nothing happened. (*Official Records of the Union and Confederate Armies,* Vol. XLVIII, Part I, pp. 937-939, 1166-1167, 1276-1279; Part II, pp. 122, 457-463.)

head high in the accomplishment of this defense of free
institutions; he may ally his name with those of Washington, Jefferson, and Jackson. Under the magic of
Blair's words defeat takes on the aspect of victory.

On January 16, Blair returned to Washington on the
Don, the flagship of the Potomac flotilla. The reporters
found him "silent but in good humor." [149]

[149] *New York Tribune,* January 17, 1865.

CHAPTER V

The Hampton Roads Conference

One reason for the elder Blair's taciturn good humor may have been the impression, which he had gained during his visits to Richmond, of affairs in the Confederate States of America. The Southern capital was, in truth, a city of sorrows and waning hopes. Every day the Federal armies were drawing nearer to the heart of the Confederacy and were taking in their march a fatal toll of men and of territory. Every day the resources of the Confederacy were being whittled away; and each dispatch from the various fronts seemed to tell the tale of a new and inescapable disaster. As if to increase the gloom which enshrouded the Southern cause, there was a spell of miserable weather. There were incessant rains; falling snow was turned into slush or ice by rapid alternation in the temperature. Even the clear days were robbed of their promise by the news which seeped in from defeated armies.

But the Confederacy was not in danger solely because of attacks from without. Such simply gave occasion and emphasis to the real causes of disintegration—the personal dislikes and the political differences within the Southern states. That internal dissensions should appear when a nation is threatened with disaster is a truism. But these dissensions were peculiarly dangerous for the Confederacy because that government was based upon a belief in the principles of separation and state individuality. Disunion, therefore, always had a theoretic justification and it would seem as if secessionists could not justly complain when various Southern states, in turn, talked of independent state action.

In this respect January 1865 witnessed one more step in the difficulties which the central government had had with North Carolina. In that state discontent with the Civil War had been brewing ever since 1862. There were plans for peace negotiations to be undertaken by North Carolina alone, and for a convention to carry North Carolina out of the Confederacy and back into the Union. People of this belief, denominating themselves "conservatives" and their opponents "destructives," were led by W. W. Holden, the editor of the *Raleigh Standard*. In 1862, the conservative party had helped to elect as Governor of the state, Zebulon B. Vance, whose wholesale allegiance to the cause of his creators was sometimes a matter of doubt.[1] But gubernatorial indecision could not stand in the way of the rising tide of peace sentiment. Holden, the shrewd and variable editor, who had once supported secession to the last ditch, had caught the drift of the current and converted himself into an earnest advocate of peace. His paper "took" like wildfire, and his subscription list increased enormously. Jonathan Worth, Public Treasurer of the state, was "for peace on *almost any terms*." By January, 1864, there were open mass meetings for a peace convention—irrespective of what the central government might do—and petitions were circulated for the same end.

---

[1] Rowland, Dunbar (Editor): *Jefferson Davis, Constitutionalist, His Letters, Papers, and Speeches*, Vol. IX, pp. 329-330. D. K. McRae to Jefferson Davis, January 16, 1885.

But the possibilities of state action were checkmated by the rival political ambitions of Holden and Vance, both of whom ran for governor. Ultra-loyal Confederates saw little to choose between the two candidates, but rallied around Governor Vance as the less of two evils. His successful reëlection, however, did not make him appreciably less sensitive to the strength of the peace element. Indeed, he could not well ignore it, for its violence and intensity were uncontrollable. By the end of 1864 he was writing Jefferson Davis that it would be impossible to remove the "sources of discontent" in North Carolina, "except by making some effort at negotiation with the enemy.[2]"

But the ablest advocate of independent state action was Georgia. To the supporters of the administration all the greatest malcontents of the South seemed to have gravitated to that particular region. There was Robert Toombs, "shifted from Secretary of State to subordinate General, and then to a militia officer under suspended Court Martial," there was Governor Joseph E. Brown and Judge Linton Stephens, and finally there was Alexander H. Stephens, Vice President of the Confederacy, who was disappointed because "he had been a cypher, when he expected to be the counsellor and brains of the Confederacy."[3] Even the loyal support of Benjamin H.

---

[2] Hamilton, J. G. deR. (Editor): *The Correspondence of Jonathan Worth,* Vol. I, pp. 245-258, 282-287, 303-308, 330-342; Rowland, Dunbar (Editor): *Op. cit.,* Vol. IX, pp. 330-331, Vol. VI, pp. 141-142, General Z. B. Vance to Jefferson Davis, December 30, 1864.

[3] Rowland, Dunbar (Editor): *Op. cit.,* Vol. X, p. 10, an article by Henry W. Cleveland which he sent to Jefferson Davis, November 25, 1887. Henry W. Cleveland "worshipped him [Stephens] as most Georgians did," and, as chief editor of the *Augusta Daily Constitutionalist,* gave him able support. Stephens, after the war, invited Cleveland to aid him in the composition of the "War Between the States." All

Hill, Senator from Georgia, could not compensate the administration for such disaffection.[4] But Stephens did not explain his differences with the administration policy on the basis of personal pique or thwarted ambition. Rather, he placed it on the high ground of theory. The *a priori* grounds on which Stephens had based his feeble allegiance to the secession cause were violated by his fellow secessionists. Stephens' primary devotion had always been to the civil rights which the Federal constitution had embodied and consecrated; and, when he left the Union, he tried to the best of his ability to secure the perpetuation of those principles in his state and in the new nation. But he soon beheld in the Confederacy either the actuality or the possibility of conscription, impressments, suspension of *habeas corpus*, military arrests, and imprisonments, and the operation of martial law. The adoption of these arbitrary methods for the conduct of the war was clearly unnecessary in view of the exigencies of the conflict; their use could augur, therefore, only the intention of Jefferson Davis to create a centralized, consolidated, military despotism or to establish a personal dynasty. Stephens was "wretched" at this perversion of Confederate war aims. It seemed to him that the ambition and zeal of the Southern President alone stood in the way of peace, and that, if he were willing to surrender the attain-

went smoothly until Stephens attempted to blame Davis for the "failure of the war"—a procedure against which Cleveland protested. As a result of his protest, Stephens employed another secretary-author and Cleveland lost thereby $10,000 and the "fame of it." (Rowland, Dunbar (Editor): *Op. cit.*, Vol. IX, pp. 603-605, H. W. Cleveland to Jefferson Davis, November 25, 1887.)

[4] Hill, Benjamin H. Jr.: *Senator Benjamin H. Hill of Georgia. His Life, Speeches, and Writing*, pp. 44-45; *Speech of Benjamin H. Hill before the Georgia Legislature, December 11, 1862*, pp. 252-272.

ment of Southern independence and his own continuation in power, the guarantees of the civil and political rights which were so dear to the heart of Stephens, could once again be secured within the Federal Union.[5]

By the early summer of 1863 Stephens, whose rôle in the Confederacy had become one of habitual criticism, saw an opportunity to stay the march of the South toward the inevitable goal of a military despotism. Difficulties had arisen with the North over the exchange and treatment of prisoners and Stephens believed that he would be a fit emissary for the conduct of negotiations to bring about the amelioration of the situation. But this question of prisoners was only a minor point—an excuse for the discussion of the greater question of peace. "I am not without hope that *indirectly* I could now turn attention to a general adjustment upon such basis as might ultimately be acceptable to both parties and stop the further effusion of blood in a contest so irrational, unchristian, and so inconsistent with all recognized American principles." [6] Although Stephens was unable to give any reasons for his optimistic faith in the possibility of peace, Davis was willing to adopt his suggestion. The dispatch of Stephens on a peace mission would at least serve to quiet the flood of his criticism and the victorious march of General Lee into Pennsylvania might fittingly be attended with the

[5] Stephens, Alexander H.: *Recollections of Alexander H. Stephens; His Diary kept when a prisoner at Fort Warren, Boston Harbour, 1865; giving incidents and reflections of his prison life and some letters and reminiscences*, pp. 148, 165-170, 326-332. These observations were written while Stephens was a prisoner at Fort Warren after the war and while his views of Jefferson Davis, the author of so much misfortune, were not yet mellowed by the charity of time.

[6] Rowland, Dunbar (Editor): *Op. cit.*, Vol. V, pp. 513-515, A. H. Stephens to Jefferson Davis, June 12, 1863.

proffer of peace to a vanquished foe. But Davis' acceptance of Stephens' proposition hedged it about with so
many restrictions that the Vice President would be power-
less to effect any harm to the campaign of the Confederacy for independence. The Southern President thrusts
the whole burden of seeking peace upon Stephens for in
his own letter he says not a word about the larger aspects
of the proposed mission, but simply details the problems
connected with the question of prisoners. If Stephens
talks of peace terms, it will evidently be upon his own
responsibility. As a credential for his errand, Davis gave
Stephens a letter addressed to Lincoln. Every effort was
made to cast this letter in a form which would be acceptable to the Northern President. Pains were taken to fore-
stall a refusal to receive Stephens on the ground that such
a reception would "involve a tacit recognition of the Confederacy," and the letter was drawn up in duplicate, one
copy of which was addressed to Abraham Lincoln as Commander-in-Chief of the land and naval forces of the
North, and the other addressed to him as President, with
the idea that the more acceptable form should be used.
But here concession stopped. The letter to Lincoln as
President of the United States was signed by Davis as
President of the Confederate States. If the North should
refuse this recognition, the whole idea of a conference
must be abandoned. Such a "conference is admissible
only on the footing of perfect equality," and Stephens
was instructed to take care that "the equal rights of the
Confederacy be always preserved." [7]

[7] Rowland, Dunbar (Editor): *Op. cit.,* Vol. V, pp. 515-519, Jefferson
Davis to Alexander H. Stephens, July 2, 1863, Jefferson Davis to
Abraham Lincoln, July 2, 1863.

Losing no time, Stephens proceeded by the steamer *Torpedo,* a vessel of the Confederate navy, to City Point. Once there, he applied to Admiral S. P. Lee for permission to proceed to Washington to deliver a letter from Jefferson Davis to Abraham Lincoln. Stephens neglected to state the object of his mission. The receipt of this request was the occasion for confusion at Washington. There were two cabinet meetings which served to air a quarrel between Welles and Stanton as to which Department should be the medium of communication with the Southern emissary, to disclose the President's inclination to despatch someone to Fortress Monroe to discover Stephens' purposes, and finally to show the great diversity of opinion among members of the cabinet. Probably everyone was more interested in the news which came from Vicksburg and from Gettysburg. At last on July 6, a telegram was dispatched which stated that Stephens' request was inadmissible and that the regular "agents and channels are adequate for all needful military communication . . ." The Vice President returned disheartened and perplexed to the Confederacy.[8]

The events of the summer and fall were not such as to strengthen his waning belief in the success of the Confederate cause. The last six months of that year unrolled before the South an unwelcome vista of military defeat. Gettysburg and Vicksburg were followed by Chattanooga and Missionary Ridge. Under Stephens' guidance, Georgia became a center of rising dissatisfaction. In March,

[8] *Official Records of the Union and Confederate Armies,* Series II, Vol. VI, pp. 79-80, 84-85, 94; Welles, Gideon, *Diary of Gideon Welles,* Vol. I, pp. 358-363. At the cabinet meeting on July 5, Seward, Stanton, and Chase opposed any recognition of Stephens. Blair was in favor of receiving Stephens' communication, and Welles inclined to the same view.

1864, the Vice. President of the Confederacy delivered a remarkable address before the Georgia Legislature.   It rehearsed his customary opposition to conscription and to the suspension of the right of *habeas corpus;* stated that he would not trust the "dictatorship" of the country to the President or anyone else; and implied in conclusion that Georgia might well assert its sovereignty rather than submit to a new "master." [9]   As a result of this extraordinary attack upon the President and his policies, the Georgia Legislature passed resolutions, sponsored by Linton Stephens, a brother of Alexander, on the suspension of *habeas corpus* and on the question of peace.   The latter series, which were far more revolutionary in tone, asserted the general right of secession and attacked the Lincoln administration as despotic and tyrannous.   This was a form of appeal to the peace party of the North. The resolutions then went on to state that on a favorable opportunity the state organizations and the central government of the South should make an offer of peace to the North on the basis of the Declaration of Independence. Such an offer would have a desirable effect in the North, for, even if it were refused, the peace party of the North would be encouraged and strengthened.   In the South efforts for peace are thwarted only by men, "whose importance, or whose gains, would be diminished by peace, and men whose arbitrary designs would need cover under the ever-recurring plea of the necessities of the war." [10]

[9] Cleveland, Henry: *Alexander H. Stephens, in Public and Private, with Letters and Speeches, before, during, and since the War,* pp. 761-786.   Speech on the State of the Confederacy, delivered before the Georgia Legislature at Milledgeville, Georgia, March 16, 1864.

[10] Waddell, James D.: *Biographical Sketch of Linton Stephens, containing a selection of his Letters, Speeches, State Papers, etc.,* pp. 269-275.

If any new stimulus to Stephens' distrust of the administration was needed, it came from Sherman's march into Georgia, the capture of Atlanta, and the threat which the Federal army presented to Georgia and to the Confederacy. Sherman, to be sure, did his best to capitalize the discontent of the state which he had invaded and sent a hearty invitation to Governor Brown and Stephens to confer with him as to the possibilities of peace.[11] Both refused but with reservations. Brown expected that the last paragraph of his answer "as looking to a possible contingency, in which Mr. Davis would not be recognized as superior" would be attacked by administration supporters;[12] and Stephens, perhaps influenced by Toombs,[13] refused to participate in negotiations largely on the ground that he possessed no power to do so.[14] Although they might refuse a conference with a Federal general, they still dallied with the idea of separate state action, perhaps in conjunction with other states, as a means to circumvent the obstacles which Davis had placed in the sure way toward peace.[15]

[11] *Official Records of the Union and Confederate Armies*, Series I, Vol. XXXIX, Part II, p. 381.

[12] Philips, U. B. (Editor): "The Correspondence of Robert Toombs, Alexander H. Stephens, and Howell Cobb," *Annual Report of the American Historical Association*, 1911, Vol. II, p. 653, Joseph E. Brown to Alexander H. Stephens, September 30, 1864.

[13] *Ibid.*, pp. 652-653, Robert Toombs to Alexander H. Stephens, September 23, 1864. Toombs wrote, "Do not by any means go to see Sherman, whatever may be the form of his invitation. It will place you in a wrong, *very wrong* position."

[14] Cleveland, Henry: *Op. cit.*, pp. 196-197, Alexander H. Stephens to William King, October 1, 1864. William King was the medium of General Sherman's communication.

[15] Philips, U. B.: *Op. cit.*, p. 653, Joseph E. Brown to Alexander H. Stephens, October 17, 1864; Johnston, Richard M., and Browne, W. H.: *Life of Alexander H. Stephens*, pp. 473-475, Alexander H. Stephens

If the President and Vice President had hitherto veiled their hostility to each other from a sense of dignity as to what was becoming in the two leading executives of the Confederacy, that restraint was cast aside by the end of the year. In October Davis paid a visit to the Southern armies and on his return made an address at Augusta, Georgia, the heart of the enemy's country. He attacked the croakers who saw no hope in the Confederate cause, repudiated for himself any idea of negotiation except on the basis of a recognition of Southern independence, apologized for the harshness of Confederate legislation on the plea of necessity, and advised those who "can plan in their closets the campaigns of a general and write the State papers of an executive " to "go to the front and there give us the benefit of their services." [16] But Jefferson Davis could not stay in Georgia to excite the enthusiasm of the mob. He had to return to Richmond. Stephens remained on the job. The election of Lincoln swept away, once for all, his delusive hopes of peace through a victory of the Northern peace party. In a letter published in the *Augusta Constitutionalist*, he implied that Davis preferred the election of Lincoln to McClellan—a statement which carried the further implication that Davis preferred war to peace. Linton Stephens introduced into the Georgia House of Representatives resolutions urging the calling of a convention of states to negotiate peace. This movement Davis met in a letter to certain members of the Georgia Senate. Any such step, as envisaged by the

to Linton Stephens, October 9, 1864, Alexander H. Stephens to Linton Stephens, October 18, 1864.

[16] Rowland, Dunbar (Editor): *Op. cit.*, Vol. II, pp. 356-361, Speech of Jefferson Davis delivered in Augusta, on October 5, 1864 as reported in the *Richmond Despatch*, October 10, 1864.

resolutions, seemed to Davis a logical absurdity. If a convention of all the states should assemble for the purpose of negotiating peace, it would meet under one of two conditions, for either the decisions of such a body would be binding upon all the states, or they would not be binding. In the former case, the South would be at the mercy of the North; in the latter case, the North would indirectly admit the right of the South for independence. Furthermore, a convention meeting simply for the purpose of negotiating peace, without any previous agreement as to whether or not its decisions would be binding, is a cumbersome method, infinitely inferior to individual negotiators. Jefferson Davis then strips the proposal of all its pretences and places his finger upon the real difficulty in the Stephens plan of negotiation—a difficulty parallel to that which bewildered northern Democrats—that is the unwillingness of the North to advance peace propositions acceptable to the South.[17]

Stephens, meanwhile, had left Georgia for Richmond in order to assume his duties as presiding officer in the Senate. He was in a gloomy mood. The further suspension of the writ of *habeas corpus* seemed likely to be sanctioned by the House of Representatives and Stephens thought he might even resign the vice presidency and thus wash his hands clean from all complicity in the acts of the Davis dynasty.[18] His temper, moreover, was not improved by the correspondence with the President over

[17] Rowland, Dunbar (Editor): *Op. cit.*, Vol. VI, pp. 403-406, Jefferson Davis to Messrs. A. R. Wright, Y. L. Guerry, J. M. Chambers, Thos. E. Lloyd, Fredk. W. West, R. B. Nesbit, Senators of Georgia, November 17, 1864.

[18] Johnston, Richard M., and Browne, W. H.: *Op. cit.*, pp. 475-476, A. H. Stephens to Linton Stephens, December 23, 1864.

Stephens' accusation that the former preferred the election of Lincoln rather than McClellan. Each epistolary contestant found the activities of the other "strange" and Davis, on January 8, closed the controversy with the chiding statement that he would like to see Stephens "devoting your great and admitted ability exclusively to upholding the confidence and animating the spirit of the people to unconquerable resistance against their foes." [19]

The dissatisfaction with the course of the war could not be confined to state capitals or to state politics. The craving for peace which had grown so rapidly in North Carolina and Georgia surged up to Richmond. January bore heavy witness to a gradual sapping of the Confederate morale by the personal bitterness and the petty bickerings of a discontented and apprehensive people. The croakers, hitherto somewhat restrained, increased in numbers and outspokenness. The discontent of this opposition found an expression, in the first place, in an attempt by the Confederate Congress to take the control of policy away from the President. There had always been a party of opposition to Davis; it had become more restive after the disasters of the summer of 1863; now it determined to save the country from the misfortunes of his rule. It first attempted to interfere with the conduct of military affairs; a resolution was passed requesting the President to appoint Robert E. Lee, general-in-chief of all the Confederate armies, and to restore Joseph E. Johnston to the command of the army of the Tennessee. In civil affairs there was a similar interference. The Virginian delega-

[19] *Official Records of the Union and Confederate Armies,* Series IV, Vol. III, pp. 834-840, 1000-1004, A. H. Stephens to Jefferson Davis, December 13, 1864, Jefferson Davis to A. H. Stephens, January 6, 1865.

tion in the House of Representatives in an address to the
President expressed a want of confidence in the cabinet
and, as a result of their action, Seddon, Secretary of War
and a Virginian, felt compelled to resign.

From another direction pressure was exerted to compel the President to make peace. The reassembling of
Congress saw a flood of resolutions on the subject in the
House of Representatives. In this movement Henry S.
Foote, a Representative from Tennessee and a member of
the Committee on Foreign Affairs, was a leader. Foote
was an explosive person who had never been on completely
friendly terms with Jefferson Davis. There had been
personal differences in the old days when Davis and Foote
were both Senators from Mississippi in the Federal Senate,[20] and during the Civil War, especially in the later
years, the latter "blew clouds of vituperative gas at President and Cabinet." [21] On December 1, 1864, Foote introduced a resolution calling for a convention of the
Southern states in order either to devise measures for the
more efficient prosecution of the war or so to alter the
treaty-making powers of the government as "to secure as
early a cessation of hostilities and restoration of peace as
would be compatible with honor, safety, and the permanent happiness of the people of the said Confederate
States." This motion was laid on the table. Two weeks
later, Josiah Turner, Representative from North Carolina and likewise a member of the Committee on Foreign

[20] Rowland, Dunbar (Editor): *Op. cit.,* Vol. VII, p. 395, note 1,
Memorandum of A. W. Venable, August 8, 1874.
[21] De Leon, T. C.: *Four Years in the Rebel Capitals: An inside view
of life in the southern Confederacy, from birth to death, from original
notes collected in the years 1861 to 1865,* p. 319; Foote, Henry S.:
War of the Rebellion; or Scylla and Charybdis, pp. 346-368.

Affairs, introduced a resolution whose object was the appointment of thirteen commissioners, one from each of the Confederate states, who were to propose to the North a convention for the purpose of negotiating peace. After debate, the House referred this resolution, with others offered as amendments, to the Committee on Foreign. Affairs.[22] These resolutions were only the surface indications of the forces which were working underground in the House of Representatives. Baldwin of Virginia was restive; Colyar, Atkins, and Menees, all of Tennessee, were of the same opinion as their colleague Foote. They determined, if possible, to influence the deliberations of the Committee on Foreign Affairs in the direction of resolutions looking toward peace.[23] Foote, however, could not harness his excitable nature to any more deliberate measures. The possibility of the passage of the act to suspend the writ of *habeas corpus* drew from him a threat to resign the seat which he occupied in the Confederate Congress.[24] Fleeing from Richmond, he wrote a letter on December 24 from "the bank of the Potomac, in sight of the Birthplace of Washington," to the Speaker of the House, in which he resigned his seat and announced his intention of departing for the Northern capital to make peace.[25] On this journey he was accompanied by his wife. For some reason

[22] *Journal of the Congress of the Confederate States of America, 1861-1865*, Vol. II, *Journal of the House of Representatives*, pp. 312-313; *Ibid.*, Vol. VII, pp. 317, 360, 363-364.

[23] Foote, Henry S.: *Op. cit.*, p. 375; Rowland, Dunbar (Editor): *Op. cit.*, Vol. VIII, pp. 30-31, A. S. Colyar to R. M. T. Hunter, January 3, 1877; Vol. VIII, pp. 213-215, James Lyons to W. T. Walthall, June 10, 1878.

[24] Jones, John B.: *A Rebel War Clerk's Diary at the Confederate States Capital*, Vol. II, pp. 359-360.

[25] Foote, Henry S.: *Op. cit.*, pp. 383-386.

she was allowed to pass through the Federal Lines; [26] her husband, not so fortunate, was arrested by the Confederate military authorities and imprisoned at Fredericksburg. Jefferson Davis referred the question of privilege involved to the House of Representatives.[27]

The insurgents, meanwhile, had won a partial victory in the House of Representatives. On January 12, 1865, John A. Orr of Mississippi, Chairman of the Committee on Foreign Affairs, introduced into secret session a series of resolutions which expressed a desire for peace, suggested as a method of negotiation a convention of all the states—a convention which was merely to deliberate upon means for peace and make no final agreement, and finally called upon the President to allow the House, voting by states, to select three commissioners to proceed to Washington and there discover if such a convention could be assembled. If this method of peace making was unacceptable, the commissioners were to discuss other methods and particularly the possibility of a joint action to uphold the Monroe Doctrine in return for a "prompt recognition of the independence" of the Confederacy. By a narrow majority of four, the consideration of these resolutions was postponed until the disposal of a bill dealing with the military organization of the Confederacy. The debate on these resolutions, revived by an article in the *Sentinel* which denounced them as "treason!" again demonstrated the closeness of sentiment in the House and the fact that

[26] *New York Tribune*, January 14, 1865. Mrs. Foote's arrival in Washington was the occasion of great interest. Secretary Seward took her under his particular charge.

[27] *Journals of the Congress of the Confederate States of America, 1861-1865*, Vol. VII, Journal of the House of Representatives, p. 454; Jones, John B.: *Op. cit.*, p. 385.

its members were still unwilling to force the President's
hand in the matter of peace negotiations.[28]   In the Senate, the chief ally of the discontents was naturally Alexander H. Stephens.   He was privy to their desire to push
through the lower House resolutions in favor of a peace
convention.   He may even have been the author of the
resolutions which were presented on January 12.[29]   In
the Senate he lost no opportunity to express his dissatisfaction with the conduct of the administration.   The debate over the suspension of the writ of *habeas corpus* was
so manipulated as to prevent a statement of his views, an
act which almost led him to resign.   But the Senate
assuaged his injured feelings by a resolution, passed
unánimously, which requested him to present his opinions
on the state of the country.   In a long extempore address
on January 6, he gave them his views "very freely." [30]
Only a brief condensation of those frank remarks now
remains.   He advocated, however, that the policy of the
administration "should be speedily and thoroughly
changed" and, as suggestions for this revolution, proposed a Fabian military policy and a cultivation of the
peace element in the North by means which are not at all

[28] *Journal of the Congress of the Confederate States of America,
1861-1865,* Vol. VII, Journal of the House of Representatives, pp. 451-
452, 457; *New York Tribune,* January 20, 1865, an excerpt from the
Sentinel of January 17, 1865.

[29] Johnston, Richard M., and Browne, W. H.: *Op. cit.,* pp. 480-483,
A. H. Stephens to Linton Stephens, January 6, 1865; Rowland,
Dunbar (Editor): *Op. cit.,* Vol. VIII, p. 31, A. S. Colyar to R. M. T.
Hunter, January 3, 1877. Colyar claims that the resolutions included
the names of the commissioners who were to be appointed—Stephens,
Hunter and Campbell. There is nothing to substantiate this claim in
the resolutions published in the Journals.

[30] *Ibid.,* p. 483, A. H. Stephens to Linton Stephens, January 6, 1865.

explicit in his report of his own oration.[31] Probably he
advocated peace negotiations as a means for showing the
North the real purpose of the Lincoln administration and
the Northern President's desire to create a military despotism. Stephens saw in Presidents North and South
nothing but dynasties and despotisms.

While the ferment of this discontent was brewing,
Francis Preston Blair, Sr., paid his first visit to Richmond and read his editorial appeal to Jefferson Davis.
Every aspect of the situation in the Confederate capital
seemed to impel the President to consider favorably
Blair's suggestions. The obstacle to previous negotiations—the question of Southern independence—was
adroitly concealed by the Mexican project and, therefore, Davis could not be accused of inconsistency if he
again entered upon negotiation. Thus, on the one hand,
he was sheltered from the southern fire-eaters. On the
other hand, by making a sincere effort at peace, he
could quiet the clamor of the peace crowd and ease the
pressure which it was bringing to bear upon him. If, in
the course of negotiations, it should again develop that
the North would make no concession to Southern self-government, there would be renewed enthusiasm for the war.
In any case the possibility of an armistice would be of
military advantage. Accordingly, Davis assented to the
"dreams of an old man." F. P. Blair, Sr., on his return
to Washington, carried with him a note written to him by
Jefferson Davis. In it the Southern President asserted his
willingness to dispense with forms and to send or receive

---

[31] Stephens, Alexander H.: *A Constitutional View of the Late War
between the States; its causes, character, conduct, and results. Presented in a series of colloquies at Liberty Hall*, Vol. II, pp. 587-589.

commissioners.   But the closing words ran, "That not-withstanding the rejection of our former offers, I would, if you could promise that a commissioner, minister, or other agent would be received, appoint one immediately, and renew the effort to enter into conference, with a view to secure peace to the two countries." [32]   In his report to Lincoln, Blair had to give not only the results of his visit to Richmond, but also the first account of the proposals which he had laid before the Confederate President. With the Mexican project, as Blair had drawn it up, Lincoln would have nothing to do; [33] but he was in other respects willing to continue negotiations.   In turn he wrote a letter to Blair.   This letter authorized him to tell Jefferson Davis that "I have constantly been, am now, and shall continue ready to receive any agent, whom he, or any other influential person now resisting the national authority, may informally send to me with the view of se-curing peace to the people of our one common country." [34] On the 20th of January Blair left Washington for Rich-mond on the *Don.*

Blair was soon back in Secessia, for on the 21st he presented Lincoln's reply to Jefferson Davis.   There was still some ambiguity over the Mexican project, but Blair spoke of the President's reticence in that matter as due to his difficulties with the extremists in Congress; an armis-tice to carry out the objects which Blair and Davis had

[32] *Official Records of the Union and Confederate Armies,* Series I, Vol. XLVI, Part II, p. 506, Jefferson Davis to F. P. Blair, Sr., Jan-uary 12, 1865.
[33] Nicolay, John F., and Hay, John: *Abraham Lincoln, a History,* Vol. X, pp. 107-108.
[34] *Official Records of the Union and Confederate Armies,* Series I, Vol. XLVI, Part II, p. 506, A. Lincoln to F. P. Blair, Sr., January 18, 1865.

previously discussed would have, therefore, to be arranged by some military convention between Lee and Grant.[35] Whatever may have been the actual situation, Davis was apparently left under the impression that the Mexican expedition was still a possibility.   On January 25, Blair returned from his second visit to the Confederacy.   He had had quite a sojourn at Richmond and the nature of his errand was a subject of great curiosity and speculation there.   It was known that he came on the question of peace and the extremist press viewed with great alarm the cordiality with which, it was rumored, he was received by the President.   The *Richmond Examiner* thought that Blair was either a spy or a propagandist, a fit person in any case to be excluded from the country; and advised Jefferson Davis, if he must interview such persons, to depart permanently for the other side of the Potomac.[36] The *Whig* lamented the increased power which Blair's mission gave to the Confederate peace crowd and dreaded a repetition of the "peace mania" which last summer "brought us to the verge of ruin." [37]   The *Sentinel*, the

[35] Davis, Jefferson: *Op. cit.,* Vol. II, pp. 616-617; *Official Records of the Union and Confederate Armies,* Series I, Vol. XLVI, Part II, p. 506, Memorandum of A. Lincoln, January 28, 1865; *New York Tribune,* January 21, 1865.

[36] *New York Tribune,* January 16, 1865, quotation from *Richmond Examiner,* January 13, 1865; *Ibid.,* January 21, 1865, quotation from *Richmond Examiner.*

[37] *Ibid.,* January 17, 1865, quotation from the *Richmond Whig,* January 14, 1865. The Niagara peace negotiations had not been a pleasant morsel for the fire eaters of the Confederacy. The *Richmond Examiner* of July 26 for once approved of a state paper of Mr. Lincoln—his letter "To Whom It May Concern." "When officious individuals go creeping round by back doors asking interviews with Lincoln for a full interchange of sentiments, it gives us sincere gratification to see them spurned, yes, kicked, from the said back door. To Abraham we deliberately say 'Bravo,' or, if he likes it better, 'Bully.' Think of an

fiercest opponent of compromise, pictured peace on Northern terms as involving universal confiscation of property and judicial murders, and asserted that "All the dark and malignant passions of a vindictive people, drunk with blood and vomiting crime, will be unloosed upon us like bloodhounds upon their prey."[38]

Blair enjoyed the greatest freedom in Richmond and he did not confine himself to conversation with Jefferson Davis. His acquaintance with Southerners was extensive and with this acquaintance, including as it did many officials of the Confederacy, he talked about the desirability of peace. The resources of the North, he pointed out, were overwhelming and there were vast reserves of man power in Europe which could be utilized if the North promised European recruits a portion of Southern confiscated lands. The South might well submit before it was utterly exhausted. It is doubtful whether Blair had any closer connection with the Southern peace movement than that of general encouragement. Robert Ould, Commissioner of Exchange for prisoners, at whose home Blair spent his first visit in Richmond, testifies to the propriety

ex-Senator from Alabama and a Virginian Member of Congress, for we say nothing of the third negotiator, exposing themselves, gratuitously, idly, and unbidden to receive such an ignominious rebuff at the hands of the truculent buffoon of Illinois." (Severance, F. H.: "The Peace Conference at Niagara Falls in 1864," *Buffalo Historical Society Publications*, Vol. XVIII, pp. 90-91.) Secretary Benjamin felt called upon to assert that the commissioners opened their correspondence without any authority from their government. (*Official Records of the Union and Confederate Navies*, Series II, Vol. III, p. 1194.) And Clay from Canada sadly despairs of the Confederacy if such an editorial is an earnest of its wisdom. (Report of C. C. Clay to J. P. Benjamin, August 18, 1864.)

[38] *New York Tribune*, January 24, 1865, quotation from the *Sentinel*, January 20, 1865.

of Blair's conversation and one of those who thought him a spy bears witness to Blair's silence rather than his loquacity.[39]

Blair, meanwhile, had returned to Washington. On January 28 he gave the final report of his mission to Lincoln and he had again to utilize his gift for reconciling difficult situations. It was necessary to convince Lincoln that Davis would enter into negotiations with the purpose of uniting the two warring sections. Such had been the implication of the words at the end of Lincoln's letter of January 18—"securing peace to the people of our one common country." Davis had written earlier that negotiations should be entertained to "secure peace to the two countries." If the Civil War was to be brought to a conclusion, one of these two conceptions would have to surrender. Without the promise of such a surrender, negotiations would be fruitless. But this discrepancy between the two letters did not daunt Blair. He told Lincoln that Davis had read the letter of January 18 twice and "at the close of which he (Mr. Blair) remarked that the part about 'our one common country' related to the part of Mr. Davis' letter about 'the two countries,' to which Mr. Davis replied that he so understood it." [40]

When Blair had departed from Richmond, Davis consulted Stephens concerning the advisability of entering into negotiations and concerning the personnel of the

[39] Rowland, Dunbar (Editor): *Op. cit.,* Vol. VIII, pp. 129, 212, 601, Robert Ould to Jefferson Davis, May 9, 1881; *New York Tribune,* January 17, 1865, quotation from the *Dispatch,* January 14, 1865; Jones, J. B.: *Op. cit.,* Vol. II, p. 386.

[40] *Official Records of the Union and Confederate Armies,* Series I, Vol. XLVI, Part II, p. 506, Memorandum of Lincoln, January 18, 1865.

peace commission. Davis expressed himself as fully convinced that the administration would support Blair's proposals but he doubted the wisdom of making a military
agreement which might result in reunion. Stephens was
naturally in favor of a conference under any condition.
The joint attack upon Mexico might not result in reunion; if it did, reunion would be on terms which would
recognize the theoretical position of the Confederacy.
Anyway, an armistice would be advantageous. Then
Stephens turned to the question of emissaries. He first
proposed Jefferson Davis himself, and then, when the
President refused, suggested John A. Campbell, Assistant
Secretary of War, General Henry L. Benning, ex-Justice
of the Supreme Court of Georgia, and Thomas S.
Flourney, a Virginian who was well known to President
Lincoln. The qualifications of these men were their ability and the fact that their absence from the Confederacy
would not attract attention. Just why Stephens had suddenly devised this latter criterion, after previously urging
the departure of Jefferson Davis, is a problem. The interview terminated as members of the cabinet arrived to
discuss, for the first time, the same situation.[41]

The next day, January 28, the Vice President of the
Confederacy was pained to learn that Davis and his cabinet had not seen fit to follow his advice as to the member-

[41] Rowland, Dunbar (Editor): *Op. cit.*, Vol. VIII, pp. 27-28, Jefferson Davis to Dr. E. L. Drake, 1877; Vol. VIII, p. 212, James Lyons
to W. T. Walthall; Stephens, Alexander H.: *A Constitutional View of
the Late War between the States*, Vol. II, pp. 590-594. Davis says
that he early conferred with Stephens on the subject of the mission;
Lyons tells a story of Stephens being informed of his appointment as
commissioner before Blair's departure. Stephens, on the other hand,
says he learned of the whole mission the day after Blair's departure
from Richmond.

ship of the commission. To be sure, there was agreement as to Judge John A. Campbell, but the other members were Robert M. T. Hunter and Alexander H. Stephens. Stephens was in despair for Hunter and himself did not fulfill the qualification of being inconspicuous. Hunter was President *pro tempore* of the Senate, and he himself was Vice President and the presiding officer of the upper House. Their absence from Richmond would be sure to attract attention and arouse comment. He urged upon the President the advisability of changing so undesirable an arrangement, but Davis was obdurate.[42] The selection of Stephens, displeasing as it was to him, should have been no surprise. The President's acceptance of Blair's proposition was in part determined by the desire to answer the complaints of the malcontents and the critics of the administration. If that purpose were to be fulfilled and if there were to be no charges of bad faith, it was important to entrust the conduct of negotiations to the proponents of peace.[43] Of these Stephens was certainly the most outstanding.

Another of Stephens' colleagues, John Archibald Campbell, was also an advocate of peace. Campbell, appointed in 1853 to the Supreme Court of the United States, had resigned this position at the outbreak of the war and sadly followed Alabama, his native state, in its withdrawal from the Union. Under the Confederacy he held no office until

[42] Stephens, Alexander H.: *A Constitutional View of the Late War between the States,* Vol. II, pp. 594-595; Rowland, Dunbar (Editor): *Op. cit.,* Vol. VIII, p. 28, Jefferson Davis to D. E. L. Drake, 1877.
[43] Rowland, Dunbar (Editor): *Op. cit.,* Vol. VIII, p. 28, Jefferson Davis to Dr. E. L. Drake, 1877; pp. 30-32, A. S. Colyar to R. M. T. Hunter, January 3, 1877; p. 218, Barksdale to Jefferson Davis, July 20, 1878; pp. 246-247, Barksdale to W. T. Walthall, August 3, 1878.

1862 when he was appointed Assistant Secretary of War and placed largely in control of the relations of that Department with civilians.   One of the motives which induced him to accept this position was the hope that he would be in a more influential position for promoting peace.   By the end of 1864 he was pointing out the exhaustion of the Confederacy and urging members of Congress to take measures for negotiation.   Finally in December, 1864, with the approval of Hunter, Seddon, and even Jefferson Davis, he sent a letter to an old colleague of his in the North, Judge Nelson.   Campbell, asserting his belief that an "honorable peace" might be made, announced himself ready to confer informally for that purpose with Nelson or with Ewing of Ohio, Judge Curtis, or Secretary Stanton.   Campbell would naturally be wholly unaccredited; his sole object was "simply to promote an interchange of views and opinions which might be productive of good and scarcely do harm."   This letter Nelson showed to Stanton who gave a qualified approval of the project, but said that nothing could be done until the scheme of President Lincoln and of Francis P. Blair had been tried.[44]

The third member of the commission, Robert Mercer Taliaferro Hunter, possessed a mellifluous name and the usual experience of a Virginian politician.   He came from a family of the Virginian aristocracy—the F. F. V.'s— and his political career in that state had been shaped by this influence.   Before the Civil War he had been first a

----

[44] Conner, Henry G.: *John Archibald Campbell, Associate Justice of the United States Supreme Court, 1853-1861*, pp. 151-164; Rowland, Dunbar (Editor): *Op. cit.*, Vol. V, pp. 98-99, J. A. Campbell to Jefferson Davis, May 7, 1861.

Representative and then a Senator in the national Congress. There, as an exponent of Calhoun's views on state's rights, he became more and more in sympathy with the ideas of such men as Jefferson Davis and Robert Toombs. It was logical, therefore, that in the Baltimore Convention of 1860 he should advocate the support of Breckinridge and Lane, that he should think it advantageous for Virginia to secede if the cotton states left the Union, and that he should become Secretary of State in Davis' cabinet. In 1862 he left this office to his successor, Judah P. Benjamin, and entered the Confederate Senate as a member from Virginia.[45] His life during the remainder of the war was not a happy one. Financial difficulties, always serious, were increased when Federal troops in 1863 burned down the mill on his plantation and drove away his horses and cattle. Earlier he had been embittered by the loss of his eldest son. By 1865 he seemed to have become convinced that the further prosecution of the war was impossible. Mrs. Hunter was despondent, the remarks of F. P. Blair, Sr., transmitted to Hunter by another Confederate Senator, made a deep and gloomy impression, the conscription of boys as young as sixteen and the enrollment of negroes in the army were unpleasant prospects, the military situation of the Confederacy was increasingly unfavorable. In January Hunter was a frequent caller on Judge Campbell. A partisan observer explained the sudden activity of so fat a man as due to a desire to obtain news of approaching disasters in time to

[45] Ambler, Charles H. (Editor): "Correspondence of Robert M. T. Hunter, 1826-1876," *Annual Report of the American Historical Association for the year 1916*, Vol. II, pp. 8-9, 344-352; Washington, L. G.: "Hon. R. M. T. Hunter, An Address," *Southern Historical Society Papers*, Vol. XXV, pp. 196-201.

save somehow the remnants of his fortune.[46]   But Campbell and Hunter more likely were discussing means to obtain their common desire, the initiation of peace negotiations.

On the afternoon of January 28, the three commissioners met President Davis.   He told them of the project which F. P. Blair, Sr., had presented to him but gave them no very exact account of how the joint arrangement as to Mexico was to be carried out.[47]   Then, on the night of the same day, Mr. Washington of the State Department delivered to Campbell the money for the expenses of the journey and the commissioners' letters of appointment.   As he received them, Campbell remarked that their last sentence closed with the phrase, "the purpose of securing peace to the two countries," while the letter of Lincoln to F. P. Blair, Sr., which was to serve as their passport, spoke of "one common country." [48]   Campbell's observavation disclosed the dilemma which confronted Davis. On the one hand, he desired the peace mission in order to silence the clamor of his foes and perhaps to salvage something by the delay of an armistice.   It is inconceivable that he really believed that Lincoln would consent to disunion.   On the other hand, Davis was determined to accept nothing short of independence for the Confed-

[46] Hunter, Martha T.: *A Memoir of Robert M. T. Hunter,* by Martha (his daughter), pp. 77, 115, 122; Rowland, Dunbar (Editor): *Op. cit.,* Vol. VII, pp. 572, R. M. T. Hunter to J. W. Jones, 1877 (?), 579-582; Vol. VIII, pp. 66, Jefferson Davis to General G. W. C. Lee, January 4, 1878, pp. 128-129; Jones, J. B.: *Op. cit.,* Vol. II, pp. 379-382, 387, 400-401.

[47] Campbell, John A.: *Reminiscences and Documents relating to the Civil War during the year 1865,* pp. 4-5.

[48] Rowland, Dunbar (Editor): *Op. cit.,* Vol. VII, pp. 584-585, J. A. Campbell to R. M. T. Hunter, October 31, 1877.

eracy. Such had been the upshot of his conversation with Stephens, such were his verbal instructions to the commissioners by which they were allowed to make any sort of treaty other than one providing for the reconstitution of the Federal Union,[49] such had been the difficulty with Benjamin over drawing up the letter of appointment. The Confederate Secretary of State had foreseen the unwisdom of being too explicit and had advocated vagueness and generalities. He had written, "In compliance with the letter of Mr. Lincoln, of which the foregoing is a copy, you are hereby requested to proceed to Washington city for conference with him upon the subject to which it relates." To this form of appointment, Davis objected because it might apparently be misconstrued to be a confession that Davis was willing to sacrifice independence. The President rewrote the letters so as to read, "for informal conference with him upon the issues involved in the existing war, and for the purpose of securing peace to the two countries."[50] In truth there was no other course open with honor to the Confederate President. He had taken his oath of office to maintain and defend the government of the Confederacy. He could not violate that oath. As long as the army existed in the field and the people gave any support, he was determined to fight on. If the course of events had changed the determination of the people whom he represented he "should have bowed to their will, but would never have executed it."[51]

[49] Campbell, J. A.: *Op. cit.*, p. 4.
[50] Rowland, Dunbar (Editor): *Op. cit.*, Vol. VII, pp. 570-571, J. P. Benjamin to Jefferson Davis, May 17, 1877.
[51] Rowland, Dunbar (Editor): *Op. cit.*, Vol. VIII, pp. 28-29, Jefferson Davis to Dr. E. L. Drake, 1877; Vol. VIII, p. 247, Barksdale to W. T. Walthall, August 3, 1878; Reagan, John H.: *Memoirs, with*

It is interesting to speculate as to what the commissioners thought of the instructions which practically reduced their mission to an effort to secure an armistice and discover Northern peace terms. What did this delegation of confirmed peace men think of the proposal of no peace without independence? Stephens was convinced that they had no power to accomplish anything except the securing of an armistice, but whether he was pained at this limitation of their functions is problematical. His own thinking on the subject of peace seems somewhat akin to Horace Greeley's in its confusion. He had certainly envisaged, however, the possibility of reunion with eagerness and complacency. Campbell admits that a short while after the conference, he was in favor of reunion. Hunter's attitude seems a piece of his usual uncertainty. In a later controversy with Jefferson Davis he announced that no one of the commissioners was in favor of reunion, and that a peace drawn up on that basis had no chance of acceptance. Yet seven years earlier, he states that he was of the opinion that abolition and reunion should be accepted, and the best possible terms secured on the other points at issue.[52] But whatever may have been their personal feelings, the commissioners accepted their appointment, and on January 29 reached the lines in the vicinity of Petersburg.

special reference to secession and the Civil War, Edited by Walter F. McCaleb, p. 171.

[52] Stephens, Alexander H.: *Recollections of Alexander H. Stephens, His diary kept when a prisoner at Fort Warren, Boston Harbour, 1865, giving incidents and reflections of his prison life and some letters and reminiscences,* p. 265; Conner, Henry G.: *Op. cit.,* p. 160; Rowland, Dunbar (Editor): *Op. cit.,* Vol. VII, p. 574, R. M. T. Hunter to J. W. Jones, 1877 (?); Vol. VIII, pp. 212-213; Lee, Fitzhugh: "The Failure of the Hampton Conference," *The Century Magazine,* Vol. LII, p. 478, R. M. T. Hunter to J. M. Mason, September 19, 1870.

The scene now shifts to the Northern army. Under a flag of truce, Lieutenant Colonel Hatch of the Confederate forces asked permission for three peace commissioners, on their way to Washington, to cross the lines "in accordance with an understanding claimed to exist with Lieutenant General Grant." Through the regular military hierarchy this request eventually reached headquarters only to find General Grant absent from the army and Major General E. O. C. Ord, Commander of the Army of the James, the ranking officer on the spot. That afternoon the latter forwarded the despatch to Washington for instructions. Stanton, in reply, expressed no knowledge of any such arrangement and forbade the passage of the commissioners until the telegram had been acted upon by the President.[53] The President then formulated his course of action. As a result of an evening conference,[54] he reached a decision to send a special messenger to the lines in order to examine the instructions of the Confederate commissioners and see if they were really authorized to make peace on the conditions which he had proposed. This decision showed that the President had not taken too seriously the assurances of the elder Blair, for only the previous day the latter had reported that Davis had understood Lincoln's position and accepted the phrase "our one common country." Admirers of Stanton have wished to see in the President's caution in admitting the Confederate commissioners another evidence of the great War

[53] *Official Records of the Union and Confederate Armies,* Series I, Vol. XLVI, Part II, pp. 290-291, O. B. Willcox to Major General Parke (received 3:30 P.M.); pp. 267, 292; p. 291, E. O. C. Ord to J. G. Parke, January 29, 7.15 P.M.; p. 292, Stanton to E. O. C. Ord, January 29, 10 P.M.

[54] *Ibid.,* Series I, Vol. XLVI, Part II, pp. 506-507.

Secretary's influence. Undoubtedly Stanton, reflecting the extremist position, disliked all overtures for peace and distrusted all persons who thought peace was possible. He may have felt with other extremists that the President was too apt to be swayed by the dictates of leniency and lovingkindness; [55] he certainly did not trust the Blairs. By 1865, however, Lincoln was unquestionably master of his own administration and his own grasp of peace possibilities, a grasp, strengthened by the previous peace negotiations, is sufficient to account for his unwillingness to embark upon further peace efforts without a definite clarification of the Southern independence issue.

The bearer of the President's instructions was Major T. T. Eckert. Eckert had worked his way into the War Department through a knowledge of the telegraph. Stanton had made him a Major, given him a horse and carriage for his official duties, and placed him in complete charge of the telegraphs in the war offices. Over the telegraph Stanton loved to exercise a despotic control; and for this purpose Eckert, his grateful appointee, was an excellent instrument. Some of the latter's activities, indeed, seem those of an offensive busybody. On one occasion he took the liberty of withholding from transmittal communications from a certain New York politician to McClellan and of showing them to Stanton. At another time he delayed, on his own responsibility, the despatch of the order for the removal of General Thomas until news of a victory by Thomas' army arrived.[56] On the morning

[55] Flower, Frank A.: *Op. cit.*, pp. 257-258; Bates, David H.: *Lincoln in the Telegraph Office; Recollections of the United States Military Telegraph Corps during the Civil War*, pp. 327-328.
[56] Bates, David H.: *Op. cit.*, pp. 103-105, 136-137, 315-318.

of January 30 Eckert was given his instructions. He was
to deliver to the commissioners a copy of Lincoln's letter
to F. P. Blair, Sr., and to ask if they accepted its terms.
If the answer was in the affirmative, the Confederates were
to pass through the lines where they would be met for the
purpose of an informal conference by a commissioner or
commissioners from the North. If they did not accept
these terms, Eckert was to refuse them safe conduct.[57]

[57] *Official Records of the Union and Confederate Armies*, Series I,
Vol. XLVI, Part II, pp. 507-508. The days of January 30 and 31
were bewildering in their peace perplexities. General J. W. Singleton,
a prominent member of the Sons of Liberty in Illinois and an ardent
advocate of peace (*Official Records of the Union and Confederate
Armies*, Series I, Vol. XLV, Part I, p. 1082; Series III, Vol. III, p.
501) had gone on a self-imposed peace mission to Richmond. Rumor
has enshrouded the conditions of his departure with uncertainty. It
was said that he was invited by the authorities in Richmond (*New York
Tribune*, January 13, 1865) and that he was dispatched by Clay and
Thompson in Canada. (*New York Tribune*, January 16, 1865.) His
character and his errand could not have been peculiarly dangerous,
however, for he was allowed to depart by the administration. He
lingered for two weeks in Richmond, enjoying a Confederate hospitality
which paid his hotel bills and having interviews with President Davis,
General Lee, and other members of the administration (*New York
Tribune*, February 6, 1865, A Letter from W. C. Jewett, February 4,
1865.) From this pleasant sojourn, he returned with four ladies and
the conviction that the South would not lay down its arms without independence. This news he gave to the President on January 30 (*New
York Tribune*, February 1, 1865).

At about the same time Henry S. Foote had at last succeeded in
escaping from the Confederacy. He had returned to Richmond after
his first arrest, delivered a scathing attack upon the administration in
the House (Jones, J. B.: *Op. cit.*, Vol. II, p. 392), and escaped ex-
pulsion from that body by a narrow margin (*Journal of the Congress
of the Confederate States of America, 1861-1865*, Vol. VII, pp. 490-
492). He then made his way without mishap into the Federal lines
and from Lovettsville, on January 30, 1865, he wrote Seward a letter
in which he says that Jefferson Davis is the only obstacle to the reunion of the North and South and asserts that peace would be possible if there were an offer by Lincoln of complete amnesty and the
proposal of either voluntary or gradual emancipation of the slaves.

But meanwhile affairs were taken out of the hands of
Eckert and the Washington authorities by the return of
Lieutenant General Grant to the headquarters of the
army. Arriving on the morning of January 31, he was
uninformed as to the previous correspondence between his
subordinates and Washington, and confronted with a personal letter which the restless Confederate commissioners
had dispatched to him the previous evening. This letter
reiterated the desire of the commissioners to go to Washington to discuss terms of peace upon the basis of the
letter of F. P. Blair, Sr., "of which we presume you have
a copy"; and then added that, if this procedure is impossible, they wished to see Grant in person and confer with
him on the subject of peace. Grant at once dispatched
this note to the President and coupled it with the information that he had sent a staff officer to admit the Confederates.[58] In accordance with Grant's instructions, Lieutenant Colonel Babcock of Grant's staff met the commissioners almost at sunset at the Petersburg lines. The
commissioners walked across no man's land, covered with
its mute testimony of the long battle which had been
waged there, amid cheering by soldiers of both armies.
As they boarded the train for City Point, there was again
cheering. It was late when they reached their destination.
Babcock led them to the door of a log cabin, then knocked,

The receipt of this letter was acknowledged on January 31 and Foote
was informed that it had been shown to the President. (Foote, Henry
S.: *Op. cit.*, pp. 388-395.)
    [58] *Official Records of the Union and Confederate Armies*, Series I,
Vol. XLVI, Part II, p. 298, A. H. Stephens, J. A. Campbell, R. M.
T. Hunter to Grant, January 30, 1865; pp. 311-312, Grant to Stanton,
January 31, 1865, 7.30 P.M., and Grant to Lincoln, January 31, 1865,
10 A.M.; p. 319, E. O. C. Ord to Grant, January 31, 1865, 3.30 P.M.

and, when a voice replied, "Come in," opened the door and ushered in the commissioners. A plainly attired man was busy writing by the light of a kerosene lamp. The Confederates could hardly believe that they were in the presence of the commander of the Federal forces.[59]

Grant's dispatch of the early morning, meanwhile, had arrived at Washington and had compelled an alteration in the plans for the treatment of the commissioners. Eckert, who had not yet departed, was, nevertheless, sent on his mission [60]—a mission considerably attenuated by the fact that the commissioners had passed through the Union lines without his preliminary scrutiny; and Seward was despatched to Hampton Roads to confer with the peace emissaries once they were admitted. The President evidently believed that the reception of the envoys by Grant was sufficient credential. The instructions to the Secretary of State were definite and a trifle peremptory. He was to lay down three indispensable conditions of peace: "1st. The restoration of the national authority throughout all the States. 2d. No receding by the Executive of the United States, on the slavery question, from the position assumed thereon in the late annual message to Congress and in preceding documents. 3d. No cessation of hostilities short of an end of the war and the dis-

---

[59] *Official Records of the Union and Confederate Armies,* Series I, Vol. XLVI, Part II, p. 317, Parke to Willcox, January 31, 1865, 1.20 P.M., Willcox to Webb, January 31, 1865, 6.50 P.M.; *New York Tribune,* February 3, 1865; Stephens, Alexander H.: *A Constitutional View of the Late War between the States,* Vol. II, pp. 596-597; Roland, Dunbar (Editor): *Op. cit.,* Vol. VIII, p. 131, account of R. M. T. Hunter; Jones, J. B.: *Op. cit.,* Vol. II, p. 406.

[60] *Official Records of the Union and Confederate Armies,* Series I, Vol. XLVI, Part II, p. 311, Lincoln to Grant, January 31, 1865, 1.30 P.M.

banding of all forces hostile to the government." The
Secretary was to hear what the commissioners had to say
and then report to the President. He himself was authorized to take no action of any kind.[61]

On February 1, the Confederate commissioners passed
the day pleasantly on one of General Grant's dispatch
boats. They had conversations with many officers, among
whom were General Meade and General Grant, and they
found that the desire for peace was prevalent.[62] In the
afternoon, however, they were annoyed by the arrival of
Major Eckert, who delivered his message from President
Lincoln. The answer which the commissioners framed
and which they handed to Eckert at six o'clock did not
satisfy his matter of fact mind. The commissioners, indeed, had found it difficult to reconcile the discrepancy
between Lincoln's letter and their instructions. Stephens
observed that neither letter was correct as really thirty-

[61] *Official Records of the Union and Confederate Armies*, Series I,
Vol. XLVI, Part II, p. 509. In his message of the previous December
the President had written: "In presenting the abandonment of armed
resistance to the national authority on the part of the insurgents as
the only indispensable condition to ending the war on the part of the
government. I retract nothing heretofore said as to slavery. I repeat
the declaration made a year ago, that 'while I remain in my present
position I shall not attempt to retract or modify the Emancipation
Proclamation, nor shall I return to slavery any person who is free by
the terms of that proclamation, or by any of the acts of Congress.'"
"If the people should, by whatever mode or means, make it an executive duty to re-enslave such persons, another, and not I, must be their
instrument." (Lincoln, Abraham: *Complete Works of Abraham Lincoln,* Edited by John G. Nicolay and John Hay (Edition 1905), Vol. X,
p. 310.)

[62] Rowland, Dunbar (Editor): *Op. cit.,* Vol. VIII, p. 131, account of
R. M. T. Hunter; Meade, George D.: *The Life and Letters of George
Gordon Meade, Major General United States Army,* Vol. II, pp. 258-
260; Grant, U. S.: *Personal Memoirs of U. S. Grant,* Vol. II, pp. 420-
422.

six countries were involved. But theoretical distinctions aside, the difficulty had to be met. In their reply, therefore, the commissioners included a statement of their instructions and then said that "Our earnest desire is that a just and honorable peace may be agreed upon, and we are prepared to receive or to submit propositions which may possibly lead to the attainment of that end." Eckert, however, was able to see only the difference between "one common country" and "two countries." He refused to let them go further.[63]

General Ulysses Simpson Grant, however, had an independent nature. Already he had admitted the Confederate commissioners within his lines in a manner which was above quibbling about technicalities and instructions from Washington. In fact, he seemed positively eager to meet the commissioners, and they, on their side, were equally eager to arrange matters with him personally. A partial explanation of Grant's actions can be found in the fact that the Blairs had taken him into their confidence in the matter of their peace efforts. Old Blair had arranged with Grant the means by which the Mexican foray was to be carried out.[64] In Richmond he had hinted to Jefferson Davis of the possibility of a military convention between

[63] Rowland, Dunbar (Editor): *Op. cit.*, Vol. VIII, pp. 131-132, account of R. M. T. Hunter; Campbell, J. A.: *Reminiscences and Documents relating to the Civil War during the year 1865*, p. 9, J. A. Campbell to R. M. T. Hunter, October 31, 1877; *Official Records of the Union and Confederate Armies*, Series I, Vol. XLVI, Part II, pp. 341-342, Eckert to Stanton, February 1, 1865, 10 P.M., Eckert to Lincoln, February 1, 1865, 10 P.M., p. 512, Stephens, Campbell, and Hunter to Eckert, February 1, 1865. Eckert did not see fit to transmit either to Lincoln or to Stanton the whole reply of the commissioners. Lincoln did not see that reply until he reached Hampton Roads.

[64] Bigelow, John: *Op. cit.*, Vol. IV, pp. 51-52.

Lee and the Federal commander.   And then there was
Mrs. Ulysses Simpson Grant, née Julia B. Dent, a de-
scendant of an old Maryland family and a resident of
St. Louis, whence the Blairs came.[65]   An officer told
Hunter that Mrs. Grant thought that her husband ought
to arrange an interview for the commissioners; that they
were "good men" and their "intentions were praisewor-
thy"; that a conference with Mr. Lincoln might accomplish great good, especially if Seward were excluded.   He
would be likely to prevent a settlement by his "wily tac-
tics."   This advice has a ring reminiscent of the Blairs.
It is no wonder that the commissioners were as impressed
by the friendliness of Mrs. Grant as they were by that of
her husband.   Both seemed eager for the conference to
take place.[66]

The commissioners, disappointed by Eckert, naturally
turned their next efforts toward General Grant.   At eight
o'clock that evening he received a note from them which
stated that "We desire to go to Washington City to confer
informally with the President personally, in reference to
the matters mentioned in his letter to Mr. Blair of the
18th of January ultimo, without any personal compromise on any question in the letter.   We have permission to
do so from the authorities in Richmond."   Eckert was
shown this note but he again gave his refusal and then
dashed to the telegraph office to transmit his reports to

[66] Grant, Arthur H.: *The Grant Family, A Genealogical History of
the Descendants of Matthew Grant of Windsor, Conn., 1601-1898,* p.
142; Marshall, Edward C.: *The Ancestry of General Grant and their
Contemporaries,* p. 173.

[66] Rowland, Dunbar (Editor): *Op. cit.,* Vol. VIII, p. 132, account of
R. M. T. Hunter; Stephens, Alexander H.: *A Constitutional View of the
Late War between the States,* Vol. II, pp. 597-598.

Stanton and Lincoln. He closed the latter message with the statement that since he had complied with his instructions, he would return to Washington on the next day. As far as he was concerned the incident was closed. A half hour later, Grant, in a circumspect telegram to Stanton, said that, as a result of his conversations with Hunter and Stephens (Campbell was ill), he was convinced that the "intentions" of the commissioners were "good" and "their desire sincere to restore peace and union." Although he recognized the difficulties in the way of receiving them, he did not think it wise to have them go back to Richmond without meeting some one of authority. In fact, he was "sorry that Mr. Lincoln cannot have an interview" with them. As for their instructions, their letter to Grant was all the President had asked for, even if they had used different language to Eckert.[67]

On the morning of February 2 the various participants in this negotiation transferred their activities to Fortress Monroe. First of all went Eckert in consequence of a

---

[67] *Official Records of the Union and Confederate Armies,* Series I, Vol. XLVI, Part II, pp. 342-343, Grant to Stanton, February 1, 10.30 P.M. The nature of the relations between Grant and Eckert during this negotiation seems to have altered during the course of forty years. A perusal of the telegrams sent at the time substantiates the belief that Grant brushed Eckert aside and took matters pretty much into his own hands. There is some evidence that Eckert and Grant worked in harmony although it is not conclusive. (*Official Records of the Union and Confederate Armies,* Series III, Vol. IV, p. 1164; Series I, Vol. XLVI, Part II, p. 353.) On February 2 he telegraphed Grant that Seward "expressed his satisfaction of course pursued in reply to letters received yesterday." He would not be likely to give Grant such pleasant information if they were at odds. Yet in 1907, Eckert gave a narrative of affairs which shows him continually balking and thwarting Grant. Eckert seems greater in power than all kinds of generals. (Bates, D. H.: *Op. cit.,* pp. 335-338.)

command sent by Seward on the previous evening; [68] and then followed the commissioners. Grant, without waiting to hear from Washington, had determined to send them since "they have accepted the proposed terms"; [69] but, before their departure, a telegram arrived from Washington saying that Lincoln would be a party to the conference. Grant, showing his gratification at the good news, announced the President's determination to the commissioners, and soon afterwards the *Mary Martin*, a dispatch boat, headed away from City Point for Hampton Roads. There the commissioners arrived in the course of the afternoon. Lincoln, meanwhile, had about made up

[68] *Official Records of the Union and Confederate Armies*, Series I, Vol. XLVI, Part II, p. 342, Seward to Grant, February 1, 1865, 11.30 P.M.; p. 353, Eckert to Grant, February 2, 1865, 11.30 P.M.

[69] *Ibid.*, Series I, Vol. XLVI, Part II, p. 352, Grant to Seward, February 2, 1865, 9 A.M. (Dispatched Hour.) Just what induced Grant to take a step much more vigorous than any envisaged in his cautious telegram to Stanton on the evening of February 1, is uncertain. Since Grant had dispatched that telegram, he had learned of Seward's arrival at Fortress Monroe "to meet the persons from Richmond." (*Official Records of the Union and Confederate Armies*, Series I, Vol. XLVI, Part II, p. 341, Seward to Grant, February 1, 1865, 11.30 P.M.) This definite news may have precipitated his action. Then again, some time during February 2, another note addressed to Eckert had been coaxed out of the Confederate commissioners. This time they expressed their willingness to discuss peace on the basis of Lincoln's letter to Blair or "upon any other terms or conditions that he may hereafter propose, not inconsistent with the essential principles of self-government and popular rights, upon which our institutions are founded" and, after a reiteration of their desire for peace, they add "that in accepting your passport, we are not to be understood as committing ourselves to anything, but to carry to this informal conference the views and feelings above expressed." This note was delivered by Lieutenant Colonel Babcock to Eckert at Fortress Monroe at 4.30 P.M. February 2, 1865, when he arrived with the commissioners. (*Official Records of the Union and Confederate Armies*, Series I, Vol. XLVI, Part II, p. 512.) Perhaps this note enabled Grant to say, "they have accepted the proposed terms."

his mind to recall both Seward and Eckert in view of the
latter's report, when he received Grant's telegram of the
night before. The news it contained not only led him to
alter his decision in regard to the recall of Seward, but
also induced him to join the latter at Hampton Roads.
With an attaché of the White House, the President left
by train for Annapolis where he boarded the *Thomas
Colyar*. Late that evening he arrived at Fortress Monroe
and went at once aboard the *River Queen*, the vessel by
which Seward had come down earlier and upon which he
was now awaiting the arrival of his chief.[70]

On the morning of February 3, occurred the Hampton
Roads Conference. The Confederate commissioners went
on board the *River Queen*, which was decked with flags
and anchored about fifty rods from the shore, and were
ushered into the cabin where the actual meeting was to
take place. Seward and the President entered soon after.
These five men, with the addition of a colored servant who
came in occasionally with refreshments and with things to
smoke, were the only ones present at the famous Hampton
Roads Conference.

The conversation [71] opened with an exchange of pleas-

[70] *Official Records of the Union and Confederate Armies,* Series I,
Vol. XLVI, Part II, p. 352, Lincoln to Grant, February 2, 1865, 9
A.M. (Dispatched Hour), Lincoln to Seward, February 2, 1865, 9
A.M., Seward to Stanton, February 2, 1865, 7 P.M., Eckert to
Stanton, February 2, 1865, 11.30 P.M.; p. 511; *New York Tribune,*
February 6, 1865; Stephens, Alexander H.: *A Constitutional View of
the Late War between the States,* Vol. II, p. 598.

[71] In the account of the conference, given in this chapter, no attempt
is made to follow the exact sequence of the various topics of conversation. The different reports of the conference have different chrono-
logical orders. Accordingly the material will be grouped under the
headings into which it logically falls; Blair's Mexican project, reconstruction, confiscation, slavery, etc.

antries between Stephens and Lincoln. They recalled the
old days when they were members of a club to secure the
election of Taylor; Lincoln asked after various acquain-
tances in the Confederacy; both talked of their services
in Congress. These reminiscences served as a graceful
reminder of the former days of harmony and good feeling,
and eased the conversation into a discussion of how they
might be restored. Lincoln, at the outset, demanded the
unequivocal restoration of the Union and at once Stephens
tried to divert the consideration of this point by alluding
to Blair's Mexican project. The President replied that,
while Blair meant well, he had no official authority whatever. The project could not be carried out by granting
an armistice unless a previous pledge was given that the
Union would be restored. This pledge the commissioners
were not able to give. Then, in accordance with a previous understanding among themselves to ferret out the
possible bases for peace even if they could not secure an
armistice, Campbell asked what the terms for reconstruction of the Union would be. The immediate pursuit of
this subject was prevented by Seward who asked Stephens
to elaborate his Mexican project as it had a "philosophical
basis."

Stephens then developed his favorite theory as to how
such a joint operation would serve to unite the two countries. There would first be a secret military agreement
between the North and South providing for the location
of troops, the division of tariff receipts, and for other
necessary arrangements. Then the two nations would
turn their common forces upon the enemy. Such a proceeding would have the practical value of uniting the two
sections in one common purpose; it would also have the

theoretical value of stressing the principle of the Monroe
Doctrine—the right of self-government—a principle
which would gradually be recognized as the correct one
for the settlement of the differences between the North
and the South. "This great law of the System would
effect the same results in its organization, as the law of
gravitation in the material world"; it would pull the states
together. The other commissioners, less abstruse, thought
that the joint assertion of the Monroe Doctrine would
approximately result in the end foreseen by Stephens.
Campbell said that such a project would bring about reunion; and Hunter, although he thought Southern independence might still be retained, believed a close military
and commercial alliance would eventuate. Seward and
Lincoln spoke for the Union. Although they both disliked the presence of the French in Mexico, their objections to the Mexican project were fundamental and
numerous. The former attacked Stephens' reasoning on
practical grounds. The right of self-government violated
the law of self preservation. For instance, could the
whole United States allow Louisiana, which controlled the
mouth of the Mississippi, to govern itself independently
to the extent of forming an alliance with foreign countries? Then there were the details of the military
arrangements. Lincoln saw that the formulation of an
agreement would lead to bickering and jealousy and besides he had no power to make such an agreement. The
right to declare war lay with Congress; the Senate had a
share in the making of treaties. In any case he had no
intention of making such a convention without first securing an unconditional recognition of the Union. To do

otherwise would be to recognize the Confederacy and the justice of their status in rebellion against the national authority. Hunter, who had been much pained by Stephens' earlier remarks, now broke into the conversation. The South was not a unit in support of the proposed Mexican procedure. As for himself, he did not lay claim to the whole country or entirely approve of a war waged for policy rather than for honor as the Mexican project envisaged. Hunter, in fact, was under the impression that the commissioners were not empowered to enter into any agreement involving the coöperation of Northern and Southern arms, for the subjugation of Mexico.

The discussion now returned to the bases of a possible reconstruction. Seward opened the question by quoting from the President's message of the previous December the parts which reiterated his purpose to end the war only on the acceptance of the Congressional and Executive acts in regard to emancipation. Campbell replied with a query about confiscation. Seward answered that this was a question for the courts, but that Congress would be liberal in restoration and indemnity. Hunter raised the question of the status of West Virginia. Would it continue to be independent or would it be reunited with Virginia? Lincoln leaned to the former opinion.

Then arose the question of the Southern slave and the real effect of the emancipation proclamation upon him. As to the application of the proclamation, Lincoln felt that it was a war measure and as such it would be inoperative in time of peace. As far as he could tell, it applied only to the number of slaves which had already been freed by it—a number which Seward estimated at 200,000.

Although the proclamation would not be withdrawn, its applicability was to be determined by the courts and the courts might do anything. Then Seward produced the thirteenth amendment.[72] The commissioners deduced from his conversation that he did not take it very seriously. Stephens believed that Seward thought that, if the Southern states made peace and reëntered the Union they could defeat the amendment by their votes. Campbell said Seward thought the amendment was a war measure and the demand for it would cease with peace although the extremist sentiment in the North was growing. Lincoln had a different proposal. He began by admitting that the emancipation proclamation had been forced upon him; that he had adopted it solely as a war measure. His own belief was that the government in time of peace had no power over slavery except in the territories. He, nevertheless, did believe in the rightfulness of eventual emancipation everywhere. Even then it would cause suffering, but that suffering was inevitable. To Hunter, Lincoln's attitude and the story of the Illinois farmer and the hogs, which he told to illustrate it,[73] seemed harsh and ruthless. Then Lincoln advised

[72] It occurred to Campbell later that the amendment was passed during the preliminaries of the conference and that the *Philadelphia Inquirer* had stated that Seward urged its immediate passage on the ground that he wished to use it in negotiations with the commissioners. On his way to Hampton Roads Seward stopped at Annapolis, persuaded the Governor to call the Legislature and to submit the amendment to it. The lower House passed the amendment within an hour and then Seward went on to the conference. (Campbell, J. A.: "The Hampton Roads Conference," *Transactions of the Southern Historical Society,* Vol. I, in *Southern Magazine,* Vol. XV, p. 188.)

[73] "An Illinois farmer was congratulating himself with a neighbor upon a great discovery he had made, by which he would economize upon much time and labor in gathering and taking care of the food

Stephens to return to his native state, and induce it to withdraw active support from the war and ratify the thirteenth amendment *"prospectively,* so as to take effect— say in five years." But whatever method of freeing the slaves was followed, all the commissioners, Northern and Southern, recognized the evils of immediate emancipation.

The discussion of the main points at issue was now concluded and attention was directed informally to various aspects of the peace situation. The commissioners thought that Lincoln should make some preliminary agreement with the Southern states in case they should wish to return to the Union. Hunter said there had been precedents for such an action. Charles I had made a treaty with rebels. Lincoln referred the question of history to Seward and replied that "all he knew of Charles I was that he lost his head." Hunter remarked with intensity that to give up all arms and all guarantees of fair treatment was "unconditional submission." Seward replied that they did not use that word; the South would have all the safeguards of the constitution and the courts. Lincoln said that in the exercise of powers delegated to him by the various confiscation and penal acts, he would be very lenient. As for the readmission of the states into

crop for his hogs, as well as trouble in looking after and feeding them during the winter.

"'What is it?' said the neighbor.

"'Why, it is,' said the farmer, 'to plant plenty of potatoes, and when they are mature, without either digging or housing them turn the hogs in the field and let them get their own food as they want it.'

"'But,' said the neighbor, 'how will they do when the winter comes and the ground is hard frozen?'

"'Well,' said the farmer, 'let 'em root!'" (Stephens, Alexander H.: *A Constitutional View of the Late War between the States,* Vol. II, p. 615.)

the Union, he could not tell what Congress would do; he disapproved of their policy in regard to the already reconstructed states. For himself, moreover, he would be willing to be taxed in order to compensate owners for their freed slaves; the North was as much responsible for slavery as the South. Some had even proposed $400,000,000 as a proper amount. But the President could not answer for others as to such compensation. As for Seward's attitude on the same subject, the commissioners derived different impressions. Stephens thought that Seward was in favor of compensation; but the other two Southerners inferred that Seward regarded the military expenditures of the North as enough of a debt to incur in behalf of abolition.[74]

The conference had now lasted for four hours and there was a pause in the conversation. The commissioners arose and talked over matters of smaller import, such as the exchange of prisoners. Stephens asked the President to reconsider the possibility of an armistice and received a noncommittal answer. Lincoln and Seward left the cabin; Babcock escorted the Confederates to their boat. In the afternoon the President left for Annapolis and Washington; the commissioners departed for City Point and Richmond. The Hampton Roads Conference was over.

The Southern commissioners returned very much

---

[74] Stephens, Alexander H.: *A Constitutional View of the Late War between the States*, Vol. II, pp. 599-619; Campbell, J. A.: *Reminiscences and Documents relating to the Civil War during the year 1865*, pp. 6-17, 23-26; Rowland, Dunbar (Editor): *Op. cit.*, Vol. VIII, pp. 133-136, account of R. M. T. Hunter; *Official Records of the Union and Confederate Armies*, Series I, Vol. XLVI, Part II, p. 513.

sobered. Stephens realized the grave military situation
of the South, intensified by the loss of Fort Fisher, which
protected the Confederacy's last outlet to the world, and
saw that the cause of the country was lost without peace.
There should be another mission to the North for which
the possibilities of success would be greater if it were less
public.[75] Campbell saw the impossibility of another campaign and thought that the Conference had offered some
terms less bitter than total subjugation.[76] But the opinions of Hunter differed slightly from those held by his
confrères. The Hampton Roads Conference had angered
him, for Lincoln's terms, involving as they did complete
submission, seemed unnecessarily harsh. Still even his
uncertain nature realized the difficulties in the way of
military success. For the moment, it was a question which
road—peace or war—led to the less gloomy prospect.[77]
He seemed willing to be influenced in either direction.

But these differences and timidities of opinion found no
replica in the mind of Jefferson Davis. Conscious of his
own severe sincerity of purpose and of act, he could not
ascribe a similar quality to Lincoln. Lincoln, he thought,
had acted in bad faith; the statements of the Southerners,
especially as regards the Monroe Doctrine, would be used
by the Northern commissioners to create international

[75] Stephens, Alexander H.: *A Constitutional View of the Late War
between the States,* Vol. II, pp. 619-621.
[76] Campbell, J. A.: "The Hampton Roads Conference," *Transactions
of the Southern Historical Society,* Vol. I, in the *Southern Magazine,*
Vol. XV, p. 188, Campbell to G. W. Mumford, August 6, 1874.
[77] Lee, Fitzhugh: *Op. cit.,* p. 478, R. M. T. Hunter to J. M. Mason,
September 19, 1870; Rowland, Dunbar (Editor): *Op. cit.,* Vol. VIII,
p. 575, R. M. T. Hunter to J. W. Jones.

hostility against the South.[78]   Such considerations, however, were purely secondary ones.   The vital fact was that
the North offered to the South at Hampton Roads unconditional submission.   Jefferson Davis could not in honor
accept such a termination to the war.   The only choice
was a continuation of the struggle.   To further such a
purpose the Hampton Roads Conference could be utilized.
The first difficulty was the report [79] to be made by the
commissioners.   Two of them were certainly unwilling to
participate in a design to lead the South into a new war
fury.   Besides, the conference had been confidential.   The
result of this conflict was a simple statement signed by all
three commissioners.   It said that Lincoln's bases for

[78] Stephens, Alexander H.: *A Constitutional View of the Late War
between the States,* Vol. II, p. 619; Jones, J. W.: "The Peace Conference of 1865," *The Century Magazine,* Vol. LXXVII, p. 68, Jefferson
Davis to J. W. Jones, September 1, 1885.

[79] The question of this report is an extremely controversial one.
Stephens asserts that he was unwilling to make any report because
the conference had been confidential and because publicity would render
abortive any further attempts at negotiations.   He was induced to
submit a report by the insistence of his colleagues and of Jefferson
Davis.   (Stephens, Alexander H.: *A Constitutional View of the Late
War between the States,* Vol. II, pp. 621-622.)   Henry W. Cleveland
gives an exactly opposite explanation.   He says that Stephens wanted
to give a full report, but was held in check by Campbell, Hunter, and
Davis because a full report would increase the disaffection in the
South.   (Rowland, Dunbar (Editor): *Op. cit.,* Vol. IX, p. 603, H. W.
Cleveland to Jefferson Davis, November 25, 1887.)   Jefferson Davis, in
turn, complains of the meagerness of the report which the commissioners
rendered and adds that Stephens insisted that "a mere statement would
be more effective to rouse and convince the country." (Lee, Fitzhugh:
Op. cit., p. 477, Davis to J. M. Mason, June 11, 1870.)   In view of
Stephens's and Campbell's professed yearnings for peace, it is not likely
that they cared to arouse the country for war.   If they had to make
a report at all, they probably preferred one which would be fairly noncommittal and release them from all responsibility for the use which
was made of it.

peace were unaltered from those laid down in his December message to Congress; no treaty or armistice could be granted to the Confederate states; Lincoln would use the powers entrusted to him liberally; and "during the conference the proposed amendment to the Constitution of the United States, adopted by Congress on the 31st ult., was brought to our notice." Although this report omitted several qualifications of importance, it did not prejudice the case for peace or for war. The Presidential message which transmitted the report to the Senate and the House of Representatives of the Confederate States, however, infused color and vigor into its matter of fact assertions. The North refused to give any terms or guarantees other "than those which the conqueror may grant, or to permit us to have peace on any other basis than our unconditional submission to their rule. . . ." [80]

On the evening of the same day, February 6, occurred a gigantic mass meeting at the African Church. Over two hours before the speaking was scheduled to begin, every seat was taken and fears were entertained as to the safety of the galleries. General Smith of Virginia opened the meeting and then came Davis. For three quarters of an hour he held his audience mastered. Newspaper accounts of the speech are inadequate, for they give no hint of his eloquence, of his emotion and of his magnetic power. He hurled defiance at the North, and said that as far as he was concerned, he would rather give up a thousand lives than independence. Carried away by the enthusiasm of the President, the audience adopted resolutions spurning

[80] Rowland, Dunbar (Editor): *Op. cit.*, Vol. VI, pp. 465-467, Report of the Commissioners, February 5, 1865, Message of Jefferson Davis, February 6, 1865.

"with indignation due to so gross an insult" the terms
which Lincoln proffered, declaring the circumstances
under which the terms were offered "add to the outrage
and stamp it as a designed and premeditated indignity to
our people," and asserting "that in the presence, and in
the face of the world, reverently invoking thereto the aid
of Almighty God, we renew our resolve to maintain our
liberties and independence; and to this we mutually pledge
our lives, our fortunes, and our sacred honor." The
press, which during the week of negotiations had held its
judgment in suspense, now unleashed all its fury. The
Enquirer said "the prospects of war are much brighter—
cannot be darker than those of peace." The *Examiner*
saw the Confederacy with three unconquered armies, an
uncaptured capital, and an almost uninvaded country.
The *Whig* concluded that "To talk now of any other arbitrament than that of the sword is to betray cowardice
or treachery." [81] But the deep tragedy of those days
when the President and his followers were determined upon
immolating their cause and their country was made still
deeper by the fact that the South was not a united nation.
Stephens refused to address the meeting at the African
Church, had a last interview with Davis, and then returned sadly to Georgia.[82] Campbell's voice was silent.
As for Hunter, his easily influenced nature allowed him to
be the presiding officer at a second meeting in the African

[81] *New York Tribune*, February 10, 1865, quotations from the *Richmond Enquirer*, February 7, 1865, from the *Richmond Examiner*, February 7, 1865, from the *Richmond Whig*, February 6, 1865; Stephens,
Alexander H.: *A Constitutional View of the Late War between the
States*, Vol. II, pp. 603-604; Jones, J. B.: *Op. cit.*, Vol. II, p. 411.

[82] Stephens, Alexander H.: *A Constitutional View of the Late War
between the States*, Vol. II, pp. 605-606.

Church.[83]   A day or two later, he had again become convinced that peace was necessary and he turned savagely upon the administration.[84]

The Hampton Roads Conference had delivered the Southern cause into the hands of those who were bent upon the perpetuation of the war for Southern independence. In the North the negotiations had dangerously strengthened the extremist element.   When the elder Blair moved to and fro on his missions of intrigue and reconciliation, when commissioners from the Confederacy crossed the Federal lines, when Lincoln himself finally departed for Hampton Roads, the radicals in the Republican party became thoroughly alarmed.   The Committee on the Conduct of the War saw that the Union cause was betrayed and that their own influence was diminished.   Stanton was rumored to be disturbed by these new peace efforts.   In Baltimore, Beecher addressed a great audience.   He

[83] *New York Tribune,* February 13, 1865, quotation from the *Richmond Despatch.* Judah P. Benjamin was the chief speaker. His address was not a challenge like that of Davis, but a complaint against the war weariness of the South. He advocated the hanging of the Congressional croakers.

[84] The activities of Hunter after his return from Hampton Roads do not give a favorable impression of his constancy. Before and after the conference he undoubtedly wished and urged peace, and yet he did not have the courage to break entirely with Davis. So he presided at the African Church mass meeting. For details of his post war controversy with Davis, consult Lee, Fitzhugh: "Failure of the Hampton Roads Conference," *The Century Magazine,* Vol. LII, p. 478, R. M. T. Hunter to J. M. Mason, September 19, 1870; and Rowland, Dunbar (Editor): *Op. cit.,* Vol. VIII, pp. 575-578, R. M. T. Hunter to J. W. *Jones,* 1877 (?); pp. 123-128, Davis to J. W. Jones, March 27, 1878. Hunter claims that he finally broke with Davis when a confidential conversation on peace, which he had had with the President, was being reported around Richmond by the President's aides, and when he was described by them as "thoroughly conquered." Davis rather conclusively disposes of this legend.

painted a picture of a procession of justice "with male-
factors of the blackest dye, criminals against a nation's
life and against humanity, marching to the gibbet, and
broken into by people who would stay the execution and
let the criminals loose." A voice in the audience shouted
"Blair, Blair," and the crowd became riotous with indignation.[85] The radicals were organizing opposition to the
leniency of the President.

On February 3, Lincoln had left Hampton Roads for
Annapolis. There were crowds at the railroad station in
the latter place, eager to learn the results of the negotiation.[86] On the 4th of February, Lincoln was back in
Washington. The next day there was a cabinet meeting.
Lincoln proposed an offer of $400,000,000 for the slaves
of the Confederates if armed resistance would cease before
April. This sum was to be divided into two portions, the
first to be paid on April 1, and the second on July 1, if
the slavery amendment was adopted. All political offenses
were to be pardoned and all property subject to confiscation was to be freed from that liability. But this offer was
disapproved by the cabinet. Congress could not pass
such an act before adjournment, and an offer of compensation should not be made until the war was ended by
force of arms.[87]

Until the war was ended by force of arms was the result
in the North, as it was in the South, of the Hampton

[85] *New York Tribune*, February 2, 3, 1865.

[86] Bates, David H.: *Op. cit.*, pp. 341-342, Eckert had an opportunity
for another display of his terrific rectitude. He refused a check for
$100,000, offered to him by a prominent official in return for some hint
as to the outcome of the negotiations.

[87] Fessenden, F. P.: *Op. cit.*, Vol. II, p. 365; McClure, A. K.: *Colonel
Alexander K. McClure's Recollections of Half a Century*, pp. 293-298.

Roads Conference.   On February 4, Stanton had telegraphed Grant, at the direction of the President, that
nothing should prevent the continuance of his "military
plans or operations." [88]   In Congress the radicals were
jubilant.   The Hampton Roads Conference had put an
end to the talk of peace by negotiations and determined
that peace should come only by military victory.   In
response to the demands of Congress, Lincoln submitted
a report on the preliminaries to the negotiations and on
the conference itself.   On the former point the report was
well documented and explicit; on the latter, it was brief.
Lincoln and Seward had acted only on the points laid
down in the President's memorandum to his Secretary of
State.   The Southerners were evasive on the question of
reunion and desired a postponement, "which course, we
thought, would amount to an indefinite postponement.
The conference ended without result." [89]   But no event
passes without some result.   The Hampton Roads Conference was the last considerable effort to make peace by
agreement and to end the war by negotiation.   But the
President of the crumbling Confederacy could not bring
himself to make the sacrifice of the ideals and of the cause
of the South which such a peace involved.   He elected to
take a last desperate chance for success or failure.   Humiliating as the Northern terms must have seemed, it
would have been the part of wisdom, if not of honor, to
have yielded.   His decision increased the strength of the
extreme group in the North by furnishing renewed evidence of the unrighteousness of the Confederacy; and, by

[88] *Official Records of the Union and Confederate Armies*, Series I,
Vol. XLVI, Part II, p. 365.
[89] *Ibid.*, pp. 505-513.

assenting to a continuation of the war, he made a military peace inevitable. Thus Lincoln's task of reconciliation, of "malice toward none; with charity for all" was made extremely difficult. It is interesting to speculate as to the course of events if Lincoln had returned from Hampton Roads with the definite acceptance by the Confederate commissioners of his terms of peace. But such speculation is idle. For Appomattox Court House, the tragedy at Ford's Theater, and the days of reconstruction were to determine the peace terms of the American Civil War.

BIBLIOGRAPHY

There have naturally been some great reservoirs of material which have been useful throughout the whole of this present work. Of these the most important is the government publication, *The War of the Rebellion; a compilation of the Official Records of the Union and Confederate Armies* (Washington, 1880-1901). This work, cited throughout as the *Official Records of the Union and Confederate Armies,* consists of one hundred and twenty-eight volumes. These are divided into four series; the first of which deals with military operations according to campaigns and theaters of operations; the second deals with prisoners of war; the third and fourth series contain documents respectively of various kinds "not relating specially to the subjects of the first and second series." This loose classification has permitted the publication of nearly every kind of document, often in the strangest places. *The Official Records* are indispensable to any study of the Civil War. Next in importance is John G. Nicolay and John Hay, *Abraham Lincoln, a History.* Ten volumes (New York, 1890). This work is practically a history of the Civil War written by the private secretaries of the President. Its judgments and generalizations are invalidated by the undiscriminating admiration of the authors for their subject. It must be pointed out, moreover, that for so extensive a work there are often mysterious and baffling lacunæ. In spite of these defects, the volumes contain documents and material which cannot be obtained elsewhere. There are memoranda and notes of the secretaries, there are manuscript letters to the President, and there are unpublished letters and memoranda of the President. These volumes should be supplemented by John G. Nicolay and John Hay (Editors), *Complete Works of Abraham Lincoln,* **Twelve** volumes (New York, 1905). Of the newspapers, the *New York Tribune* has been most frequently consulted. Its news reports are voluminous, its special correspondents furnish information otherwise unattainable, and its quotations from other papers—especially Southern ones—are extensive.

Works Relating to Chapters I and III

The political background for the peace negotiations has been built up from various scattered sources. For the general history of national politics *The American Annual Cyclopædia and Register of Important Events* (New York, 1862-1866), gives a yearly summary. Two works of source value are Horace Greeley, *The American Conflict: A History of the Great Rebellion in the United States of America, 1860-'64.* Two volumes (Hartford, 1864), and Edward McPherson, *The Political History of the United States of America, during the Great Rebellion* (Washington, 1865). For the national conventions, there are M. Halstead, *Caucuses of 1860* (Columbus, Ohio, 1860); C. W. Johnson, *Proceedings of the First Three Republican Conventions of 1856, 1860 and 1864* (Minneapolis, 1893); *Official Proceedings of the Democratic National Convention Held in 1864 at Chicago* (Chicago, 1864).

The following essays and works have been peculiarly useful for some phases of the general political situation. William E. Dodd, "The Fight for the North-west, 1860," *American Historical Review,* Vol. XVI, pp. 774-789 (New York, 1911); W. A. Dunning, *Essays on the Civil War and Reconstruction and Related Topics* (New York, 1898); C. R. Fish, "The Decision of the Ohio Valley," *Annual Report of the American Historical Association for the Year 1910,* pp. 155-164 (Washington, 1912); E. D. Fite *The Presidential Campaign of 1860* (New York, 1911); Mary Scrugham, "The Peaceable Americans of 1860-1861," *Studies in History, Economics, and Public Law,* edited by the Faculty of

Political Science of Columbia University, Vol. XCVI, No. 3 (New York, 1921).

There have been numerous studies of state politics during the Civil War period, most of them undertaken by graduate students at Columbia University and published in its *Studies in History, Economics, and Public Law.* Of this series the following have been utilized: S. D. Brummer, *Political History of New York State during the Period of the Civil War* (New York, 1911); H. M. Dilla, *The Politics of Michigan, 1865-1878* (New York, 1912); G. H. Porter, *Ohio Politics during the Civil War Period* (New York, 1911); E. E. Ware, *Political Opinion in Massachusetts during Civil War and Reconstruction* (New York, 1916). Volume Three of the *Centennial History of Illinois, The Era of the Civil War, 1848-1870* (Springfield, Illinois, 1919), is by Arthur C. Cole.

Autobiographies, reminiscences, memoirs, biographies, personal narratives of all varieties, furnish material of diverse value. For an understanding of the details of Republican policy, the following works are enlightening: Frederic Bancroft, "Seward's Attitude toward Compromise and Secession, 1860-1861," *The Atlantic Monthly,* Vol. LXXIV, pp. 597-609 (Boston, 1894); T. W. Barnes, *Memoir of Thurlow Weed* (Boston, 1884); John Bigelow, *Retrospections of an Active Life,* Five volumes (Garden City, New York, 1913); John Cochrane, *Memories of Incidents Connected with the Origin and Culmination of the Rebellion* (New York, 1879); M. D. Conway, *Autobiography, Memoirs, and Experiences,* Two volumes (Boston and New York, 1904); Francis Fessenden, *Life and Public Services of William Pitt Fessenden,* Two volumes (Boston and New York, 1907); F. A. Flower, *Edwin McMasters Stanton, the Autocrat of Rebellion, Emancipation, and Reconstruction* (Akron, Ohio, 1905); J. M. Forbes, *Letters (Supplementary) of John Murray Forbes,* Three volumes (Boston, 1905) and *Reminiscences of John Murray Forbes,* Three volumes (Boston, 1902); G. V. Fox, *Confidential*

Correspondence of Gustavus Vasa Fox, Two volumes (New York, 1918); G. C. Gorham, *Life and Public Services of Edwin M. Stanton,* Two volumes (Boston and New York, 1899); A. B. Hart, *Salmon Portland Chase* (Boston and New York, 1899); S. F. Hughes, *Letters and Recollections of John Murray Forbes* (Boston and New York, 1899); G. W. Julian, *Political Recollections, 1840 to 1872* (Chicago, 1884); A. K. McClure, *Colonel Alexander K. McClure's Recollections of Half a Century* (Salem, Massachusetts, 1902); Charles Moore, "A Sketch of the Life of Sullivan M. Cutcheon," *Collections and Researches made by the Michigan Pioneer and Historical Society,* Vol. XXX, pp. 96-109 (Lansing, Michigan, 1906); H. G. Pearson, *The Life of John A. Andrew, Governor of Massachusetts, 1861-1865,* Two volumes (Boston and New York, 1904); A. G. Riddle, *The Life of Benjamin F. Wade* (Cleveland, 1888) and *Recollections of War Times, Reminiscences of Men and Events in Washington, 1860-1865* (New York, 1895); J. W. Schuckers, *The Life and Public Services of Salmon Portland Chase* (New York, 1874); N. W. Stephenson, *Lincoln. An Account of his Personal Life* (Indianapolis, 1922); Lindsay Swift, *William Lloyd Garrison* (Philadelphia, 1911); R. B. Warden, *An Account of the Private Life and Public Services of Salmon Portland Chase* (Cincinnati, 1874); Thurlow Weed, *Autobiography of Thurlow Weed* (Boston, 1884); Gideon Welles, *Diary of Gideon Welles,* Three volumes (Boston and New York, 1911).

Particular phases of the policy of the Republican party have been made the subject of special investigation. There is a precise discussion of the Confiscation Acts in James G. Randall, *The Confiscation of Property during the Civil War* (Indianapolis, 1913). An idea of the enforcement of these acts can be obtained in the report of the Secretary of the Treasury on the finances for 1864 printed in *House Documents,* Thirty-eighth Congress, Second Session, Executive Documents, Vol. VII, No. 3 (Washington, 1864), and from a report on the captured and forfeited cotton which came into the hands of the Treasury Department printed in *House Documents,* Thirty-ninth Congress, Second Session, Executive Documents, Vol. XI, No. 97 (Washington, 1867). There is an admirable essay on the Committee on the Conduct of the War in W. W. Pierson, "The Committee on the Conduct of the Civil War," *American Historical Review,* Vol. XXIII, pp. 550-577 (New York, 1918). *The Reports of the Joint Committee on the Conduct of the War* (Washington, 1863, 1865), have been published under that title. Some idea of the reactions of military men to this Committee can be traced in W. B. Franklin, *A Reply of Maj.-Gen. William B. Franklin to the Report of the Joint Committee of Congress on the Conduct of the War* (New York, 1863), and in George Meade, *The Life and Letters of George Gordon Meade,* Two volumes (New York, 1913).

The material for a knowledge of the Democratic party during the Civil War is very meager. Apparently leading Democrats were not as literary as Republicans or else preferred to forget their part in the conflict. The Chairman of the Democratic National Committee has left some "selected" documents in August Belmont, *Letters, Speeches, and Addresses of August Belmont* (1890). "The Diary of a Public Man," *The North American Review,* Vol. CXXIX, pp. 125-140, 259-273, 375-388, 484-496 (New York, 1879), gives the reactions of a Douglas Democrat at the outbreak of the war. Although G. B. McClellan has been given extensive notice in the general military histories and in separate biographies, his political activities have escaped detailed treatment. The only account, outside of the newspapers, is a brief two pages in B. C. Birdsall, "McClellan and the Peace Party," *The Century Magazine,* Vol. XVII, pp. 638-639 (New York, 1890). An understanding of McClellan and his difficulties can be obtained from two books, opposite in character. J. H. Campbell, *McClellan—A Vindication of the Military Career of General George B. McClellan* (New York, 1916), successfully dispels many impressions about its subject and creates some new

misimpressions. McClellan's failures are laid at the door of
Stanton and the radicals. George B. McClellan, *McClellan's
Own Story* (New York, 1887), is an unfortunate apologia. It
prints the General's letters to his wife, the perusal of which does
not leave a very happy impression of his intelligence and
discernment. The material on Vallandigham is very unsatisfactory. C. L.
Vallandigham, *The Record of Hon. C. L. Vallandigham* (Columbus, Ohio, 1863), stops short before the crucial year of 1864, and
James L. Vallandigham, *A Life of Clement L. Vallandigham*
(Baltimore, 1872), is written by the great Vallandigham's brother
and is both obscure and discreet. The best account of Vallandigham's activities can be pieced out from scattered references
in the *Official Records of the Union and Confederate Armies.*

The secret orders in the North still await an adequate secondary account. Mayo Fesler, "Secret Political Societies in the
North during the Civil War," *Indiana Magazine of History,* Vol.
XIV, No. 3, pp. 183-286 (Bloomington, Indiana, 1918) utilizes
the unpublished Bickley Papers, in the Judge Advocate General's
office, which deal with the origin of the secret orders, but the
account is often guilty of inaccuracies. There is a very good
narrative in W. D. Foulke, *Life of Oliver P. Morton,* Two volumes (Indianapolis and Kansas City). The most rewarding
sources for material are again the *Official Records of the Union
and Confederate Armies.* These contain Confederate correspondence and the reports of Northern investigators, Federal military
commanders, and special investigators. Many of these reports
have been reprinted separately. There is a great deal of unsus-
pected material in the *Official Records of the Union and Confederate Navies in the War of the Rebellion* (Washington, 1921).
Series II, Vol. II, contains the correspondence of the Navy Department of the Confederate States with its agents abroad, and
Volume III of the same series contains papers of Jefferson Davis
and the correspondence of the State Department with its diplo-

matic agents. A most valuable source is John B. Castleman, *Active Service* (Louisville, Kentucky, 1917). Castleman was on active service with the Confederate commissioners in Canada, and, in writing this book, had access to the offical journal of the commissioners. F. G. Stidger, *Treason History of the Order of Sons of Liberty* (Chicago, 1903), publishes various documents and supplements them with a narrative of his activities as a Federal agent who became a member of the secret orders. There is interesting testimony in the case of George St. Leger Grenfel which is published in *House Documents,* Thirty-ninth Congress, Second Session, Executive Documents, No. 50 (Washington, 1867). Other material has been utilized from William Bross, *Biographical Sketch of the Late Gen. B. J. Sweet. History of Camp Douglas* (Chicago, 1878); T. H. Keefe, "How the Northwest Was Saved," *Everybody's Magazine,* Vol. II, pp. 82-91 (New York, 1900); John A. Marshall, *American Bastile* (Philadelphia, 1870); Benn Pitman (Editor), *The Trials for Treason at Indianapolis* (Cincinnati, 1865).

Works Relating to Chapter II

For an understanding of Horace Greeley only two sources are necessary: the one, a file of the *New York Tribune,* and the other Horace Greeley, *Recollections of a Busy Life* (New York, 1868). The *Recollections,* while they are often silent as to important episodes in the author's life, throw a flood of light on his activities, interests, beliefs, whims, virtues, and vices. In short, they give a complete picture of Greeley's personality. The background of Greeley's life in politics and in journalism can be built up from the works of S. D. Brummer and of Thurlow Weed, cited above and from the following: H. M. Field, *The Life of David Dudley Field* (New York, 1898); Parke Godwin, *A Biography of William Cullen Bryant* (New York, 1883); L. D. Ingersoll, *The Life of Horace Greeley, Founder of the New York Tribune* (Chicago, 1873); J. S. Pike, *First Blows of the Civil War* (New York, 1879). *Proceedings at the Unveiling of a Memorial to Horace Greeley at Chappaqua, N. Y.* (Albany, 1915), contains little new information but prints an extensive bibliography of Greeley's works.

The material on the activities of the Confederate Commissioners in Canada has already been discussed in connection with the works on the secret orders (pages 264-265). Of the works there cited the *Official Records of the Union and Confederate Armies and the Official Records of the Union and Confederate Navies* print reports, documents, investigations, etc. John B. Castleman, *Active Service*, continues to be of great service. The peace activities of W. C. Jewett are all too elaborately detailed in the various pamphlets which he published. The following are the abbreviated titles of his works: *An Appeal to the Governors and People of the Northern States of America and Representative Vallandigham* (London, 1863 ?); *The Friendly American Mediation Move of the Emperor of France* (Portland, Maine, 1862); *Mediation Address to England* (London, 1863 ?); *Mediation in America* (no date); *Mediation Position of France in Connection with the Congress of Nations* (London, 1863 ?); *National Appeal in Connection with the Independent Peace Mission of William Cornell Jewett* (London, 1863 ?); *A National Appeal to the American People and the Church Universal* (New York, 1864).

The details of the preliminaries to the Niagara Conference and of the Conference itself must be collected from the *Official Records of the Union and Confederate Armies*, from John G. Nicolay and John Hay, *Abraham Lincoln, a History*, and from the *New York Tribune*. There is an account in W. R. Thayer, *The Life and Letters of John Hay*, Two volumes (Boston and New York, 1914), based largely upon excerpts from Hay's diary. This account, as well as that in Nicolay and Hay's *Lincoln*, is most unfair because of its intense anti-Greeley animus. There is a secondary narrative in F. H. Severance, "The Peace Conference at Niagara Falls in 1864," *Buffalo Historical Society Publications,* Vol. XVIII, pp. 79-94 (Buffalo, New York, 1914).

For the Jaquess-Gilmore Mission to Richmond, with the exception of a few documents in the *Official Records of the Union and Confederate Armies,* the only full accounts are those given by James R. Gilmore. Unfortunately his published reports do not give an impression of strict reliability. The first published accounts of the mission by Gilmore are "Our Visit to Richmond," *Atlantic Monthly,* Vol. XIV, pp. 372-383 (Boston, 1864); and "Our Last Day in Dixie," *Atlantic Monthly,* Vol. XIV, pp. 715-726. These accounts omit all discussion of the preliminaries to the despatch of Jaquess and Gilmore to Richmond. Later additions, elaborations, and revisions were made in James R. Gilmore, "A Suppressed Chapter of History," *Atlantic Monthly,* Vol. LIX, pp. 425-448 (Boston, 1887); and in James R. Gilmore, *Personal Recollections of Abraham Lincoln and the Civil War* (Boston, 1898).

Works Relating to Chapter IV

Until the papers of the Blairs are made accessible to historical students, a knowledge of the activities of that family must be derived from many scattered and inadequate sources. That lack is made good by only a few speeches and letters which have been published. In the preparation of this chapter, the following have been consulted: F. P. Blair, Sr., *Republican Documents, Letter from Francis P. Blair to My Neighbors, September 17, 1856* (?); and *A Voice from the Grave of Jackson! Letter from Francis P. Blair, Esq., to a Public Meeting in New York, held April 29, 1856* (Washington, 1856 ?). By Francis P. Blair, Jr., there are: *Remarks of F. P. Blair, Jr., of St. Louis, in the House of Representatives of Missouri on the Repeal of the "Jackson Resolutions," February 1, 1853* (City of Jefferson, Missouri, 1853);

Remarks of Mr. Blair in Joint Session, January 10, 1855, in reply to Mr. Steward, Senator from Buchanan; Remarks of Mr. Blair, of St. Louis, in reply to Mr. Goode, delivered in joint session, Friday, February 2nd, 1855; Remarks of Hon. F. P. Blair, Jr., of St. Louis, in Joint Session of the General Assembly of Missouri, upon the subject of the senatorial election, November 3, 1855; Speech of Hon. F. P. Blair, Jr., of Missouri, on the acquisition of territory in Central and South America, to be colonized with free blacks. . . . Delivered in the House of Representatives on the 14th day of January, 1858, with an appendix (Washington, 1858); *The Destiny of the Races of this Continent. An Address delivered before the Mercantile Library Association of Boston, Massachusetts, on the 26th day of January, 1859* (Washington, 1859); "*Fremont's Hundred Days in Missouri*" . . . *delivered in the House of Representatives, March 7, 1862* (Washington, 1862). By Montgomery Blair there are: *Comments on the Policy Inaugurated by the President in a Letter and Two Speeches* (New York, 1863); *Speech of the Hon. Montgomery Blair, Postmaster-General of the United States, at the mass meeting of the Loyal National League, in Union Square, New York . . . April 11, 1863* (New York, 1863); *Speech of Hon. Montgomery Blair (Postmaster-General) on the Revolutionary Schemes of the Ultra Abolitionists, . . . delivered at the Unconditional Union meeting, held at Rockville, Montgomery Co., Maryland, on Saturday, October 3, 1863* (New York, 1863); *Speech of the Hon. Montgomery Blair, on the Causes of the Rebellion . . . delivered before the Legislature of Maryland, at Annapolis, on the 22nd of January, 1864* (Baltimore, 1864). There are a few letters, mostly on the subject of colonization, in Francis P. Blair, Sr. and Jr., and Montgomery: "Letters of Edward Bates and the Blairs, Frank P.—Sr. and Jr.—and Montgomery, from the private papers and correspondence of Senator James Rood Doolittle, of Wisconsin. Edited by Duane

Mowry," *Missouri Historical Review,* Vol. XI, pp. 123-146 (Columbia, Missouri, 1917).

No adequate biographies of the Blairs have ever been written. There are brief sketches, somewhat inaccurate, in *Appletons' Cyclopædia of American Biography, Six volumes* (New York, 1887-1889). D. G. Croly, *Seymour and Blair, their lives and services* (New York, 1868), is a campaign biography, as is *The Lives and Services of Horatio Seymour and Frank P. Blair, Jr.* (Philadelphia, 1868). There are two meandering accounts in George Baber, "The Blairs. Outlines of a Virginia and Kentucky Family of Notable Civilians and Heroes," *Register of the Kentucky State Historical Society,* Vol. XIV, No. 42, pp. 37-49 (Frankfort, Kentucky, 1916); and Gist Blair, "Annals of Silver Spring," *Records of the Columbia Historical Society,* Vol. XXI, pp. 155-194 (Washington, 1918). The latter article is a reminiscence by a son of Montgomery Blair and he quotes from a manuscript life of F. P. Blair, Sr., by Montgomery Blair. The extensive and important relationship of the Blairs can be traced in the following genealogical works or articles: H. P. Andrews and P. P. Wiggins, *The Descendants of John Porter, of Windsor, Conn., . . . with some account of the families into which they married* (Saratoga Springs, New York, 1882); T. M. Green, *Historic Families of Kentucky* (Cincinnati, 1889); W. R. Hollister and Harry Norman, *Five Famous Missourians* (Kansas City, 1900); Edmund J. Lee, *Lee of Virginia, 1642-1842* (Philadelphia, 1895); Charles L. Woodbury, "Memoir of Hon. Levi Woodbury, LL.D.," *New England Historical and Genealogical Register,* Vol. XLVIII, pp. 10-15 (Boston, 1894).

For the part which the Blairs played in national politics, especially before the Civil War, the following works and articles have contributed incidental information: J. S. Bassett, *The Life of Andrew Jackson,* Two volumes (New York, 1911); "Blair of the Globe," *The United States Magazine and Democratic Review,* Vol. XVII, pp. 10-14 (New York, 1846); Gist Blair, "Lincoln,

Jefferson Davis, and Francis Preston Blair," *Register of the Kentucky State Historical Society,* Vol. XV, No. 44, pp. 35-40 (Frankfort, Kentucky, 1917); James Buchanan, *The Works of James Buchanan* (Philadelphia, 1910); C. M. Clay, *The Life of Cassius Marcellus Clay* (Cincinnati, 1886); Lewis Clephane, *Birth of the Republican Party, with a brief history of the important part taken by the original Republican Association of the National Capital* (Washington, 1889); W. C. Clephane, "Lewis Clephane: A Pioneer Washington Republican," *Records of the Columbia Historical Society,* Vol. XXI, pp. 263-277 (Washington, 1916); Charles Gibson, "Edward Bates," *Missouri Historical Society Collections,* Vol. II, No. L, pp. 52-56 (St. Louis, 1900); J. W. Gordon, *The Hon. Edward Bates, of Missouri, Is He Fit . . . Is He Available, as the Republican Candidate for the Presidency?* (Indianapolis, 1860); G. M. Grouard, *A Practical Printer's Answer to Mr. Kendall's Tract No. 5, on the Public Printing* (Washington, ?, 1844); O. J. Hollister, *Life of Schuyler Colfax* (New York, 1886); Amos Kendall, *Autobiography of Amos Kendall.* Edited by his son-in-law, William Stickney (Boston, 1872); Horatio King, *Turning on the Light* (Philadelphia, 1895); J. K. Polk, *The Diary of James K. Polk, during his presidency, 1845-1849.* Edited and annotated by Milo Minton Quaife, Four volumes, (Chicago, 1910); N. S. Shaler, *Kentucky. A Pioneer Commonwealth* (Boston, 1885); Gideon Welles, "Mr. Lincoln and Mr. Seward," *The Galaxy,* Vol. XVI, pp. 518-530, 687-700, 793-804 (New York, 1873).

The importance of Missouri in the Blairs' history has already been emphasized. The activities of Frank Blair in its politics before the Civil War can be traced from his speeches and from the following works: S. B. Harding, *Life of George R. Smith, Founder of Sedalia, Mo.,* (Sedalia, Missouri, 1904); C. M. Harvey, "Missouri from 1849 to 1861," *Missouri Historical Review,* Vol. II, pp. 23-40 (Columbia, Missouri, 1907); C. P. Johnson, "Remarks on the Occasion of the Presentation of the Portrait of Oliver D. Filley . . .," *Missouri Historical Society Collections*, Vol. II, No. 6, pp. 1-12 (St. Louis, 1906); P. O. Ray, *The Repeal of the Missouri Compromise* (Cleveland, 1909).

Most of the works on the Civil War period are unsatisfactory because they fail to deal with events in Missouri after Fremont assumed command of the Western Department. The battle of Wilson's Creek seems to have been a convenient stopping point for historical treatment. In the books which have been written, it is difficult to obtain a clear and accurate knowledge of what really happened, so great are the complexities of Missouri politics and so partisan are the writers on the subject. The *Official Records of the Union and Confederate Armies* and Nicolay's and Hay's *Abraham Lincoln* are of fundamental importance. These should be supplemented by James Peckham, *Gen. Nathaniel Lyon, and Missouri in 1861* (New York, 1866), an extreme glorification of Lyon which, nevertheless, contains valuable letters, too often abbreviated; by T. L. Snead, *The Fight for Missouri from the Election of Lincoln to the Death of Lyon* (New York, 1886), a book extremely fair to the Union cause although its author was an aide-de-camp of Jackson who eventually became a member of the Confederate Congress; and by W. B. Stevens, "Lincoln and Missouri," *Missouri Historical Review*, Vol. X, No. 2, pp. 63-119 (Columbia, Missouri, 1916), which interrelates national and state politics during the whole war. Additional information can be obtained from G. S. Grover, "Civil War in Missouri," *Missouri Historical Review*, Vol. VIII, pp. 1-28 (Columbia, Missouri, 1913); Nathaniel Lyon, *The Last Political Writings of Gen. Nathaniel Lyon, U. S. A.* (New York, 1861); H. C. McDougal, "A Decade of Missouri Politics—1860 to 1870 —from a Republican Viewpoint," *Missouri Historical Review*, Vol. III, pp. 126-153 (Columbia, Missouri, 1909); John McElroy, *The Struggle for Missouri* (Washington, 1909); J. C. Moore, *Missouri, Confederate Military History.* Edited by Clement A. Evans, Vol. IX, Part II (Atlanta, 1899); L. W. Reavis, *The*

Life and Military Services of Gen. William Selby Harney (St. Louis, 1878); R. J. Rombauer, *The Union Cause in St. Louis in 1861* (St. Louis, 1909); Ashbell Woodward, *Life of General Nathaniel Lyon* (Hartford, Connecticut, 1862). For the Fremont episode the best accounts are in Gustave Koerner, *Memoirs of Gustave Koerner (1809-1896)*, Two volumes (Cedar Rapids, Iowa, 1909), an unprejudiced account written by an Illinois German; and the *Report of the Joint Committee on the Conduct of the War, 1863)*, Three parts (Washington, 1863), which contains the testimony of Fremont, F. P. Blair, Jr., and Montgomery Blair. J. M. Schofield, *Forty-six Years in the Army* (New York, 1897), is also useful. Typical attacks upon the Blairs are: William Brotherhead, *General Fremont, and the Injustice Done Him by Politicians and Envious Military Men* (Philadelphia, 1862); J. P. C. Shanks, *Vindication of Major-General John C. Fremont . . . in the House of Representatives, Tuesday, March 4, 1862* (Washington, 1862); J. S. Thomas, *The Case of General Fremont. Remarks . . . in the House of Representatives,* March 7, 1862 (St. Louis, 1862).

The material on the political situation in Maryland, the other Blair constituency, is very meager. Some notion of the situation can be derived from H. W. Davis, *Speeches and Addresses delivered in the Congress of the United States and on Several Public Occasions* (New York, 1867); and D. C. Steiner, *Life of Henry Winter Davis* (Baltimore, 1916), which, although it duplicates the *Speeches and Addresses,* has valuable notes at the ends of the chapters. There are two other works of value: Lew Wallace, *Lew Wallace, an Autobiography,* Two volumes (New York, 1906); and W. S. Myers, "The Maryland Constitution of 1864," *Johns Hopkins University Studies in Historical and Political Science,* Series XIX, Nos. 8-9 (Baltimore, 1901).

The best report of the Blair Peace Mission to Richmond is the Blair memorandum, printed by Nicolay and Hay from a manuscript. This memorandum is printed in full in their article on the "Mexican Project and the Hampton Roads Conference" in *The Century Magazine,* Vol. XVI, pp. 839-844. It is given in an abbreviated form in their *Abraham Lincoln, a History,* Vol. X, pp. 96-106. Another account, a conversation with F. P. Blair, Sr., is given in John Bigelow, *Retrospections,* Vol. IV, pp. 50-52. The narrative in Jefferson Davis, *The Rise and Fall of the Confederate Government,* Two volumes (New York, 1881)adds little new. There is another record of a brief conversation with Blair on this subject in G. P. Lathrop, "The Bailing of Jefferson Davis," *The Century Magazine,* Vol. XXXIII, pp. 636-640 (New York, 1887).

Works Relating to Chapter V

Rowland Dunbar (Editor), *Jefferson Davis, Constitutionalist. His Letters, Papers, and Speeches,* Ten volumes (Jackson, Mississippi, 1923), is the most valuable single source for the material in this chapter. Not only does the editor publish the documents, correspondence, speeches, and messages at the time of the war, but he also includes the material incident to the war which the Confederates fought in after years with each other in reminiscence and in controversy. In this contest, the material bearing on the Hampton Roads Conference was contributed largely in 1877 and 1878—twelve or thirteen years after the events had transpired. Memories are apt to be fickle after so long an elapse of time. For a further understanding of the political situation in the Confederacy in 1864-1865 and of the peace movement, the following works are useful: Varina Davis, *Jefferson Davis. . . . A Memoir by His Wife,* Two volumes (New York, 1890); T. C. De Leon, *Four Years in Rebel Capitals* (Mobile, Alabama, 1892); J. G. de Roulhac Hamilton, *The Correspondence of Jonathan Worth,* Two volumes (Raleigh, North Carolina, 1909); John B. Jones, *A Rebel War Clerk's Diary at the Confederate States Capital,* Two volumes (Philadelphia,

1866); E. A. Pollard, *The Last Year of the War* (New York, 1866); Sarah A. Putnam, *Richmond during the War* (New York, 1867). Proceedings in Congress can be surmised from the *Journal of the Congress of the Confederate States of America, 1861-1865*. Seven volumes (Washington, 1904).

Of the commissioners appointed to the Hampton Roads Conference, the material is satisfactory only in respect to Alexander H. Stephens. He has left his own record in A. H. Stephens, *A Constitutional View of the Late War between the States*, Two volumes (Philadelphia, 1870) and in *Recollections of Alexander H. Stephens* (New York, 1910). Both are interesting documents. The former is Stephens' reasoned apologia "presented in a series of colloquies at Liberty Hall." The latter is Stephens' diary kept while he was imprisoned in Fort Warren, Boston Harbor, in 1865. Stephens was subject during his incarceration to indigestion and fears of death and he was not particularly charitable toward Jefferson Davis, whom he regarded as responsible for all his misfortunes. The recollections flit around in the most engaging manner on all subjects from Stephens' health to his opinion of the classics. These two works should be supplemented by Henry Cleveland, *Alexander H. Stephens, in Public and Private* (Philadelphia, 1867); R. M. Johnston and W. H. Browne, *Life of Alexander H. Stephens* (Philadelphia, 1884); and J. D. Waddell, *Biographical Sketch of Linton Stephens* (Atlanta, 1877). U. B. Philips (Editor), "The Correspondence of Robert Toombs, Alexander H. Stephens, and Howell Cobb," *Annual Report of the American Historical Association for the Year 1911*, Volume II (Washington, 1913), is more complete for the earlier war period than for the period 1864-1865.

The other commissioners are treated in H. G. Connor, *John Archibald Campbell, Associate Justice of the United States Supreme Court, 1853-1861* (Boston and New York, 1920); Martha P. Hunter, *A Memoir of Robert M. T. Hunter . . . with an address on his life . . . by Col. L. Quinten Washington* (Washington, 1903); C. H. Ambler (Editor), "Correspondence of Robert M. T. Hunter, 1826-1876," *Annual Report of the American Historical Association for the Year 1916*, Volume II (Washington, 1918). Neither Hunter's *Correspondence* nor Martha Hunter's *Memoir* of her father is particularly valuable for the Civil War period. A much better understanding can be obtained from Rowland Dunbar's *Jefferson Davis*.

The preliminaries to the Hampton Roads Conference can be studied in the works cited for the Blair Mission in Chapter IV and in the *Official Records of the Union and Confederate Armies*. In addition some details are added by David H. Bates, *Lincoln in the Telegraph Office* (New York, 1907), and in U. S. Grant, *Personal Memoirs of U. S. Grant*, Two volumes (New York, 1886). The accounts of the Conference necessarily pay some attention to the steps which led up to it. Of these accounts there are five of major importance. There is the very brief one submitted by Abraham Lincoln to the House of Representatives on February 10, 1865, in the *Official Records of the Union and Confederate Armies*, Series I, Vol. XLVI, Part II, pp. 505-513, and the even more brief account despatched by Seward on February 7, 1865, to C. F. Adams in the *Official Records of the Union and Confederate Armies*, Series III, Vol. IV, pp. 1163-1165. The Southern accounts are more elaborate. Stephens' account can be found in snatches throughout his *Recollections* and finally in his *War Between the States*, Vol. II, pp. 599-626. The latter is the fullest and the best ordered account of the Conference. Hunter's account first appeared in 1877 in the *Philadelphia Weekly Times*. It was republished in the *Southern Historical Papers*, Vol. III, No. 4, pp. 168-176, and can be found also in Rowland Dunbar's *Jefferson Davis*, Vol. VIII, pp. 128-136. The controversy which Hunter had with Davis over this report can be traced in the same work. The earliest Southern account is John A. Campbell, "The Hampton Roads Conference," *Transactions of the Southern Historical Society*, Vol. I, in the

Southern Magazine, Vol. XV, pp. 187-194 (Baltimore, 1874), and John A. Campbell, *Reminiscences and Documents Relating to the Civil War during the Year 1865* (Baltimore, 1887). These two accounts are practically identical. They are based upon a memorandum of the Conference which Judge Campbell wrote out very soon after it took place.

INDEX